PATHWAY TO PIAGET

A VOLUME
IN THE
POSTGRADUATE INTERNATIONAL
BEHAVIORAL SCIENCE SERIES

Edited by
Jerome J. Platt

Editorial Consultant for this Volume
Robert J. Wicks

PATHWAY TO PIAGET

A Guide for Clinicians,
Educators, and Developmentalists

Hugh Rosen

POSTGRADUATE INTERNATIONAL, INC.
Cherry Hill, New Jersey

First Edition

Copyright © under the Universal Copyright
and Bern Convention

© 1977 by Postgraduate International, Inc.

Library of Congress Catalog Card Number: 77-077571

Printed in the United States of America

ISBN 0-918924-00-6

To
SUSAN BALIS
for Helping Me to Decenter

CONTENTS

PREFACE

Today there exist several excellent introductory texts on the work of Jean Piaget. Nevertheless, throughout many years of teaching his developmental psychology to students and colleagues in the helping professions, I have not been able to locate a suitable one for our purposes. Clinically oriented people raise questions and express interests that are either not covered in extant books or are not dealt with adequately if they are covered. I have often been approached by colleagues who profess an interest in knowing more about Piaget, for certainly they sense the significance of his work for any serious student of human growth and behavior. However, they find the prospect of ranging though his difficult material dismaying, and they yearn for a book directed toward their own interests in individual, inter-personal, and psychopathological development. In this book I have attempted to respond to those interests without com-promising the depth and complexity of Piaget's system. The present book strives toward a unique integration of theory and research covering a wide spectrum of literature derived primarily from the cognitive-developmental psychology of the Geneva School founded by Piaget. All that appears in this volume appears elsewhere; but nowhere else will this particular synthesis of con-ceptual and empirical material be found in a single endeavor. Although the major emphasis is on Piaget's own work, I have sought to make generous use of theoretical and research efforts by others who have adopted his work as a point of departure. The credit for any errors in this book, however, should un-equivocally be accorded to me.

By stating that this book is oriented toward members of the helping professions, I do not mean that it instructs the practitioner on how to apply cognitive-developmental psychology to conducting psychotherapy. I do assume, however, that the clinician will not only be interested in Piaget's basic ideas regarding how knowledge of the physical world is constructed, but that he will also be greatly concerned with the implications that this has for the realms of moral development, interpersonal communication, and developmental psychopathology.

The first five chapters of the book are dominated almost exclusively by Piaget's own work. Chapter 1 is a touchstone to all that follows, as it offers an introduction to the conceptual framework of the Piagetian system. Chapter 2 presents an extensive exploration of egocentrism and its decline throughout each major developmental period. Egocentrism is a central concept which severely limits each developing individual's capacity for acquiring a knowledge of reality based upon objectivity, reciprocity, and relativity. In the chapter on conservation the reader is familiarized with one of the most important and highly researched Piagetian tasks. An in-depth comprehension of conservation will illuminate the meaning of operational thinking, which reflects the characteristic intelligence toward which development tends. In the chapter on cognition and language, the notion that thinking is necessarily dependent upon words is dispelled. It is hoped that in becoming acquainted with Piaget's controversial position on this matter, the structure of this cognitive-developmental theorist's work will become increasingly more clear to the reader.

There are two chapters on moral development. One is an exposition of Piaget's only work on the subject. The other is a critique and presentation of some replicated studies, including the contemporary work of Lawrence Kohlberg, which expands greatly upon the earlier findings of Piaget. Considerable attention has been devoted to moral judgment in the belief that professionals whose work involves them intimately in helping other individuals choose "the good life" should themselves be thoroughly acquainted with the relevant findings of present-day cognitive developmental theory and research.

In a sense, the last three chapters go beyond Piaget, although they are firmly rooted in his work. A burgeoning literature has

been pointing the way toward applying Piaget's radical constructivist epistemology to areas involving effective communication and interpersonal relationships. Drawing from the extant
literature, Chapter 7 traces the complex stages that the child
moves through in acquiring the ability to recognize the relativity
of his own viewpoint and to see things from another's point of
view. Chapter 8, Adaptive Communication, pursues the centrality
of this role-taking capacity, as it is called, to the enhancement
of communication between speaker and listener. As a capstone to
the entire book, I have provided a chapter which surveys a
spectrum of the works available in English which approach psychopathology from the Piagetian perspective. In this chapter
alone, I fully anticipate that many of the questions originating
with my students and colleagues will be dealt with, perhaps
even to their satisfaction, despite the embryonic stage of cognitive-
developmental psychopathology as a comprehensive field of study.

I have approached Piaget's work with respect, but not with
reverence. The system he advanced should be viewed as open-
ended in that each hypothesis must withstand the rigors of
empirical validation, proving to be either confirmed or dis-
proved. In the case of the latter, the hypothesis should be either
eliminated or subjected to appropriate modification. Alternately,
however, the system may be viewed as a closed one in that it is
comprised of a set of interlocking concepts and postulates, each
component being difficult to understand without grasping the
whole; while at the same time the total system cannot be comprehended without a knowledge of its parts. It is in the very
nature of the material that careful exposition of it will warrant
a certain amount of repetition. Yet it is hoped that each repetition
will impart a slightly different perspective and provide a moderately
novel insight to an aspect of the material. As dreams were said
by Freud to be a royal road to the unconscious, I hope this book
will prove to be an enlightening pathway to Piaget.

Finally, I would like to acknowledge the assistance I have
received from several sources. I am indebted to Dr. William
Adamson, Chief of Child and Adolescent Psychiatry, Education
and Training in the Department of Mental Health Sciences at

Hahnemann Medical College and Hospital. His thoughtful reading of the manuscript and constructive comments were most helpful. The persistent curiosity and questions of my students have been an impetus without which this book may never have been written. The task of typing the manuscript was carried out by Barbara Cunningham, whose patience and loyalty sustained me through some trying moments. A word of thanks also goes to my sister, Susan Warner, who provided help when time became of the essence.

PATHWAY TO PIAGET

1

GENETIC EPISTEMOLOGY: BASIC CONCEPTS AND OVERVIEW

INTRODUCTION

Clinicians in the helping professions are invariably familiar with the field of human development. Nevertheless, their grasp of psychosexual and social development is rarely matched by an equal understanding of the evolution of cognitive competencies. Much interest mixed with awe is often expressed concerning the formidable work of Jean Piaget, who is undisputably this century's most productive and prominent developmental psychologist. His work comprises a highly complex and interdependent system which is difficult to comprehend in depth and, therefore, keeps many motivated but busy practitioners from studying it. The purpose of this chapter is to provide a theoretical foundation for the remainder of this book and to facilitate the process of comprehension in the more ambitious reader who may wish to turn to original Piagetian sources.

The ultimate goal of all Piaget's professional efforts has been to advance a science of genetic epistemology. Epistemology is a well-established discipline in the tradition of Western philosophy. However, Piaget has gone far beyond the unvalidated speculations of philosophers and has rooted his pursuit of this science in empirical studies. The realm of epistemology embraces an examination of the nature of knowledge and the manner in which it is acquired.

Such a view encompasses the relationship between knower and known. The qualifying term genetic is not a reference to the hereditary transmission of cognitive characteristics, but refers to the individual's own historical process in the acquisition of knowledge. The "genesis of knowledge" is perhaps a phrase which aptly captures the appropriate meaning.

At age ten Piaget published his first paper, a one-page description of a partly Albino sparrow which he had observed in the park. During adolescence he published many papers on the subject of malacology, a branch of zoology. Born in 1896, Piaget was awarded a doctorate in 1918 at the University of Neuchâtel for his studies in the natural sciences and his thesis on mollusks. Previous baccalaureate work had already exposed him to such significant areas as psychology, logic, and the scientific method. All of these subjects, including his biological studies, were later to merge in a vast interrelated network of theory and research which were to become the Piagetian system. Postdoctorate studies involved Piaget in two psychological laboratories and Bleuler's psychiatric clinic in Zurich. Following the one-year experience in Zurich, he attended the Sorbonne for two years where he pursued courses in such subjects as psychopathology, logic, and the philosophy of science. All of this eventuated with an experience standardizing Burt's reasoning tests in work with Parisian children at a grade school which was host to one of Binet's laboratories. Although he was interested in the correct answers given by the children, Piaget was fascinated by their mistakes. Discerning that the wrong answers were possibly governed by a developmental pattern, Piaget embarked upon the science of genetic epistemology. In brief he sought to discover the reasoning behind the answers rather than to focus merely on the answers themselves. Evans (1973) contains Piaget's autobiography and expands upon these comments.

METHODOLOGY

The Piagetian methodology has varied over the years. A consistent thread has been its reliance upon direct work with children in contrast to Freudian methodology. As is well known, Freud's developmental psychology was based primarily on reconstructions from the verbalization of his adult patients, relying heavily upon fantasy, associations, and memory. Both giants of psychology, however, utilized a clinical method. Piaget's first five books primarily center on discussions between the investigator and the children, the former posing questions which the latter attempt to answer. A standardized approach is deliberately avoided as the questioner is prepared to delve further into the child's line of reasoning, being sure to follow the cues of the child. Applying the method properly is the key to fruitful results and Piaget maintains that at least a year of training is necessary to acquire proficiency in its use.

The following period of Piaget's studies concentrated mainly upon the growth of intelligence during infancy and was based heavily upon direct observation, embellished by the ingenious use of objects placed in the environment for the child to manipulate. Piaget's approach to observing infants is akin to Darwin's meticulous accumulation of minute bits of data which were integrated to produce a theory of evolution. The richness of detail captured by Piaget is extraordinary, and one must read the original source material to fully appreciate it (Piaget 1936/1963; Piaget 1936/1971; Piaget 1946/1962).* It has become commonplace to criticize Piaget's infancy studies because he employed a sample of only three babies, all of whom happened to be his own offspring. Significantly, however, there have been replicated studies, one of which utilizes a sample of ninety babies, essentially validating Piaget's own findings (Décarie 1965).

A third period of Piaget's work introduced an experimental method in which the child is presented with materials and assigned a problem-solving task. The child's subsequent actions are observed and, in addition, he is asked to provide explanations for what he is doing. Studies utilizing this method have led to

*First date refers to original version in non-English. Second date refers to English source utilized by the author. References at the end of this book are arranged by English date in chronological order. (The double date reference system used here is in accord with the Publication Manual of the American Psychological Association).

the formulation of highly complex logico-mathematical models. Piaget has never been interested in assigning quantitative measurements to intellectual attainment. He has consistently concentrated upon a qualitative assessment of the mental mechanisms underlying developing cognitive competencies. Furthermore, he has not sought to overwhelm with massive statistical data. Instead, his qualitative findings have served to generate innumerable hypotheses which have been experimented with cross-culturally around the world. The frequency with which replicated studies have confirmed his findings has been great. Criteria for a good theory embrace its potential for a fertile production of hypotheses. In this respect, Piaget's theories meet the test with consummate vigor.

FUNCTION AND STRUCTURE

In Piaget's view, intelligence is not an entity of the mind set apart from the body. It is an integral part of the person and is subject to some of the same biological processes governing the material aspects of all human and other organisms. These processes, specifically adaptation and organization, are known as functional invariants. They are called invariant because they continue to function in the same manner throughout the developmental stages in contrast to cognitive structures which undergo qualitative changes over time. Before clarifying the functional invariants further it will be useful, indeed necessary, to expand upon the nature of structures, as the two are so interrelated that one set cannot exist without the other. Although Piaget has shown great inventiveness in postulating theories about structures, he is actually part of a much broader contemporary movement known as structuralism. Prominent among the structuralists are Noam Chomsky, a world renowned linguist, and Claude Levi-Strauss, a towering figure among anthropologists. Gardner (1972) in speaking of all three researchers, Chomsky, Levi-Strauss, and Piaget, has stated the following:

> Each of these scholars focuses particularly on Man, seeing him as a constructive organism, with generative capacities, who nonetheless is preordained to follow certain paths in his intellectual

development and achievement because of the structure of his own brain and the regulating forces in the human environment (p. 242).

In another chapter he makes the following concise and illuminating statement:

> In short the structuralists sought underlying arrangements of elements which determined overt forms of behavior and thought, could be expressed in logical formal language, and reflected the biological attributes of human beings (p. 40).

Despite the immense similarity of their thought, Piaget differs significantly from both Chomsky and Levi-Strauss in at least one major area. Piaget is a radical constructivist. Unlike the other two scholars, he does not believe that structures are innate. Chomsky, for example, points to the existence of inborn, linguistic structures which enable a child of even only average intelligence to exercise a set of universal rules for dealing creatively with and learning relatively quickly any language his environment exposes him to. Although these structures permit the child to creatively generate an infinite variety of sentences with his newly acquired language, they are static in the sense that their essential character is not modified as the child develops. In sharp contrast, Piaget asserts that cognitive structures are not innate. At the beginning of infancy there exist only primitive reflexes, such as sucking and grasping. Gradually the reflex behavior becomes refined and coordinated and the child, through continued interaction with his environment, constructs a progressively more complex network of structures which provides cognitive competencies enabling increasingly more successful problem-solving and adaptation. Before identifying the major periods of development, it will be necessary to elaborate upon the functional invariants.

ADAPTATION AND ORGANIZATION

Adaptation is basically the organism's relation to the external world, and organization is essentially an internal matter. Assimilation and accommodation are the twin processes which interact together to form adaptation. The former is conservative as it is a process in which the cognitive structure does not change. What occurs is that the external stimulus, input from the outside, is received and interpreted from the standpoint of the existing structure. The external world is not received as a mere copy of reality. Instead, what is "out there" is modified to conform to the present character of the mental structures at the time of the interaction between organism and environment. For example, in the case of a very young child whose contact with four-legged, furry creatures has been confined to small dogs, a drive in the country exposing him to cows and horses may lead to exclamations about the extra large "dogs." The classificatory schema (structure) for four-legged, furry creatures is presently simple and globular. However, in the course of interacting with the environment over time, the child will attempt to alter the existing schema to conform to the unique or differentiating features of the new stimuli. Continued exposure to horses will lead to the recognition that they have their own way of running and that they are capable of kicking strongly. Since dogs neither gallop nor kick, the child will modify his mental structure in order to differentiate between horses and dogs. Eventually his classification schemas will become sufficiently sophisticated so that he will not only be able to differentiate among four-legged, furry creatures, but will be able to deal with them in a hierarchical and inclusive relationship. In other words, he will recognize that horses and dogs are two of many types of creatures, all of which may be classified as animals.

The emergence of new mental structures and the modification of preexisting ones are brought about by attempts to accommodate the existing structures to the contours of the external reality. Because it involves change, accommodation is viewed as progressive in contrast to assimilation which is conservative, since in the latter there is no alteration of structure. These twin processes are of singular importance as reflected in the following comment by Flavell (1963): "Assimilation and accommodation constitute the most fundamental ingredients of intellectual functioning. Both functions are present in every intellectual act, of whatever type and developmental level" (p. 58). Nevertheless, the relationship between these two processes will vary throughout development. Generally, when intelligent functioning is present there will be an equilibrium, a balance, between assimilation and accommodation. On the one hand, equilibrium avoids an excessive and slavish conformity to the external and surface appearance of reality while on the other, it avoids constantly fitting external stimuli into one's own subjective schemas, regardless of the new features of the stimuli which do not appear to fit. Hence, the complex events in a child's life do not simply make an imprint upon a passive mind, but are actively constructed by him in an internal meaning system which continuously develops into a rich, highly organized and interlocking network of cognitive structures. Commenting on what he sees as Piaget's main epistemological thesis, Flavell (1963) states: "The cognizing organism is at all levels a very, very active agent who always meets the environment well over halfway, who actually *constructs* his world by assimilating it to schemas while accommodating these schemas to its constraints" (p. 71).

Organization, one of the two functional invariants, plays a vital role in the internal meaning system of the human organism. Examples of this can be observed during infancy. At first the baby will suck reflexively. If the hand happens to fall into the mouth, sucking will be activated. But shortly after birth, the infant begins to coordinate the placement of his thumb into his mouth with the sucking behavior. Within a few months such separate schemas as looking and grasping are organized into a single schema manifesting such behavior as grasping an object which then is brought closer and visually examined. The term schema (schemas) does not stand simply for a single act; it refers primarily to an abstract structure which covers a whole class of similar behaviors. It is, in a sense, an internal design for action. Advanced and more complex structures are no longer called schemas, but operations. An example of organization at a later developmental period may be enlightening. Movement into the concrete operational period is usually initiated by the emergence of classificatory and seriating operations. Classification at this point involves not only the ability to arrange objects in a proper hierarchy, but also the competence to recognize and understand the inclusion relationships obtaining. Seriation is the capacity to place a group of different-sized objects in appropriate order, without trial and error, ranging in a progressive series from the smallest to the largest, or vice versa.

The cognitive competency for dealing properly with number tasks always follows the arrival of classification and seriation and never precedes it. Piaget's explanation (Piaget 1941/1965) for this empirical fact is that the two earlier operations are organized to form a number operation. In other words, the ability to grasp number depends upon classification and seriation because by its very nature it is made up of these operation. For example, to grasp the nature of the number five, it is necessary to understand that it is inclusive of a particular group of individual units each treated alike, regardless of other differences (i.e., color, shape, weight), much as when one assigns individual items to a class. In this instance, the class is the cardinal number five. In addition, to truly grasp the nature of five it must be understood that five is simultaneously greater than four and less than six. The capacity manifested here to see the relational nature of five in either direction is one form of reversibility, a cornerstone of intellectual attainment, and it is precisely this ability that enables seriation to emerge. Explained in this way, it is possible to see that an ability to fully comprehend numbers will never precede the development of classificatory and seriation structures, as the logic of the situation dictates the inevitable sequence. Not surprisingly, independent research continues to find the same sequence of development discovered earlier by Piaget in this and other areas.

DEVELOPMENTAL PERIODS

The thought processes of children differ substantially from those of adults, just as they do between very young children and older children. These differences are not simply a matter of having less intelligence when younger and more when older. Rather, they are qualitative and are attributable to the mental structures which change over time through adaptation and organization. Piaget's research has revealed four major developmental periods, each one made up of numerous stages and substages.

SENSORIMOTOR PERIOD

The sensorimotor period extends from the beginning of life to approximately eighteen to twenty-four months of age. At the beginning of this period the infant is characterized by a profound egocentrism. Egocentrism is the inability to differentiate between subject and object. It does not imply selfishness, but is a term used by Piaget mainly to denote a particular type of cognitive deficit. Each period witnesses a decline of the form of egocentrism specific to it as intellectual progress occurs, but as the child enters the next period he experiences a new level of egocentrism.

During infancy the child does not differentiate between his sensations and their external referents. Even more broadly, he does not differentiate between himself and the outside world. Piaget is willing to allow that this is narcissism, but it is such without a Narcissus (Piaget 1924/1969). The point is that at this earliest phase of development there is no differentiated sense of self to be experienced as separate from nonself. Nevertheless, throughout infancy, there is a gradual construction of schemas which enables the child to undergo a miniature "Copernican Revolution." Hence, by the close of the sensorimotor period, the child experiences himself as only one object existing among innumerable others, each enjoying spatial positions relative to one another.

In the earlier phases of the period, the child's actions tend to be body centered, but there occurs a progressive decentering as the child's actions increasingly display a differentiation between his own body and other objects. A hallmark of intelligent behavior, the adaptation of a means to achieve an end, evolves throughout this process. Goals obtained earlier only by trial and error are eventually achieved more economically, eliminating the inefficiency of such procedures. By the end of this period the goal itself can be held in mind from the beginning of a planned sequence of actions, whereas earlier a goal would first be obtained as the result of an accidental manipulation upon the environment and, subsequently, sought deliberately (Piaget 1936/1963). Keeping pace with these accomplishments the infant is also acquiring cognitive competencies in object permanence, causality, space, and time (Piaget 1936/1971). All of these developments are significant both in themselves and as precursors to more advanced intellectual achievements. Although symbolic activity does not appear until the sixth and final stage of the sensorimotor period, Piaget views this period as the foundation of intelligence because the child's overt actions so clearly manifest intelligent behavior. Further, he cites this period as sound proof for his controversial stand that language acquisition is not a necessary condition for intelligence. In fact, he believes that the development of cognitive structures are necessary to language acquisition. A growing body of research has been providing support to Piaget's position on the language-cognition controversy (Furth 1966; Sinclair-de-Zwart 1969; Cromer 1974).

The sensorimotor period is also important because it illustrates the roots of Piaget's view that all intelligence is action. (Note that he does not maintain that all action is intelligent.) It is of course more difficult to appreciate this outlook beyond the sensorimotor period. However, Piaget insists that overt, intelligent behavior during the first period of intellectual development subsequently becomes interiorized and the solutions to problems are worked out through mental actions.

PREOPERATIONAL PERIOD

The crowning achievement of the sensorimotor period is the use of the symbol. The major attainments in goal-directed behavior, object permanence, causality, space, and time are all contingent upon the use of the symbol. The sixth stage of the sensorimotor period heralds the beginning of the preoperational period which covers the child's life from approximately eighteen to twenty-four months through six or seven years of age. The first phase of the preoperational period is characterized by the development of the semiotic function (called the symbolic function in Piaget's earlier work). It is at this point in development that representational thought arrives, allowing the child to mentally leap into the past and future. He is no longer destined to be grounded within the field of the immediate present. The semiotic function is made up of two components: signs and symbols. Signs are words and symbols like those utilized in mathematics and science. They are arbitrary in that they bear no necessary or intrinsic relationship to that which they signify, and public in that they are an agreed upon convention and socially shared. Symbols (other than those employed in mathematics and science) are such elements as dream symbols, mental images, symbolic play, and deferred imitation (Piaget 1946/1962). Both symbols and signs are called signifiers, which means that they can represent objects not present to the perceptual apparatus. However, unlike signs, symbols are motivated, tend to be ego-involved, and are private. Also, symbols resemble that which is signified. For example, a mental image can represent an absent object, but to do so it must resemble that object in some way. Conversely, a word (sign) can stand for an absent object but need not resemble it at all. In interpreting Piaget, Furth (1966) points out that he uses the term "symbolic" in a more Freudian sense than in the sense of symbolic-logic. Hence, there is an element of egocentrism about it, for it does not reflect the objective comprehension which one would look for in refined logical thinking. But it is precisely the development of logical thinking that has been the primary focus of Piagetian investigations.

The preoperational period may prove to be of exceptional interest to many clinicians. Much of Piaget's early work is devoted to the child during this period, although not confined to it, and covers such areas as language and thought (Piaget 1923/ 1955), modes of reasoning (Piaget 1924/1969), the child's view of the world and causality (Piaget 1926/1960; 1927/1969), and the development of the child's moral judgment (Piaget 1932/ 1965). On the whole, Piaget stresses the limitations rather than the achievements of this period. Nevertheless, it is quite a fascinating period of growth. During this period the child centers his thinking which means that he attends to one aspect of an object or event rather than decentering and thereby taking into account two or more aspects simultaneously. For example, if two sticks of the same size are placed side-by-side horizontally, with the left and right ends aligned evenly, the child can recognize that they are the same length. However, if the top stick is moved to the left, the young child will no longer recognize the identity of length. He will usually center on the observable fact that the top stick is further to the left and will consider it as the longer of the two. He fails to recognize that while the stick is longer at the left end it is shorter at the right end. In brief, he is not decentering as he is not taking into account simultaneously both the left and right sides of the arrangement. Although the child is now able to represent absent objects in his mind, his actual reasoning tends to be perceptually rooted in that, by centering on only one aspect of what he sees, he distorts information and draws false conclusions. Later he will develop the ability to decenter and will have constructed appropriate mental mechanisms for penetrating beyond misleading visual cues. This will enable him to process information in a more accurate and adaptive fashion.

A second major limitation of the preoperational period is irreversibility. The child is unable to follow a process from beginning to end and retrace the steps back to the starting point. A very complex or even a simple procedure may be involved. In the elementary example of the two sticks given above, the preoperational child does not yet have the capacity to grasp mentally that the procedure could be reversed, and the sticks brought back into alignment. When he becomes capable of reversible thinking he reasons that were the sticks to be realigned they would again be the same size; therefore, they must now still be the same size even though they are not evenly aligned. The child's irreversible thinking subjects him to contradictory and unsystematic thinking.

A third major limiting aspect of the preoperational period

is the static character of the child's thinking. He is not attuned to transformations, but instead centers on separate states. For example, when two beakers of the same size are established as containing an equal amount of water, he believes that there is more water in a third narrower but taller beaker after the water from one of the first two vessels is poured into it. He centers on the height of the third vessel, failing to recognize the nature of the dynamic change which he has observed occurring. He lacks the operational structures which develop in the next period and enable him to deal with tasks involving transformations.

During the latter part of the preoperational period the child undergoes a transition during which he moves from centering on states toward comprehending transformations. His thinking becomes semireversible and his capacity for conceptualizing becomes more mature. At the opening of the period he functions only at a preconceptual stage. He does not have the capacity to identify a single defining common characteristic of a class and to consistently apply it to the total range of objects to which it is applicable. Instead, for example, he will start to group objects according to color (he may place together a blue circle and a blue triangle) and then shift to using shape as a defining characteristic (possibly adding a red triangle next to the blue triangle). The thinking reflected in this illustration proceeds from particular to particular and is called transductive reasoning. It is neither inductive nor deductive. Numerous instances of children's statements exemplifying transductive reasoning are provided in the book by Piaget (1924/1969) on this subject. One of these is the child stating, "I haven't had my nap so it isn't afternoon" (p. 232). Another is, "Daddy's getting hot water, so he's going to shave" (p. 231). Of course, it is possible for the conclusions arrived at this way to be correct, but they will not necessarily be so, and when they are it will not be for the right reason. The preconcept lacks genuine individuality and genuine generality. We are all familiar with the young child who mistakes any man who walks down the street, perhaps puffing a pipe as his father usually does, to be his father. The child does not have a true concept of his father as a single individual, nor does he have a true general concept of all men forming a class, in which his father is only one member. The preconcept exists on a plane halfway between the individual and the general and is responsible for fostering transductive reasoning. Piaget (1946/1962) comments, "In other words, transduction is reasoning without reversible nestings of a hierarchy of classes and relations" (p. 234). A little further he remarks, "To sum up, it is clear that transduction, which is co-ordination without a hierarchy of nestings, remains half-way between practical reasoning, which is a continuation of sensori-motor co-ordinations, and truly logical reasoning" (p. 237). In the latter phase of the preoperational period the child is able to properly arrange concrete materials in true hierarchies. However, when questioned about these his answers reveal that he does not as yet have a genuine comprehension of inclusion in the classification systems. As an example, a child dealing with twelve wooden beads, ten of which are brown and two of which are white, would persist in thinking that there are more brown beads than wooden beads. He would continue to do this even after clearly establishing that there are a total of twelve wooden beads and that the brown beads, as well as the white beads, are indeed wooden. He lacks the ability to simultaneously consider the subclass (brown beads) and the general class (wooden beads). Once separating the part from the whole, he loses sight of the fact that the subclass is nested or included within the more general class.

Egocentrism in the preoperational period offers a fascinating topic for study. Its remnants when persisting into the adult life of an individual may explain some of the irrational behavior encountered, may account for interpersonal problems, and perhaps even psychopathology (Odier 1956; Lidz 1973). Because he does not have the ability to differentiate between his own point of view and that of others, the preoperational child cannot take the role of another. He assumes that what he thinks and feels is a predominant view shared by all. This has a far-reaching effect on his speech and social interaction (Piaget 1923/1955). The child does not bother to construct sentences which will provide the information which the listener needs for comprehension.

He uses pronouns without explanatory referents, he leaves out necessary causal connections, and he does not offer logical proof of his assertions. He appears to be under the impression that he is understood regardless of these shortcomings which, of course, he is unaware of. In brief, the child is not aware of the listener's informational needs and, therefore, makes no attempt to adapt to them. The situation is rendered even more complicated when the listener is a peer, for he, too, is locked into his own egocentrism. The listener often believes he has understood the speaker, when actually he has only assimilated what he has heard into his own meaning system. Communication of this sort rarely achieves the satisfactory results sought by the speaker. Consequently, there will be frustration and friction. It is out of the crucible of social interaction, with its increasing challenges and demands for clarification and proof, that genuinely socialized speech begins to emerge. Egocentric speech, in turn, begins to decline.

There are other quite interesting and important preoperational phenomena, such as animism, realism, and artificialism which Piaget has investigated and explains by once again invoking the concept of an underlying egocentrism. These, along with the child's tendency to see chance events in the world as motivated (psychological causality) reveal a great deal about the cosmology of the child. Piaget cautions the reader against interpreting these findings as suggesting that the child has a highly integrated and systematic world view. The verbal responses of the child reflect spontaneous thoughts to questions he had never before considered. Indeed the unsystematic character of the preoperational child's thinking is one of its most striking features.

CONCRETE OPERATIONAL PERIOD

The third major epoch of intellectual development is the period of concrete operations. Much of what has occurred during the previous period has been preparatory for the achievements of the concrete plane. Marking the arrival of the concrete operational period is a systematic network of cognitive structures.

The period generally starts at about six or seven years of age and continues until about eleven or twelve. The growing child is now capable of consistent and logical thought processes which take place internally. Flavell (1963), in comparing the previous period and the one now under consideration has stated the following:

> In the preoperational period the child does possess, of course, representational actions in various states of internalization. But these preoperational actions, which Piaget sometimes labels *intuitions,* are sporadic and isolated cognitive expressions which do not coalesce into the tight ensembles we have been discussing (p. 166).

The operations of this period are called concrete because they apply to objects and not to verbal hypotheses. A wide range of physical materials has been utilized to test children in the Piagetian tasks of this period. The tasks include classification, seriation, one to one correspondences, and conservation of many kinds. Possibly because of the heavy emphasis on these materials, a notion has arisen in which it is believed that concrete operations can only be applied to objects which are visible and present in the environment. Lewis (1963) suggests a broader interpretation as found in the remarks which follow:

> In saying that all this thinking still tends to be concrete in nature, Piaget does not mean that the child's reasoning is necessarily confined to what is present to his senses. In memory and in imagination the child can transport himself in time and space. But his thinking remains concrete so long as it is bound to the actual features of a situation—present or absent—rather than free to explore and deal with new and abstract relationships or to entertain a hypothesis and reason from it (p. 169).

The logical structures of the concrete operational period are called groupings and involve both the logic of relations and the logic of class inclusion. The former has already been alluded to in the discussion on seriation, or ordering. It entails a type of reversible thinking known as reciprocity. In other words, if A is greater than B, then reciprocally B is less than A. Transitivity is still another operation which the child has constructed and which applies here. It is the ability to draw conclusions about two elements through comparison with an intermediary element. For example, if A equals B and B equals C, then it follows that A equals C. At the concrete operational period transitivity can be applied to real objects, but it is not until the formal operational period that it can be performed on a purely verbal level.

The logic of class inclusion entails reversible thinking known as negation or inversion. For example, in the grouping referred to as additive composition, the child can combine elements into a nesting of hierarchies and separate them by subtraction, thereby restoring the original position. For example, boys plus girls equal children. Children plus adults equal human beings. These additive compositions can be reversed. Adults removed from human beings leave children. Girls removed from children leave boys. In algebraic terms, $A + A^1 = B$. Negating the process, $B - A^1 = A$ (Pulaski 1971). The initial operation carried out in one direction is cancelled by reversing the operation to restore the original position. Multiple classification is also a cognitive competency arrived at in this period. Formerly only able to attend to one feature of an object at a time, the child can now attend to two features of an object simultaneously. A banana, for example, can be viewed as both yellow and long. Class multiplication of this type is called bi-univocal and constitutes another of what Piaget calls groupings. There is a total of nine groupings of logical classes and relations which actually are quite complicated. The reader who seeks to grapple with these may wish to consult Flavell (1963) or Inhelder and Piaget (1955/1958; 1959/1969).

The characteristics of preoperational thinking which have been cited as limitations are eliminated with the development of concrete operations. The child is no longer misled by perceptual cues. He does not mistake appearance for reality. The ability to decenter or attend to several aspects of a situation simultaneously, replaces centration. Thinking is no longer static but relates to transformations. Irreversibility gives way to reversibility of thought. All of these changes signifying more adaptive thinking are beautifully illustrated in conservation, a Piagetian task of singular import. Piaget's position is that all rational activity is necessarily contingent upon conservation. Conservation is the capacity to grasp that, despite certain changes in an object or set of objects, there are particular properties which remain unchanged. For example, given two balls of clay of equal amounts, reshaping one so that it is elongated will change the shape, but the two objects will still possess the same amount of clay. As another example, suppose that there is one row of ten pennies spread out evenly. Directly under each penny is a corresponding button. Will condensing one of the two rows change the number in each set? The preoperational child thinks that it will, even though he realizes that originally there were ten objects in each set. On the other hand, the concrete operational child will conserve number, knowing that changing the arrangement does not alter the actual number in either of the two rows. Conservation studies are numerous and apply to a wide range of fields including substance, weight, volume, number, length, distance, area, time, and speed. A great deal of cross-cultural research has been done utilizing conservation tasks, most of which has confirmed Piaget's findings. It has been of considerable interest to note that the conservation of substance, weight, and volume does not emerge all at once, but is found to develop sequentially over a span of years, covering the concrete operational period, in the order listed above.

In the preoperational period the child fails to conserve in all areas. Generally around the age of six or seven he shows evidence of realizing that, in the case of the two equal balls of clay, the amount remains the same even though the shape of one has been transformed. Piaget believes that this newly emerging ability is based on several operations which have been constructed through the child's interaction with the environment and his own self-regulating mechanisms. Methodologically, Piaget poses questions to the child so that he can ascertain the line of reasoning which enables the child to conclude that conservation has taken place. The conserving child generally offers one or more of several explanations. He may say that the elongated piece of clay contains the same amount as it did before, and the same amount as the remaining ball of clay, because nothing has been added and nothing has been subtracted. Piaget calls this the identity operation. An alternative explanation often presented is the assertion that the sausage-shaped piece of clay could be compressed back into its original form and, therefore, it must possess the same amount it had at the outset of the experiment. The reader will perhaps recognize this as the type of reversible thinking known as negation or inversion. Lastly, the child will sometimes use an operation called compensation, which enables him to recognize that what has been gained in length is lost in width; hence, there has been no overall change in amount. In other words, although the sausage-shaped clay is now longer than it was originally, it has become narrower, which compensates for the gain in length. Piaget also refers to this operation as reciprocity, another form of reversible thinking.

What if there were no cognitive competencies allowing for conservation in the many areas cited earlier? Science and modern technology as we know it could hardly exist. Indeed, everyday life would most likely be a chaotic affair, as the order and consistency necessary for civilization would not be possible. Yet somehow children all over the world do develop these cognitive capacities, in the same invariable sequence, even though they are rarely ever taught conservation directly. Conservation arrived at through natural interaction between the child and his environment has two outstanding characteristics. The first is its stability. It is not likely that the child will regress to a preconservation stage once he progresses beyond the initial phase of the preliminary acquisition of the relevant operations. The second is the logical certitude upon which the recognition of conservation is predicated. A child who has arrived at conservation competencies through the development of operational structures is unlikely to be misled by perceptual cues. He knows as a logical necessity that the mere reshaping of one of two objects, previously established as equal in substance, weight, and volume, will not alter the equality in those dimensions (Smedslund 1961).

FORMAL OPERATIONAL PERIOD

The period of formal operations, ranging approximately from eleven to fifteen years, is the last major cognitive epoch to evolve. Reality, with which the child's logical operations has been dealing with until now, becomes subsumed by the realm of the possible. Inhelder and Piaget (1955/1958) state the following:

> In other words, formal thinking is essentially hypothetico-deductive. By this we mean that the deduction no longer refers directly to perceived realities but to hypothetical statements, i.e., it refers to propositions which are formulations of hypotheses or which formulate facts or events independently of whether or not they actually occur (p. 251).

Operations of the concrete operational period involve real objects and, therefore, are first-degree operations. On the other hand, formal operations are second-degree operations. They go beyond the actual and the known object to employ hypotheticodeductive reasoning. Inhelder and Piaget (1955/1958) observe that

> The connection indicated by the words "if . . . then" (inferential implication) links a required logical consequence to an assertion whose truth is merely a possibility (p. 257).

The young adolescent has now become capable of pursuing hypothetico-deductive reasoning by successfully designing and executing a scientific experiment. He can assess a situation, isolate single variables while holding all other variables constant, and proceed to draw logical conclusions based upon accurate observation of what takes place. Further, he has acquired the ability to successfully solve some problems through the use of combinatorial analysis. Given a range of elements and a task of discovering which particular combinations produce a specifically desired effect, he can arrange the elements in such a way as to systematically and exhaustively test all possible combinations.

Piaget has taken the empirical findings of his long-term collaborator, B. Inhelder, and explained them in their book (Inhelder and Piaget 1955/1958), through the use of two logical models which he maintains govern the mental performance of formal operations. They are the sixteen binary operations and the INRC group. The interested reader can pursue these in greater depth by consulting Flavell (1963), and Boyle (1969). These models of logical operations which Piaget uses to explain the higher order thinking of formal operations are part of a cognitive unconscious. The complex and systematic network of mental structures which enable formal operational thought is not known to the thinker as such. The surface procedures for arriving at a solution and the solution, or end product, are what are known to the thinker. It is only Piaget and those who study his work who become familiar with the essential nature of these structures, which Piaget believes truly do exist. Perhaps this could be viewed as analogous to the psychodynamic position which holds that one can experience an affect without necessarily knowing the dynamic process which had led to it. Nevertheless, by becoming familiar with Freud's metapsychology and defense mechanisms, one can understand the nature of the underlying process which can lead to the affect. Of course, in psychodynamic theory, the same affect can be arrived at by different paths. However, in Piagetian theory cognitive performance can only be accomplished if the structures necessary to the task are present and utilized. Indeed, although it will not be pursued here, the cognitive-developmental position in general would hold that certain cognitive structures are a necessary, although not sufficient condition to the individual's unfolding emotional life.

The achievement of formal operations are not predetermined, and it does not follow that all people will attain them. Observations of some primitive tribes suggest that adult members of the entire group may not have reached the formal operational period. However, this is a debatable issue and it is entirely possible that, while formal operations are theoretically independent of the content to which they are applied, in actual practice an individual may appear to utilize them in some areas and not in others. Piaget's (1972) recent comments on this are suggestive:

> In brief, our third hypothesis would state that all normal subjects attain the stage of formal operations or structuring if not between 11-12 to 14-15 years, in any case between 15 and 20 years. However, they reach this stage in different areas according to their aptitudes and their professional specializations (advanced studies

or different types of apprenticeship for the various trades): the way in which these formal structures are used, however, is not necessarily the same in all cases (pp. 9-10).

A formal structure seems . . . generalizable as it deals with hypotheses. However, it is one thing to dissociate the form from the content in a field which is of interest to the subject and within which he can apply his curiosity and initiative, and it is another to be able to generalize this same spontaneity of research and comprehension to a field foreign to the subject's career and interest (p. 10).

The issue dealing with the applicability of formal operations to a range of content has been emphasized here because of its extreme importance to any consideration of human growth and potential. Although Piaget does not posit the development or existence of operational structures beyond the formal period, he certainly does not believe that intellectual progress stops at adolescence or early youth. Having constructed formal operations an individual can extend their application to ever widening areas and, in addition, can utilize them to gain increasing mastery in great depth over a single chosen area. Piaget's own intensive efforts and prodigious output over a long lifetime is perhaps the most immediately relevant demonstration of this potential.

Egocentrism in the concrete operational period is seen in the child's inability to differentiate between the newly achieved structures and the actual objects or content to which they are applied. As stated earlier, in the formal operational period, the newly constructed logical structures enable thinking logically within the wider realm of the possible, encompassing reality as merely one subset of what is possible. The adolescent arriving at the final period of cognitive development begins to look to the future and to experiment mentally with adult roles. He generates a multitude of abstract theories about the way society ought to be and is unmindful of the point of view which characterizes those who have been living and struggling for a much longer time in the society he hopes to reform. Highly speculative philosophical and political ventures are typical at this time in development. Inhelder and Piaget (1955/1958) comment as follows:

> The indefinite extension of powers of thought made possible by the new instruments of propositional logic at first is conducive to a failure to distinguish between the ego's new and unpredicted capacities and the social or cosmic universe to which they are applied. In other words, the adolescent goes through a phase in which he attributes an unlimited power to his own thoughts so that the dream of a glorious future or of transforming the world through Ideas (even if this idealism takes a materialistic form) seems to be not only fantasy but also an effective action which in itself modifies the empirical world. This is obviously a form of cognitive egocentrism (pp. 345-346).

Decentration from this egocentrism of adolescence is facilitated largely by the establishment of peer groups in which ideas are expressed and tested out on one another. It is within this social context that the adolescent may discover the vulnerability of his ideas. Of even greater significance in fostering the decline of egocentrism in this period is passage into an occupation or a professional training. Taking a job places the adolescent in an adult role and in doing so he undergoes a transition from idealistic reformer to achiever. However, the transition is a slow one, as the adolescent's belief in the omnipotence of thought persists for some time to come. Nevertheless, the ultimate decline of egocentrism when achieved liberates the individual's thinking so that it is characterized by objectivity and reciprocity. He can now differentiate between his own thought and reality, between his own point of view and society's; in brief, he entertains multiple perspectives simultaneously and coordinates these many viewpoints in his own mind. If there is ever to be a universal and prolonged epoch of peace, it will be forged and maintained by people who have rid themselves of cognitive egocentrism.

STAGES AND TRANSITIONS

In the foregoing exposition of Piaget's work there have been many references to the concept of stages. A review and refinement of the implications of this aspect of the system is now in order. The exquisitely detailed empirical validation of the innumerable and complex facets of human cognitive development will not be discussed here, but can be found throughout the books and articles which Piaget has authored over a lifetime of dedicated professional work. What becomes evident, however, in examining these detailed observations is that there is an invariable sequence to each stage of development. For example, if a particular competency is observed to develop in the sequence ABC, it would be predicted that it will always develop in that order and it would not be predicted that an alternate order, such as ACB would be observed. Piaget has discovered that conservation of substance, weight, and volume always appears in exactly that sequence, spanning the concrete operational period and with an interim of approximately two years between each stage. The early roots of conservation can be observed in the development of object permanence, which occurs in six invariably ordered stages during the sensorimotor period. Familiarity with these stages reveals an internal logic which makes the invariable character of their development not at all surprising. An approach to studying Piaget which will facilitate comprehension is to examine each stage of cognitive competency in relation to its preceding and subsequent stages. The principle to bear in mind is that a given stage represents an advance over the former stage and a limitation in relation to the following one. This applies to the broader periods (sometimes called stages themselves) as well. For example, as already noted, the concrete operational period is characterized by a systematic and well-integrated network of logical structures in contrast to the preoperational period which is unsystematic, not well-integrated, and lacking in the ability to apply consistently logical operations. Nevertheless, the concrete operational child can only apply logical operations to real or familiar events and lacks the ability to perform hypothetico-deductive reasoning or to engage in systematic combinatorial analysis.

Piaget's views are often misunderstood to mean that arriving at a particular level of development signifies that all cognitive functioning is characterized by that level. It is more accurate to recognize that a child, or even an adult, who has arrived at a certain level of development possesses the underlying structures needed for the type of performances typical of that level, and at times demonstrates behavior governed by those structures, but does not necessarily do so in all of his cognitive functioning. The brilliant scientist who exercises his formal operational thinking constantly in the laboratory may not evidence the same high level of cognitive functioning in his personal life and decision-making. Furthermore, certain rudiments of primitive stages of development may persist into adulthood. For example, the earliest stages of development during infancy show the child behaving in the causal sphere as if spatial contact were not necessary to produce certain effects upon objects. The infant may kick his foot in the air repeatedly as if to duplicate a previous effect of moving a rattle dangling on a string which the infant's foot had fortuitously hit a few moments before. Rudiments of this early magical stage can be seen in adults who seek to change a red light by snapping their fingers, influence the weather by carrying an umbrella on a clear day, or affect the outcome of a ballgame they may be observing, by their own body movements (Pulaski 1971).

The stage concept is often confused with the various ages that are so frequently cited in Piagetian literature. It has never been Piaget's intention to assert that specific cognitive competencies appear automatically at given ages. Such a viewpoint would be more in keeping with a maturational position. Although Piaget fully recognizes the necessity for neurophysiological maturation to occur, he does not believe that such maturation is a sufficient condition to produce the various stages which the developing child undergoes. Piaget is an interactionist and, therefore, places considerable emphasis upon the facilitative nature of the child interacting with people, objects, and events in the environment. As a result, contrary to what one would predict from a maturational view, there may be great differences in rate of development from individual to individual and perhaps even more so from culture to culture. The invariable sequence of the stages is what is universal and does not differ. When Piaget cites a certain age as the time when a problem is solved he is utilizing a statistical convention, signifying that three-fourths of the children of that age have supplied the correct answer. More fully, if a problem is said to be solved at age seven, then it also follows that one-half of the children at age six can solve it and one-third of the children at age five.

The progression from stage to stage is not really a simple matter, but is actually a complex one based on the continuing organization and integration of preceding structures. Thus each new structure, while qualitatively different from its predecessors, subsumes the previous ones into a more highly organized network of structures. Piaget (1960) states as follows:

> Inhelder and I, when considering the development of structures and of thought, speak of stages only in connexion with the formation of total structures. We include as special cases all structures observable during a given stage which integrate with the structures of the preceding stage as necessary sub-structures (p. 11).

A discussion of cognitive development through stages inevitably gives rise to the question of what the mechanism is which accounts for the transition from one stage to the next. Piaget identifies four factors influencing development which are heredity and the maturation of the nervous system, interaction with the physical environment involving the manipulation of objects, social transmission, and equilibration. It is the last of these which is most strongly emphasized in the Piagetian framework and which actually coordinates development in the other three spheres. The concepts of disequilibrium, equilibration, and equilibrium are not especially easy to grasp. Frequent exposure to them in a variety of contexts will undoubtedly increase one's familiarity with and comprehension of them. They are vital to Piaget's system and have far-reaching implications for the fields of education and psychotherapy. Langer (1969), in commenting upon the probabilistic model which Piaget adopts to explain the equilibration process, states succinctly:

The thesis is that, when the child is in a structural state of equilibrium, his assimilatory and accommodatory functions act to establish greater equilibrium. This can only come about by the performance of those actions that compensate for the perturbation and then feedback of the information obtained by these acts to the operative mental system. In this way the child changes his mental actions and develops (p. 24).

In Piaget's (1960) own words:

An apparatus which solves problems by a succession of approximations based on a series of feedbacks shows in the most decisive manner the part played by the concepts of disequilibrium and of progressive equilibration. As long as there is disequilibrium, i.e. while the problem still remains unsolved, a new negative feedback is set off, whereas the attainment of the correct solution is marked by the production of a state of equilibrium (p. 9).

In the same context Piaget (see also Flavell [1963]), elaborates an example dealing with the development of the conservation of substance. He cites the study of a child six or seven years old who, at the outset, denies the existence of the conservation of substances. A ball of clay is elongated and the child adopts the strategy that there is more substance in state B (sausage shaped) than in state A (ball shaped) because it is longer. Note that he is centering on one aspect (length) only, from which he reasons. Further elongation leads the child to the same conclusion, namely that there is even more in state C because it is "still longer." However, in the next phase the error is corrected by negative feedback, for as the clay continues to be lengthened the quality of thinness, until now disregarded, becomes prominent. In fact, during this intermediary phase, the child will now say there is less clay since he observes that it has become "too thin." Of course, he is actually still in error as he has merely substituted one centration, length, for another, thinness.

There then follows a stage of oscillation during which the child hesitatingly goes back and forth between saying first that there is more clay and then that there is less. At this time he lacks the coordination of actions which reversibility imparts. In the fourth phase, however, his strategy shifts and he attends not exclusively to one aspect of the phenomenon or another, but instead he attends to the transformation itself. In so doing, he recognizes that what is gained in length is lost in width and, hence, through this compensatory mechanism grasps that there is no overall change in the amount. In other words, the coordination of actions now takes place through a self-regulating process known as equilibration, which leads to the achievement of conservation of substance.

It is noteworthy that this has taken place with a child, age six or seven, who is already at the brink of acquiring the conservation of substance. If this procedure were to be attempted with a much younger child, it is not likely that the same outcome would occur. Similarly, if it were to be attempted with children of the same age, but using conservation of weight or volume, it would again be unlikely that there would have been the same outcome. Briefly, the developmental level of the child will determine whether or not he can meaningfully utilize new factors introduced into his environment. This gives rise to the principle of moderate novelty, which urges that to stimulate further development the new stimuli (cognitive aliment) should be neither monotonously what the child is already familiar with, nor too dissimilar from what he is presently familiar with. Inhelder, Sinclair, and Bovet (1974) in a recent work on the subject under discussion conclude their book by remarking:

> It is no less erroneous to assume that cognitive learning consists in the activation of already existing structures than to suppose that it consists in a substitution of new modes of reasoning for old. Learning is a constantly renewed process of synthesis between continuity and novelty (pp. 271-272).

Their work, reflecting years of research based on a Piagetian theoretical model, is a major breakthrough in the field of training studies designed to assist the passage of the subject from one stage of cognitive development to the next. Relatively primitive and uncoordinated schemas are not viewed as imparting mistaken or false information which must be eliminated by training or coercion. Such schemas are regarded as indicative of necessary stages which the developing child must undergo and, however inadequate at the time, they provide the "foundation for further constructions" (p. 25).

Concepts of cognitive conflict, incongruity, and subjective dissatisfaction are all relevant to Piaget's view of mental development. Inhelder, Sinclair, and Bovet (1974) have focused specifically on these areas. Their studies emphasize the kindling of the child's curiosity followed by the cognitive conflict introduced when his predictions are not matched by the events to follow in an experiment.

CONCLUSION

The full scope of Piaget's work is staggering. Beyond what has been touched upon in this overview, he has authored books on space (Piaget and Inhelder 1948/1967), geometry (Piaget, Inhelder and Szeminski 1948/1960), time (Piaget 1927/1971), movement and speed (Piaget 1946/1971), imagery (Piaget and Inhelder 1966/1971), memory (Piaget and Inhelder 1968/1973), chance (Piaget and Inhelder 1951/1975) and perception (Piaget 1961/1969). A recent publication on causality (Piaget 1971/1974) states in the foreword that about one hundred studies, already completed and prepared, on the subject of causality, will be divided into small books for later publication. Piaget is now retired from his duties as head of the Center of Genetic Epistemology in Geneva, Switzerland, although this does not mean that he is inactive.

The impact of Piaget's work has been felt in such fields as philosophy, education, psychotherapy, psychopathology, and developmental psychology. Despite earlier and still occasional references to psychoanalysis, Piaget's work has been pursued independently of Freud's and of recent psychoanalytic refinements. There are certainly differences between Freud and Piaget, but these are open to reconciliation, as their respective emphases upon affect and cognition are more complementary than antagonistic. Indeed, Piaget has asserted repeatedly his essential conviction that affect and cognition are indissociable even though he has devoted his professional life to researching and studying the latter. In a lecture given to the American Society of Psychoanalysis and later published Piaget (1973) suggested that thought be given to developing a general psychology which would integrate the findings of both psychoanalysis and genetic epistemology. He acknowledged that there are many problems yet to be solved. Perhaps it was his purpose to incite our curiosity, initiate a new cognitive conflict, and to serve as an impetus toward equilibration. This in turn would lead to coordinating psychoanalysis and genetic epistemology, structures in the history of ideas, and ultimately to the emergence of a new construction that would enable us to better understand ourselves and fellow human beings.

2

EMERGING AND DECLINING EGOCENTRISM

INTRODUCTION

Human development in the Piagetian system may be construed as a series of progressions toward objective relativism. Objective relativism, which allows for maximum adaptation to the environment, is achieved through the decline and conquest of egocentrism. The concept of egocentrism pervades Piaget's cognitive-developmental psychology and a sound grasp of it is essential to comprehending his work. Although Piaget's emphasis has been upon cognitive development in relation to the physical world, it has been proposed that egocentrism may prove to be a significant link between cognition and personality dynamics (Feffer 1967; Elkind 1974). Furthermore, since egocentrism is a negative and limiting feature of development it provides fertile grounds for exploring psychopathological phenomena in both the intrapsychic and interpersonal realms.

Despite his emphasis upon the physical world, Piaget was quite mindful of the contribution of social interaction to cognitive development and, indeed, of the contribution of cognitive structures to interpersonal relationships in both the moral and social spheres (Piaget 1932/1965; 1947/1966). Because of the potential relevance of egocentrism to clinicians in the helping professions, this chapter will examine its nature and decline in depth.

Piaget's cognitive-developmental psychology is comprised of an unvarying sequence of major periods, stages, and substages. As the child interacts with his environment, he constructs new cognitive structures over time which afford him increasingly more

33

adaptive prowess within his physical and social worlds. Each
period is characterized by a superior set of newly developed
structures which move in the direction of greater complexity
and coordination. Although development at each advanced level
introduces qualitatively different and better organized structures,
there is a common reemerging negative characteristic that stands
as a limitation at the threshold of every new period. This re-
appearing phenomenon is egocentrism. In the most general sense
it refers to a lack of differentiation between subject and object,
between knower and known. Despite this basic definition, egocentrism will be seen to take diverse forms determined by the
particular developmental period under examination.

There are fundamentally two types of egocentricity, one
existing on the ontological plane and the other on the logical
plane (Piaget 1926/1960). The former illuminates for us the
child's world view of reality and causality, whereas the latter
reveals a great deal about his judgment and reasoning. In
ontological egocentrism the child does not experience the resistance
of matter. Piaget (1926/1960) states, "Reality is impregnated
with self and thought is conceived as belonging to the category
of physical matter. From the point of view of causality, all the
universe is felt to be in communion with and obedient to the
self" (p. 167). The child's own desires and commands are felt
to reign supreme because for him there exists no other point
of view. In logical egocentrism, the child is unaware of the fact
that others may have viewpoints which differ from his. He
feels as if his own perspective is the only one possible, and,
therefore, he does not recognize a need to offer proofs or verify
his assumptions and assertions. It can be readily appreciated
that this deficiency is likely to precipitate serious social difficulties,
especially if carried over into adulthood. Underlying both types
of egocentrism is a confusion between the subject's own convic-
tions and those of others and between himself and the outside
world. Although Piaget does use the word confusion in this
context, it might be even more apt to speak of a "fusion" between inner and outer, between subject and object.

RADICAL EGOCENTRISM

During infancy there exists the most radical type of egocentrism in which self and external world are totally undifferentiated. In fact, initially there is no self at all and it is only through a gradual process of interaction with the environment that the infant simultaneously builds a self and differentiates from the objects in the milieu. Piaget (1936/1971) writes, "Intelligence thus begins neither with knowledge of the self nor of things as such but with knowledge of their interaction, and it is by orienting itself simultaneously toward the two poles of that interaction that intelligence organizes the world by organizing itself" (p. 400). The early infant does not differentiate between his own actions upon things and the independent existence of objects upon which he acts. Similarly, the sensations and perceptions he experiences are fused with the objects which are not accorded any separate permanence outside of the infant's sensating and perceiving activities. The infant takes his own activities to be the cause of effects in the environment, even though there may be no spatial contact. For example, an infant who produced the sound of a rattle by accidentally kicking it, may be observed at a later time attempting to produce the same sound by kicking his feet in the air without any striving for proximity or contact with the rattle. Although this problem is resolved on a practical level by the end of the sensorimotor period (eighteen to twenty-four months), it is the precursor of the problem of psychological causality in the following period of preoperational thought.

By surmounting the problem of object permanence in particular, the infant contributes greatly toward the decline of radical egocentrism. At the start of life he gives evidence of having no appreciation whatsoever, even on a purely practical level, that an object removed from his vision continues to exist. Through a series of six successive stages, however, he does obtain a cognitive structure or schema, as Piaget calls it, to deal with object permanence. Prior to the fourth stage, a child who has been playing with a ball which is then taken from him and hidden under a cushion will make no effort to retrieve it. At the fourth stage (eight to twelve months), the child will retrieve the ball under the condition described. However, at the time when he is just able to engage in this strategy, if he observes the ball being removed from cushion A and placed under cushion B, he will continue to seek the ball under cushion A, the place where he first found it. It is not until the fifth stage (twelve to eighteen months) that he develops the ability to cope with visible displacements, which means that he will go directly to cushion B to retrieve the ball, even though he had previously discovered it under cushion A. However, his capacity for doing this at stage five is contingent upon observing the ball as it is being moved from A to B. If in the process of the movement the ball were to be concealed in the hand of the experimenter, the child would revert to looking under cushion A and would make no attempt, upon not finding it, to look under cushion B. According to Piaget, the strategy for handling invisible displacements does not appear until the sixth stage (one and a half to two years).

There are many subtleties and substages to the development of object permanence which have not been covered in this highly schematic presentation. Nevertheless, it is hoped that the reader will derive a sense of the gradualness with which cognitive structures are constructed through stages. By the end of the sensorimotor period the child has undergone a profound evolution from primitive reflex activity, such as grasping and sucking, to the attainment of the symbolic function which permits representational thought. Developments in space, time, causality, object permanence, and means-end behavior have led to a differentiation between self and external world on a practical sensorimotor plane. The most primitive experience of egocentrism has been conquered. In the words of Piaget (1936/1971), "The elaboration of the universe by sensorimotor intelligence constitutes the transition from a state in which objects are centered about a self which believes it directs them, although completely unaware of itself as subject, to a state in which the self is placed, at least practically, in a stable world conceived as independent of personal activity" (p. 395).

ONTOLOGICAL EGOCENTRISM

In the study of the child beyond infancy we encounter another array of fascinating developments bearing on egocentrism. These are to be found mainly in Piaget's first five books (1923/ 1955; 1924/1969; 1926/1960; 1927/1969; 1932/1965).

The child before the age of seven or eight does not recognize chance in the course of events. All that occurs in nature is seen as willed. There is a constant search for justification and motivation of events which, in fact, do not permit such explanation because, as the child only later comes to recognize, they are due to chance or determined by physical laws. More positive and accurate explanations of causality emerge at seven to eight years of age and by eleven to twelve years there has developed a genuine understanding of physical causality. The child has progressively undergone a separation between self and universe. Causal sequences, which had been conceived of as occurring without intermediary links are eventually objectified, and the need for such links, rather than one's own desires or existence, are recognized as causal factors. There are as many as seventeen different types of causality in child thought as observed by Piaget. Only a few will be cited here to illustrate the manner in which the child's own subjectivity interpenetrates with his universe.

First, there is psychological causality or motivation. As an example, Piaget (1927/1969) cites the fact that children often believe God has sent them a dream because they have done something wrong. As another example, Piaget tells of a child who explained a large mountain and a small mountain by saying that the former existed for adults and the latter for children. There is also phenomenalistic causality in which two facts observed contiguously in time and space are taken to be causally related, even though there may be no actual causal relation. For example, a pebble which has sunk to the bottom of the water has done so because of its color, or the moon is suspended in the sky because it is yellow. Piaget (1927/1969) puts it succinctly: "Anything

may produce anything" (p. 259). Relationships are readily seen
between things in the universe when, in fact, none exist. Until age
four or five, children tend to believe not only that the moon
follows them, but that it is their own movements which force
the moon to move along with them. Piaget refers to this as
magical thinking. At age four or five, the child shifts from
magical to animistic thinking and believes that the moon is
following him because it is alive and willfully attempting to do
so. Artificialist causality is the belief that things are made by
humans through their own activity. Therefore, such things as
bodies of water, mountains, and the stars are viewed as products
of man's own activity. Finalistic causality is founded on the belief
that all things are created for a purpose. Relevant to the preceding
comments, Piaget (1926/1960) has written, "In fact the child
always begins by regarding his own point of view as absolute. . . .
In so far as he ignores that his own point of view is subjective
he believes himself the centre of the world, whence follow a whole
group of finalistic, animistic, and quasi-magical conceptions. . . ."
(pp. 126-127).

Animism is an intriguing aspect of child development. The
young child generally conceives of everything in the universe as
being alive or at least potentially alive. He virtually endows inanimate objects with such living properties as will, consciousness,
and purposiveness. Initially all objects may be the locus of conscious activity. Although not said to be conscious at all times,
a rock, for example, may feel nothing, but if moved may feel
something. One child queried at age eight and a half and again
a year later replied that the sun could see, a button could feel
pain if torn off material, and a twisted piece of string that was
unwinding was aware of its condition and wanted to get untwisted.
As in so many of the areas uncovered by Piaget, progress is
made through an unvarying sequence of stages. In the second stage
of animistic thinking, consciousness is ascribed only to things
which move spontaneously or whose special function it is to
move, such as clouds, rivers, and bicycles. Upon arriving at the
realization that such things as bicycles do not possess an intrinsic
capacity for motion, the child no longer ascribes consciousness

to them and reserves that attribute to things he continues to believe are capable of spontaneous motion. A child of eight years four months, in the third stage told Piaget (1926/1960) that a bicycle wasn't alive "because it has to be made to go" (p. 185), while at the same time he exclaimed that water can feel because it flows, fire because it is alive can move, and grass can feel because it is alive and it is alive because it grows.

Finally, in the fourth stage, which is not reached on the average until eleven to twelve years of age, the child restricts consciousness only to animals. One can readily discern in this progression a diminishing anthropomorphic extension of the child's own attributes to the external world. Gradually he forges a proper separation between himself and the objects populating his world. Although ages have occasionally been quoted to provide the reader with some guideposts, it is important to remember that they reflect only averages and that wide variations will be found on an interindividual, as well as intercultural basis. It is the sequences of the developmental stages in each area which are not likely to vary. Additionally, the various phenomena which have been under examination here are not found in the child in the form of an aware, carefully thought out in advance, system of thought. Piaget (1926/1960) is clear in stating, "In the child, animism is much more a general trend, a framework into which explanations are fitted than a consciously systematic belief" (p. 188).

The final concept to be examined in this section is intellectual realism which is grounded in the child's confusion between the physical and the psychical. The young child takes an essentially psychic event and ascribes to it an external reality. Names are conceived of as being an attribute of the object named, and, during an intermediary stage of development, they are believed to be dissociable from the object, but not yet accorded the status of a purely mental activity. Hence, one youngster was able to say that her cousin's name remained at the airport when the cousin boarded a plane and flew off for a trip. However, in the first stage of nominal realism, the object is virtually believed to contain the name, so that the white object which is the moon actually contains within it the name "moon." Eventually, of course, this confusion between the signs and the things signified disappears and the two are separated.

The child's early attitudes about dreams serve as still another and quite excellent example of realism. In the first stage (approximately five to six years), the child thinks the dream has originated outside of himself and even after awakening he views it as true in the same sense that other memories of his previous activities are a record of actual events. During the intermediary stage, the child (average age seven to eight years) recognizes that the dream has originated within himself, but continues to ascribe external existence to it. Finally, in the third stage (about nine to ten years), he appreciates that the dream is purely a mental event and he no longer believes that it has any objective status.

In summing up this portion of our exposition on ontological egocentrism, Piaget's (1964/1968) own words are most pertinent:

> . . . . these diverse manifestations of this early thinking are consistent in their prelogical character. They all manifest a deforming assimilation of reality to the child's own activity. Physical movements are directed toward a goal because the child's own movements are goal-oriented. Force is active and substantial because it is conceived on the model of muscular strength. Physical reality is animated and alive, while natural laws must be obeyed. In short, all of reality is construed with the self as the model (pp. 28-29).

THE LOGICAL FORM OF EGOCENTRISM

A classic example of the young child's inability to take the perspective of another is clearly illustrated in the three-mountain problem cited in Piaget's and Inhelder's book on space (1948/ 1967). Although the ultimate achievement involves a series of subtle advances, only a brief, but essential, exposition will be presented here. Placed before the child is a simulated model of three mountains, each containing such items as trees and log cabins variously situated. The task of the child is to tell what the view of the experimenter seated across from him is. In a variation of this, the experimenter places a doll at different spots around the model, with the expectation that the child will report what he thinks the doll's perspective is. The basic finding in this experimental task is that the child's capacity for accurate reporting shows a definite progression through stages as he grows older.

More striking, however, is the fact that the child in the experiment persists in describing only his own point of view even when asked to describe a variety of viewpoints as the doll is moved around the model. The opportunity to view photographs of several views from varying positions or to actually walk around the model to observe the viewpoints has no effect on the resilient egocentrism of the child. Invariably, despite being exposed to these opportunities, the child reports his own viewpoint upon resuming the task. The problem is solved as the child develops from egocentric realism in which his own viewpoint is taken as an objective absolute to a capacity to entertain multiple perspectives simultaneously and, hence, engage in relational coordination. The egocentric child tends to center on one aspect of a reality at a time and is easily misled by perceptual cues. The decline of egocentrism is related to the increasing capacity to decenter or take into account multiple perspectives simultaneously. The egocentric child lacks awareness that he holds a viewpoint which is differentiated from those of others and he ascribes a false-absolute to his personal centration. In time he constructs the cognitive structures which enable him to differentiate his own distinct viewpoint from those of others and to coordinate it with the various other perspectives. Thus, he eventually achieves objective relativity.

The inability to take the perspective of another, referred to by some as role-taking, was discussed at length in Piaget's first book (1923/1955), which was devoted to language and thought. Piaget's observations have led him to distinguish between egocentric logic and communicable logic. In the former, thinking is more intuitive than deductive and little effort is made to be explicit about the line of reasoning pursued. The child jumps in his reasoning from premise to conclusion without appropriate intermediary logical links. He does not feel constrained to verify his propositions or to offer proof of his assertions to those whom he addresses. Pronouns are freely utilized without clarity regarding the objects or people to whom they refer. In addition, causal connections such as "because" and "altogether" are rarely used properly. It is not until age seven or eight that communicable logic emerges leading to socialized speech in which a desire to be truly heard and understood becomes evident. When the child is still predominantly egocentric he lacks the desire to effectively communicate and to genuinely understand what others are attempting to communicate. The reader is cautioned to bear in mind that shades of socialized speech will gradually appear prior to the suggested average ages of seven or eight, just as egocentric speech will persist to some degree beyond those ages. The young listener also poses problems in achieving genuinely socialized communication. He frequently believes he has understood what has been conveyed to him when, in fact, he very often has not. Piaget (1923/1955) addresses this problem directly:

> When the child hears people talk, he makes an effort, not so much to adapt himself and share the point of view of the other person as to assimilate everything he hears to his own point of view and to his own stock of information. An unknown word therefore seems to him less unknown than it would if he really tried to adapt himself to the other person (p. 164).

Egocentrism is, of course, characterized by being locked into one's own perspective and an accompanying inability to take the point of view of another. Consequently, it would follow that an egocentric speaker would not be able to discern the informational needs of the listener and that this would be reflected in the paucity of his syntax. Similarly, the young listener does not realize that an alternate viewpoint is being conveyed and that he must make an effort to understand on the speaker's terms if genuine communication is to transpire. Yet speaker and listener both labor under the impression that they have been understood and do understand respectively.

Additional Piagetian contributions involving role-taking abilities can be observed in his comments on relationship. One type of common error is made when the child centers only upon himself and, hence, can recognize that he may have two brothers, but fails to see that he is also a brother to them and that, therefore, there are three brothers in the family. The young child has not yet developed a reciprocal schema (cognitive structure) which would enable him to deal with the reciprocity implied in the term "brother." In other words, if I have a brother, then I must also be a brother. He does not distinguish between the sibling and parental type of relation, in which he could have a father without, himself, being one. Younger children do not even conceive of a brother in relational terms. For example, a brother is seen in absolute terms simply as a boy who perhaps ". . . is a little person who lives with us," or, "A brother is a boy who is in the same flat" (Piaget 1924/1969).

The notion of relativity is also seen to undergo development in the area of right and left. Progress moves through three stages toward socialization as subjectification diminishes. During the first stage (five to eight years), questions regarding right and left are answered from the child's point of view. Consequently, when asked to identify the left hand of a person facing him, the child will point to the right hand of the person opposite him. In the second stage (eight to eleven years), the child is able to identify right and left in relation to a person facing him. For example, the child will answer correctly when the person opposite openly holds a coin in his hand and asks whether it is in the right or left hand. However, at this time the child still does not understand the relative nature of left and right, but conceives of them as absolute positions. It is not until the third stage (eleven to twelve years), that he grasps the actual relativity of left and right regarding objects. It is at this time that the expression "to the left of" takes on genuine meaning as opposed to merely signifying left or right as absolutes. Previously, given an array of objects A, B, and C, the child would simply state that B was in the middle. In the third stage he recognizes that B is neither to the left nor to the right in any absolute sense. What he grasps is that B is simultaneously to the right of A and to the left of C, from his position. In summary Piaget (1924/1969) states the following:

During the first (stage) the child places himself at his point of view, during the second at the point of view of others, and during the third at a completely relational point of view in which account is taken of objects in themselves. The process is therefore precisely that of the gradual socialization of thought-egocentrism, socialization, and finally complete objectivity. The curious thing is that the three stages are determined by ages which happen to correspond to the ages of important changes in the child's social life, viz. 7-8, diminution of egocentrism, and 11-12, the stages of rules and of thought which has become sufficiently formal to reason from all given points of view (pp. 112-113).

The ability to deal properly with relations is made possible when the reciprocity involved in different perspectives is realized.

EGOCENTRISM IN OPERATIONAL THOUGHT

Concrete operational thinking generally appears at around six or seven years of age. The preceding preoperational period is really a preparatory phase for the eventual emergence of concrete operations. Thinking in this period is no longer misled by perceptual cues, but instead is capable of dealing with transformations. Hence, it is decentered, nonstatic, and reversible. By this time the cognitive structures of the mind have organized into a systematic network which provides the foundation for genuinely logical thinking. The child can now deal competently with tasks involved in conservation, classification, seriation, number, and transitivity. His logical prowess, however, is confined to real objects known to him through experience. Although the preoperational period is the one generally considered the most egocentric, it will be remembered that the onset of each new period, despite its advances, is marked by a new level of egocentrism which is itself inherent in the nature of the progress made.

The concrete operational child cannot as yet apply his new found logical abilities to hypothetical situations. It is difficult for him to accept a premise for which he has no immediate verification and to reason on a deductive plane from it. To do this he would be required to psychologically take the point of view of the speaker presenting the hypothesis. The extent to which the concrete operational child can reason deductively is limited to the beliefs which he, himself, already has conviction about. It is his own world view from which he can accept premises as a point of departure for his reasoning. If, however, the child is asked to deal with a problem that assumes that dogs have six heads, he will refuse to attempt a resolution because he rejects the hypothesis.

It is only in the formal operational period that an absurd hypothesis will not be a barrier to purely deductive thought. The formal operational thinker is not rooted to empirical necessity (dogs cannot have six heads) and he, therefore, is free to make deductions from any premise. The egocentrism of the concrete operational child consists of his inability to forego his own point of view or the one salient at the moment and to place himself in the role of the other in order to accept a nonevident premise from which he may deduce logical, although perhaps nonverifiable, conclusions. Piaget (1924/1969) observes:

> It is only from the day that the child has said "I understand. Let us admit your point of view. Then if it were true . . . . this is what would happen . . . because . . . ," that a genuine hypothesis or a genuine assumption (i.e. one which is not believed in at all, but nevertheless analysed for its own sake) has really dawned in his mind. Here again it is social intercourse, but of a far more delicate order than that which we have spoken of previously, that modifies the structure of thought (p. 72).

Elkind (1974) has taken a position on egocentrism in the concrete operational period which is a modified, although still congenial, version of Piaget's work. In Elkind's view, the essence of the egocentrism is the child's confusion between empirical reality and his own assumption. The child will frequently interchange hypothesis and fact, dealing with one as though it were the other. Elkind's point is that the concrete operational child is more likely to take new evidence that runs counter to personal assumption and to attempt to make it conform to the assumption rather than to alter the assumption to match the facts. As a result, youngsters during this period hold many beliefs about people and social relations which are based only on partial information and which do not yield even when the child is presented with contradictory facts. Elkind calls these beliefs assumptive realities. The resemblance to delusions is superficial, for the assumptive realities are not characterized by either the narcissism or systematic character of delusions.

In the formal operational period (eleven to twelve years), the adolescent has at his command cognitive structures (operations) which enable him to test hypotheses in an experimental fashion and to revise his assumptive realities so that they are in keeping with any contrary evidence which is discovered. He is now capable of hypothetico-deductive reasoning and of conducting a strict scientific experiment, involving holding all variables constant except one which is tested for its effect. He is capable of combinatorial thinking which enables him to systematically and exhaustively try out all possible logical combinations of a set of elements. He has also become capable of thinking about his own thinking, as well as reflecting upon the thoughts of other people. In the most general sense, the highest achievement of the formal operational period is that reality has become a subset of the possible for the young adolescent. Where, then, is the deficiency of egocentrism amid such a powerful spectrum of intellectual tools?

The adolescent begins to think of his present and future roles in society and, in so doing, contemplates a change in a limited, or perhaps even unlimited, sector of that society. The capacity to have thought about thought leads him to construct "systems" or "theories" which to his mind can possibly be superimposed over society. The theories generated may be of a political, philosophical, aesthetic, or scientific nature and often serve to breathe life into the burgeoning reformist spirit of the adolescent. Inhelder and Piaget (1955/1958) suggest that the preceding description reflects most accurately the intellectual and student classes, whereas this development will most likely assume other forms among the adolescent working and peasant classes. The basic process will remain the same, however; it is one in which the adolescent " . . . is motivated also to take his place in the adult social framework, and with this aim he tends to participate in the ideas, ideals, and ideologies of a wider group through the medium of a number of verbal symbols to which he was indifferent as a child" (Inhelder and Piaget 1955/1958, p. 341). The formal operational adolescent undergoing this process does not fully distinguish between his own perspective as he organizes a life plan and the viewpoint of the group he anticipates reforming. The reveries and plans he forges are grandiose and usually are later abandoned. Inhelder and Piaget (1955/1958) are quite specific in explaining how their description of cognitive development in the formal operational period produces a type of egocentrism:

> The indefinite extension of powers of thought made possible by the new instruments of propositional logic at first is conducive to a failure to distinguish between the ego's new and unpredicted capacities and the social or cosmic universe to which they are applied. In other words, the adolescent goes through a phase in which he attributes an unlimited power to his own thoughts so that the dream of a glorious future or of transforming the world through Ideas (even if this idealism takes a materialistic form) seems to be not only fantasy but also an effective action which in itself modifies the empirical world. This is obviously a form of cognitive egocentrism (pp. 345-346).

Elkind (1974) has once again contributed to our understanding of egocentrism by offering the following observations about the adolescent's cognitive development. The youngster is now able to consider the thoughts of others, but he makes no distinction between his object of preoccupation and what may be of primary concern to others. Therefore, he believes that others are just as taken with the thought of him as he is himself. Put simply, while he is now taking into consideration what concerns others, he believes that it is his appearance and behavior they are concerned with. The adolescent anticipates the reactions of others to him and he expects these to be the same as the reaction he has to himself, whether positive or negative. Elkind coins the phrase *imaginary audience* to signify this phenomenon. Akin to this is what Elkind calls a *personal fable*—an untrue story which the adolescent accepts about himself. The young person believes there is a special uniqueness to his own experiences and he conveys the impression that only he can feel so deeply in love and sorrow. The strong male may believe that he will never fall ill or die and the young female may believe that she will never become pregnant, even though she engages in sexual encounters without benefit of contraceptive devices. Both have the fantasy, the personal fable, that somehow they are special enough to be exempt from these common human experiences.

THE DECLINE OF EGOCENTRISM

It is apparent from the preceding that egocentrism is a state in which the knower is centered upon one point of view only— his own. Furthermore, he lacks awareness of other perspectives as well as the fact that he is confined exclusively to his own perspective (Flavell 1963). As self and object are differentiated, the knower simultaneously becomes increasingly more aware of his own self and point of view and of the point of view of others. The process involved in no longer focusing solely upon one centration, to the exclusion of other aspects of reality, is called decentration. In decentering, the cognizer also coordinates these various viewpoints as they become known to him and he thus demonstrates a capability of entertaining multiple perspectives simultaneously. This progressive decentration at each developmental period leads to the disappearance of the egocentrism specific to the period.

Piaget sees the repetitive decentrations of the child's development as analogous to the decentrations occurring in the history of ideas, which brings to mind the often cited phrase, "ontogenesis recapitulates phylogenesis." A particularly apt example is the decline of radical egocentrism in which the child no longer experiences himself on a practical level as the center of the universe around which all else revolves, but comes to recognize that he is one of many objects in the milieu, each having positions in space relative to one another. The similarity of this achievement to the shift from the Ptolemaic system to the Copernican revolution is difficult to miss. In a stimulating comparison, Piaget (1936/1971) further elaborates the recapitulation theory by stating, "The completion of the objective practical universe (end of sensorimotor period) resembles Newton's achievements as compared to the egocentrism of Aristotelian physics, but the absolute Newtonian time and space themselves remain egocentric from the point of view of Einstein's relativity because they envision only one perspective on the universe among many other perspectives which are equally possible and real" (p. 413).

To fully understand the mechanism leading to the decline of egocentrism, it is necessary to begin with the concepts of adaptation and organization which comprise the biological substratum of the Piagetian system and are referred to as functional invariants. They are so called because they continue to perform throughout the developmental periods despite qualitative changes in the emerging cognitive structures. As noted in Chapter 1, adaptation is comprised of two processes, assimilation and accommodation. Assimilation is the incorporation of external information into the preexisting cognitive structure (schema). Functioning in its present form, it does not involve any change in the structure and, hence, represents a conservative element in the meaning system or way in which the infant or child construes things. Accommodation is the effort made by the cognitive structure to conform to the external reality which is being assimilated. Therefore, it promotes change in the structure and is considered a progressive element. Both processes are necessary for intelligent or adaptive functioning.

Initially, at the outset of infancy, the functional invariants are undifferentiated. The only existing schemas or structures are inherited or early acquired, such as suckling, grasping, and looking. Take grasping as an example. In the act of assimilating an object to his grasping schema, which is the infant's way of making sense out of his environment on a practical level, he must automatically accommodate his fingers to the shape of the object. Hence, the undifferentiated character of the infant's activity and the object. Flavell (1963) comments, "In short, agent and object, ego and outside world are inextricably linked together in even infantile action, and the distinction between assimilation of objects to the self and the accommodation of the self to objects simply does not exist" (p. 59). As a result, the infant at this point has no sense of spatial relations, independent existence of permanent objects, or causality. However, as the conservative assimilatory process attempts to reduce all of the external world to the present level of structural development, the progressive accommodatory process attempts to modify the existing structures in order to deal with novel features of the environment. For example, in exploring the physical world around him, the infant will begin to grasp objects with shapes that are new to him and which will require special accommodations to meet the demands of those contours. An opposition or antagonism, therefore, arises between assimilation and accommodation, although eventually these twin processes are fated to perform in a complementary fashion in which an equilibrium is established. In any event, the initial antagonism breaks up the undifferentiated state between assimilation and accommodation. Increasingly throughout the sensorimotor period, the infant will acquire the ability to differentiate between his own activity and the objects upon which he acts. Schemas themselves will become more and more differentiated as accommodation takes place, which in turn permits a much wider range of the child's universe to be assimilated to the newly constructed structures. The entire process is further promoted by the other functional invariant, organization.

Throughout development structures are organized into complex systems. A simple prototype, however, is the young infant's attainment of coordination of the grasping and looking schemas. Whereas they both took place separately during the very early phase of life, within only a few months the infant can be observed to grasp what he looks attentively at and to look attentively at that which he grasps. This organized property of schemas further facilitates the differentiation between subject and object on a practical or action level. Further accommodations to the environment in the area of intentional behavior also greatly promote the decline of egocentrism. In an early stage there is little differentiation between ends and means. For example, having accidentally pulled a string attached to a rattle, the infant will again pull the string to reproduce the sound of the rattle. Note, however, that the pulling of the string and the reproduction of the desired effect are performed in virtually a single act. At a later stage the infant will, when desiring to grasp an object, strike aside an obstruction, such as an experimenter's hand, in order to achieve it. In both illustrations we find a form of intentional behavior, but in the second example, which comes later in the infant's development, there is to be found a greater differentiation between the child's own actions and the objects sought.

In the area of causal development, the infant initially assimilates all cause and effect relationships to the center of his own being. He behaves as if believing that only he can create effects in his universe. Gradually as he accommodates further to the external world, he exhibits an awareness on a practical or behavioral plane that the locus of causation may reside not only in himself, but also in other people and objects. In brief, through adaptation and organization the radical egocentrism of the sensorimotor period disappears. The infant emerges onto a representational plane of development in a world that has become spatialized and objectified. As with every cognitive advance, a new form of egocentrism appears, which in turn must be conquered.

The major factor contributing to the decline of egocentrism beyond the sensorimotor period is social interaction, particularly with one's peers. The child who wishes to communicate and be understood must adapt to the informational needs of his listener. He cannot continue to assimilate reality to his own private schemas, but must also accommodate to the point of view of the other. The desire to effectively persuade and to have others accept his ideas will require this accommodation. He must, if he is to be understood, begin to identify the referents of pronouns in his speech and to link events in proper causal fashion reflected in his syntax. He can no longer juxtapose unrelated events as if these were meaningful to the listener. He can no longer make contradictory statements, as he does in the preoperational period, and yet continue to remain unaware of their contradictory nature. He will come in contact with others who will challenge, offer rebuttal, and demand clarification. Logical proof and verification will be sought in social exchange. The personal point of view of the child, adopted as universal and absolute, will not be at all evident to his peers. The desire and movement toward socialized thought not only facilitate the development of logic, but also serve to prevent the child, or even the adult, from a pathological subjectification. Piaget (1924/1969) comments as follows:

> What then gives rise for the need for verification? Surely it must be the shock of our thought coming into contact with that of others, which produces doubt and the desire to prove. If there were not other people, the disappointments of experience would lead to overcompensation and dementis. We are constantly hatching an enormous number of false ideas, conceits, utopias, mystical explanations, suspicions and megalomaniacal fantasies, which disappear when brought into contact with other people. The social need to share the thought of others and to communicate our own with success is at the root of our need for verification. Proof is the outcome of argument (p. 204).

The central role of social interaction in the decline of egocentrism persists throughout the developmental periods including adolescence, when it is well-known that youngsters in their teens seek out peer reference groups and confidantes to test with one another in endless discussion their newly generated ideas, theories, and utopias. In doing this the youngster accelerates the intellectual decentering process, for feedback from his peers will often pointedly underscore the weaknesses and limitations of his new found ideas and ideologies. Piaget identifies an even more specific source of decentration for the formal operational youngster, which is his entry into a vocation or commencement of professional training (Inhelder and Piaget 1955/1958). It is ultimately in assuming a real job that the adolescent is ushered into adulthood, and the tendency to engage in undue formal theorizing is diluted as he is brought back into the world of reality. However, although the final egocentric flight of adolescence disappears, the youngster will retain into adulthood formal operational structures which permit the creative and scientific reasoning that set him apart from all other creatures and objects in the universe.

Elkind (1974) suggests that by the time formal operations are firmly established (fourteen to fifteen years) the adolescent has used his scientific schemas to test out the concept of the imaginary audience, which is regarded as an hypothesis, and he revises it to conform with the real audience which he discovers. Henceforth, the adolescent can differentiate between his own preoccupation with self and the concerns of others. The personal fable, which may never be entirely overcome, yields to some extent to relationships of intimacy. It is through the sharing of mutual feelings, fantasies, and goals which characterizes such relationships that each participant comes to realize the illusion of his being unique in experiencing life's emotions so intensely.

CONCLUSION

It may not be apparent thus far and, therefore, will be emphasized here, that not all individuals attain the cognitive structures of the formal operational period. Further, even for those who do, there will surely be remnants of previous periods adhering to their present functioning. It is not likely that even a formal operational adult will function at that level in every area of his life at all times. It is even questionable whether this would be desirable. The various types of egocentrism which have been examined in this chapter are certainly not completely abandoned and traces of them will be found in everyone at different times. The presence of exceptionally large measures of egocentrism may well explain serious interpersonal difficulties and psychopathologies. The reader who is interested in the application to psychopathology of the Piagetian concept of egocentrism may wish to consult the following: Odier (1956), Anthony (1956, 1957), Freeman and McGhie (1957), Neale (1966), Feffer (1967), Clarke (1969), Schmid-Kitsikis (1973), Lidz (1973), Chandler, Greenspan, and Barenboim (1974), Pimm (1975), and Steinfeld (1975). Although it does not deal primarily with psychopathology, an excellent review of egocentrism and extension of the concept across the lifespan is to be found in Looft (1972).

By now, the term egocentrism has become too deeply embedded

in the Piagetian literature to be extracted successfully. Nevertheless, Piaget has voiced regrets over having adopted it because of the unfelicitous connotation of a selfish or egotistic personality which the word carries. He has, therefore, sought to disavow use of the word in that sense and to highlight his own cognitive meaning which is that of the ego centering on itself and, consequently, lacking the ability to deal with multiple perspectives simultaneously. In fact, the child is unaware of his egocentrism and, therefore, cannot recognize his own cognitive deficit.

It was stated in the opening paragraph of this chapter that Piaget conceives of human cognitive development as moving in the direction of increasingly attaining objective relativism. The concept of objective relativism and how it is acquired serves as a touchstone to understanding the basis of Piaget's system. The child's viewpoint becomes objective as he differentiates between self and external world, between psychic phenomena and the material universe, between internal, private events and the objects populating his environment. The term relativism refers to both relational or relative notions of reality and to the notion of reciprocity. The elimination of realism leads to the disappearance of the tendency to materialize and reify psychic events. As children grow older, they no longer think of such expressions as "in front of" or "behind" in terms of absolutes, which would indicate attributes of objects. Instead they begin to grasp the relational nature of subjects in the world. A term such as "foreigner" is seen not to signify an absolute property of the person, but rather a relation which is reciprocal, so that if A is a foreigner to B, then B is also a foreigner to A. In a reciprocal relationship the individual is able to see things from the other person's point of view and not only from his own. Piaget (1924/ 1969) points out that, "It is because he fails to grasp the reciprocity existing between different points of view that the child is unable to handle relations properly" (p. 134). As the child decenters he achieves multiperspectives which he then coordinates simultaneously. It is this process of decentration and coordination which leads to the decline of egocentrism and toward the achievement of objective relativism.

3

THE CONCEPT
OF CONSERVATION

INTRODUCTION

Conservation was introduced in chapter 1 of this volume. It is undoubtedly one of the most highly researched subjects within the Piagetian system and its central importance is highlighted by Piaget's assertion that it is a necessary condition to all rational activity. The genesis of conservation is in the sensorimotor period when the issue is one of conserving the object itself. Once the infant conserves the object (object permanence) he is subject during the preoperational period to an inability to conserve certain aspects of the object. For example, the preoperational child does not realize that changing the shape of a ball of clay will alter neither the amount of its substance, nor its weight or volume. The young child fails to grasp that pouring liquid from a short, wide glass into a tall, thin glass will have no effect on the amount of liquid. In both of these illustrations, which deal with continuous quantities, the child is likely to think that there will be more quantity in the sausage-shaped clay or the tall, narrow vessel than in a remaining standard to which it is being compared. The standard, it is established first, is equal in amount and perceptually appears the same as the modified object before any change is initiated. The child is limited in the same manner with respect to discontinuous quantities (a group of separate objects such as beads or marbles). Imagine a set of one hundred marbles and two separate vessels, one tall and thin, the other short and wide. The preoperational child can simultaneously place one marble in the first vessel and another in the second, repeating this until each container holds fifty marbles. The process involves a one-to-one correspondence of the marbles in the vessels. Nevertheless, the young child having undergone this procedure will claim that there are more marbles in the tall vessel than in the short one.

As the young child is perceptually rooted in the preoperational period, he centers on only one aspect of the reality. The length of the sausage-shaped clay, for example, is most salient and so, without considering the commensurate narrowing of the elongated piece, he claims it has more substance than the unchanged standard, a round ball of clay. In time, the child will decenter and will take into account that, while the changed ball of clay is longer, it is also thinner with the result that there has been no change in the amount of its substance. This ability to conserve substance appears at the beginning of concrete operations and is undergirded by a new system of integrated structures. In particular, the ability to handle length and width simultaneously is a manifestation of the structural development that permits the multiplication of relations. Within the context of the conservation task, it is generally called the compensatory operation, signifying that a change in one aspect is compensated for or balanced out by a reciprocal change in another aspect. The two other major operations enabling conservation are identity and negation. In the first of these the concrete operational child now realizes that, since nothing has been added and nothing has been taken away, despite the change in shape, the amount must remain the same. In negation, the youngster is now capable of a mental operation in which he realizes that were the sausage-shaped clay to be returned to its original state it would be the same amount; therefore, he concludes it must be the same amount now.

Conservation is an example of what is known as a horizontal décalage. A décalage literally means an unwedging or uncoupling (Flavell 1963). Applied to conservation it means specifically that competence at conservation does not immediately extend across all content areas. It actually takes several years before conservation can be equally exercised in areas of substance, weight, and volume. A horizontal décalage is generally confined to one developmental period and is a phenomenon in which the same structure is at first confined to only one area and only gradually becomes applicable to other areas. What appears to be a homogeneous concept, in the case of conservation, turns out to have a heterogeneous character in that conservation of substance is manifest at about six or seven years of age, of weight at about eight or nine years, and of volume at about eleven or twelve years.

Piaget (1941) employs the concepts of atomism, density, and compression-decompression to shed light on conservation as a horizontal décalage (Flavell 1963). The child at first comes to construe a substance such as clay as being made up of a set of discrete units which simply shift around when the shape of the clay is altered. Such a view of matter is obviously consistent with the conservation of substance. Nevertheless, he continues for a time to believe that the weight of the various particles will change as the object's position is altered. Flavell draws attention to the fact that egocentric notions of weight obstruct the child's movement toward weight conservation. The young child conceives of weight in personalized terms, defining it as the sensation produced on his skin as an object presses against him. Even after the concrete operational child has mastered the conservation of both substance and weight, he continues to believe that the density of the particles varies with change in the shape of the object. As the units shift in position they compress or decompress, hence affecting volume. It is only later that schemas eliminating this belief are developed. Piaget and Inhelder (1941) describe some rather interesting experiments dealing with atomism and density, which involve the dissolving of sugar in water and the heating of popcorn, respectively.

There are other domains to which the concept of conservation is applicable and which develop during the concrete operational period. Let us identify two of them briefly. One is the conservation involved in recognizing that the distance between two points remains the same even though an object is placed between them. The preoperational child believes that the distance diminishes when an object is placed between two points. A second example is the conservation of area. Imagine a small circumscribed area with four cubes clustered together so that they are adjacent to one another. Now separate the cubes so that they are dispersed throughout the area. The preoperational child believes that there is less area once the cubes have been dispersed than when they are adjacent to each other.

In the following sections of this chapter the reader will be introduced to aspects of conservation which are of particular importance and which, when understood, will in some instances lead to a deeper comprehension of the entire Piagetian system.

IDENTITY AND EQUIVALENCE

Elkind (1967) has distinguished between two different types of conservation in an effort to clarify the confusion which seems to typify some discussions on conservation. Conservation tasks assess both invariance of identity and of equivalence. The conservation of identity involves a change of state within a single thing. For example, a ball of clay which is transformed into a sausage shape is no longer perceptually the same, but is quantitatively identical with its previous state. When the sausage-shaped clay is judged to be quantitatively the same as a second ball of clay which had not been deformed, conservation of equivalence is brought into play. The standard conservation task is known as the conservation of equivalence. However, Elkind stresses the fact that the subject must be inferring conservation of identity when demonstrating equivalence. He would have no way of knowing that the ball and the sausage shapes were quantitatively the same if he had not first established that the original balls of clay, A and B, were the same and if he had not witnessed the transformation of B to B'. Having done so, he is able to deduce that $B'=B$ (identity) and that, therefore, since it had been established that $B=A$, it must follow that B' and A are equal quantitatively to one another despite a perceptual dissimilarity. Hence, Elkind observes that the conservation of identity is a necessary condition in the demonstration of the conservation of equivalence.

Elkind emphasizes that a serious misunderstanding stems from the fact that, although Piaget appears to be discussing the conservation of equivalence, he is actually addressing the conservation of identity. The standard conservation tasks set up by Piaget do, indeed, seem to involve equivalence, but the explanations of the children, in fact, bear upon identity between B and B′ and not a comparison between B′ and A. One can readily appreciate this by reflecting on explanations which involve operations of compensation, negation, and nothing added or subtracted. The children do not articulate the transitivity operation of B′=B, B=A, and therefore B′=A which is a necessary and sufficient condition for the conservation of equivalence. The explanations of the children deal with the invariance of identity, and it is these which Piaget focuses upon, despite the equivalence character of the tasks and the child's judgment that B′=A.

Contrary to Piaget's assumption regarding their simultaneity in time, Elkind suggests that conservation of identity developmentally precedes the conservation of equivalence. Elkind further notes that Piaget believes that children arrive at the two types of conservation at about the same age. There has emerged a considerable body of contradictory research findings pertaining to the issue of whether identity conservation precedes equivalence conservation and the ages involved. Brainerd and Hooper (1975) have drawn attention to this and have attempted to resolve the apparent contradiction. The research has been extensive, ranging across conservation in such areas as discontinuous quantity, continuous quantity (liquid and solid), length, and number. Brainerd and Hooper point out that, curiously, researchers whose findings disprove Elkind's proposal of identity preceding equivalence continue to accept his logical analysis of the subject, although they hold that for presently undetermined reasons the distinction is not developmentally observable. In reviewing the research, Brainerd and Hooper assume that Elkind was correct and that they would find procedural differences between the confirming and disconfirming studies to account for the discrepancy. Their assumption was founded upon the logical assertion that, while identity problems could be handled without equivalence, it was not true that equivalence problems could be solved without identity invariance. In addition, they cited the fact that, while identity was sometimes found to precede equivalence, equivalence was never reported to come earlier than identity, which they considered very unlikely unless identity developmentally does, in fact, precede equivalence. Careful analysis of both supportive and nonsupportive studies, led to the conclusion that identity precedes equivalence in conservation and that the discrepancy can be attributed to measurement and sampling errors. The measurement error lies in the fact that studies supporting the assumed sequence were based on a criterion of judging conservation to have taken place, without requiring the subjects to explain their reasons. On the other hand, the nonsupportive studies were based on the criteria of judging conservation to have taken place, plus requiring an appropriate explanation from the subjects. Therefore, because the nonsupportive studies used more stringent criteria than the supportive ones, it is likely that they masked the presence of identity conservation. By the time identity conservation was revealed, there appeared a simultaneity of it and equivalence.

The sampling error is related directly to age. A considerable number of the populations used in the supportive studies was of preschool age, whereas none of the subjects in the nonsupportive studies was. Brainerd and Hooper argue that one would be more likely to find synchrony of identity and equivalence in an older population and more likely to uncover a décalage in the younger population. It is precisely such a pattern that was discovered in their review of the relevant studies. It should be pointed out that Brainerd's and Hooper's analysis is significant not only because of the light it sheds on the problem under discussion, but also because of the way in which it illuminates how a rational methodological analysis, such as they have provided, can plausibly account for seemingly discrepant and confusing research findings.

Peill (1975) advances the position that Elkind may be incorrect in assuming that a deduction based on transitivity is necessary to equivalence conservation. Granting that the task logically entails deductive reasoning, she points out that psychologically the subject may simply observe after the deformation that the act was not pertinent to change in amount, for example, and, hence, may restate the initial judgment of equivalence, which had been made prior to the deformation. In support of her position she cites Smedslund (1964), who reported having found subjects who could not perform transitivity tests, but who could perform conservation of equivalence. Brainerd and Hooper (1975), however, point out that in the 1960s although several studies reported a sequence of conservation followed by transitivity, such studies tended to use more sensitive measures for conservation than for transitivity. In more recent studies which have compensated for the lack of parity in the sensitivity of measurements, a sequence of transitivity followed by conservation has emerged.

PSEUDO-CONSERVATION

Piaget (1964) has reported a phenomenon in which children's predictions involving conservation of liquid appear accurate, but which they counter upon observing a discrepancy between their expectation and the outcome. Three glasses of varying shapes are utilized. The initial glass A is three-quarters filled with water. Glass B is taller and thinner than A, while glass C is shorter and wider than A. The child is asked whether there would be the same amount to drink if the water were poured into either glass B or C and he answers yes. On the basis of his prediction, it would appear that he has acquired the conservation of liquid. When asked to indicate the anticipated water levels should water from glass A be poured into either B or C, the child points to the same level in B and C as that presently observed in A. While indicating the same water levels across the glasses, he verbalizes that the amount will always remain the same. Requested to actually pour the water from A into B and C so that each of the two glasses contains the same amount, he pours the water so that the same level is reached in both B and C, despite the considerable variation in the size of the two glasses. The child's notion of conservation, it becomes clear, is inclusive not only of amount, but level as well. Piaget contends that in view of the inadequacy of the child's notion of invariance, this must surely be considered a pseudo-conservation and not genuine conservation based upon operative structures. When the experimenter pours the original amount from A into B, the child observes the higher level in B and then claims he had been wrong, for clearly to this pseudo-conserver there is now more water in glass B because of the higher level. Lacking benefit of the operational structures which have not yet developed, the imagery of the child is unable to promote genuine conservation. In a variation of this experiment another group of children below seven years of age is able to make the correct prediction regarding water level. The imagery in these cases serves well as the children state that the water level would be higher in B and lower in C than it is in A. Yet these children fare no better than those in the other group, for when asked to pour the water so that there is the same amount in B and C, they pour it so that the level in both glasses is the same. In this case such imagery is sufficiently advanced to permit an accurate prediction, yet once again it is inadequate to provide genuine conservation for the appropriate structures have not yet developed. The children do not understand the transformation or compensation of height and width which occurs, but merely utilize an image derived from earlier exposure to witnessing a variety of pourings from vessel to vessel at mealtimes and on other occasions.

Bruner (1964) reported an experiment by F. Frank in which a screening device was used in a test on the conservation of liquid in order to rule out the water level as a cue. The screen concealed only the lower portion of the vessels so that, although the children could not observe water levels, they could see the tops of the vessels and thus were aware of differences in their sizes and shapes. Frank conducted the experiment with a sample of children ranging from ages four, five, six, and seven. There is a remarkable increase of conservation once the screening device is introduced. The shift in responses from nonconservation (pretest) to conservation (screening) is as follows: four years old from 0 percent to 50 percent, five years old from 20 percent to

90 percent, and six years old from 50 percent to 100 percent. They comment simply that it is the same water or that it has only been poured. Once the screen is removed, the four-year-old children revert to nonconservation judgments, but almost all children above four maintain the conservation response, insisting that the water is the same since it has only been poured from one place to another, even though there may appear to be a difference in amount. Several minutes later, Frank conducted a posttest without benefit of a screen. She discovered that the four-year-old children had not changed at all. However, the five-year-old children had gone from 20 percent demonstrating conservation in the pretest to 70 percent in the posttest. The six- and seven-year-old children went from 50 percent to 90 percent. It appears that without the distraction of perceptual variations in water levels which, of course, occur when two glasses of different sizes contain equal amounts of liquid, children are considerably more likely to make a conservation judgment. Further, experience at making conservation judgments while a screening device is used seems to promote a comprehension of invariance or conservation in subsequent experiences without the presence of a screen.

In the context of this discussion, it is necessary to ask whether we are dealing with genuine or pseudo-conservation. Gruen (1966) suggests that the issue centers on "methodological and definitional considerations." He points out that Bruner and those conducting research within his theoretical framework are satisfied that conservation exists when the subject makes a conservation judgment without any explanation. On the other hand, Smedslund, as well as those working out of Piaget's Geneva School, requires a satisfactory explanation before concluding that conservation exists. The reasons for this is that Smedslund and Piaget predicate the acquisition of conservation upon the development of logical operations of negation, reciprocity or compensation, nothing added or subtracted, and logical certitude. Bruner and his group at the Harvard Center for Cognitive Study do not rely upon these operations to conclude that conservation exists. Bruner cites three modes of knowing—enactive, iconic or perceptual, and symbolic. It is sufficient to Bruner to ascertain that the perceptual or enactive mode recedes and that the symbolic mode dominates, in order to conclude that the subject has acquired conservation. Hence, the Geneva School and Smedslund report that conservation first emerges at about age six or seven, whereas Bruner and the Harvard School generally find the acquisition of conservation at age five. Gruen suggests that, despite the screening device Frank utilized, had she exercised the criteria of measurement for conservation which Smedslund and Piaget employ, the children she tested would not have been found to have had conservation until later than the ages she reported. In essence, Gruen is stating that the two Schools have been examining different psychological processes and, consequently, bring to bear separate criteria of measurement. The fact of this variation accounts for some of the confusion in the literature, which can be eliminated if researchers will be explicit about defining what it is they are investigating.

CONSERVATION AND PERSONALITY VARIABLES

There have been few empirical attempts to determine the relationship between personality and cognitive development. Goldschmid (1967) first conducted research in which he discovered that boys outperformed girls on conservation tasks and that older children proved superior to younger children on each conservation task administered. Verbal ability, IQ, and MA all proved to be positively related to conservation ability. The study also suggested that among children at the same age, those with emotional disturbances were behind in conservation development when compared with children not experiencing emotional disturbances.

Goldschmid's (1968) research emphasized the relationship of conservation to environmental and personality aspects of children. He found that in describing children with high conservation scores teachers favored more positive and fewer negative adjectives. High scorers in conversation were seen by teachers as being more clever and attractive, as well as more passive and reflective. Low scorers were seen as more unsociable, as well as afraid and silly. However, the low conservers were also characterized as having more energy and physical prowess. In general, the higher conservers were preferred by their peers and teachers, were more objective in scores on self-assessment tests, and had mothers who were less dominating than those of the lower conservers. Sex and age had no bearing on these results. In conclusion, it appears that the personality and environment of a child within a given age category can account for individual differences in conservation. Goldschmid (1971) has suggested that experiments manipulating noncognitive aspects of development be conducted to explore their influence upon the child's acquisition of cognitive structures.

TRAINING STUDIES AND EXTINCTION

Training studies designed to promote the acquisition of conservation have played an important role in the field of genetic epistemology. In a Piagetian context, for conservation to have truly developed, the performance must be based on a competence derived from a grouping of operations which are systematically linked together. These operations include the two forms of reversibility, negation or inversion and reciprocity or compensation, as well as the identity operation (nothing has been added or nothing subtracted). Isolated responses specific to only one narrow area do not reflect a sufficient criterion of development.

There are several criteria which the Geneva School (Piaget 1964) advance for determining whether genuine conservation has been acquired through training experiments. One is that of durability. Conservation predicated upon the invention by the child of appropriate operational structures should continue to be manifest in a posttest administered several weeks to several months later. A second criterion is generalizability. Training received successfully in one area of conservation, if built upon the construction of new structures, should be applicable to a wider range of related tasks which call upon the same structures. A third consideration, which logically follows from the above, is that training which results in true development should move the child from his original spontaneous operational level to a higher, more complex system of hierarchical operations. In addition, Smedslund has repeatedly emphasized that genuine conservation should evidence resistance to efforts aimed at inducing extinction. It is conceivable that, even if genuine acceleration of conservation occurs in a training study, it would not necessarily follow that the natural conserver acquires conservation through the same means utilized in the study. The fact is that research in conservation training is voluminous and reflects a tapestry of diverse and often conflicting findings. Increasing refinement of research methodology and consensus of definitions must be sought to promote order and consistency in experimentation.

Modgil (1974) identifies five areas which success in training depends upon. He has based his statement on certain patterns which were manifest in an extensive analysis he made of many conservation training studies. The significant areas are as follows: "a) the child's level of development at the beginning of training, b) the training method employed, c) the particular tasks used, d) the amount of training, and e) the criteria used to evaluate success" (p. 126). Piaget has been somewhat skeptical about the desirability of artificially accelerating development and he cautions that at best there may be an optimum rate of development beyond which it may be unwise to pursue.

An exhaustive review of the research on conservation training would lead us through a maze of contrasting findings. The primary aim of this section is simply to acquaint the reader with some of the basic aspects of the field. In particular, however, because of its early influence on all subsequent studies, some of the work of Smedslund (1961) will be cited here. Additionally, an attempt will be made to bring the reader up-to-date on some of the current work emanating from the Geneva School (Inhelder and Sinclair 1969; Inhelder, Sinclair, Bovet 1974).

Smedslund (1961C) set out to train a group of children by means of external reinforcement and then to investigate the children's resistance to extinction in contrast to a control group of natural conservers. He postulated that genuine conservation should not readily be subject to extinction because it is an expression of an internal "logical" necessity. One group of eleven children showed no conservation during the pretest. They were then trained by providing them with opportunities to observe on a scale that equivalence of weight between two round pieces of clay is maintained despite the fact that one of the two pieces is transformed into a sausage shape. In this manner the subjects learned to verbalize a judgment of conservation of weight. The trained group of children and the control group of thirteen, both containing children ages five to seven, were then subject to extinction trials. The extinction efforts were conducted by the experimenter who surreptitiously removed a small piece from one of the objects after it was transformed. An original equivalence of weight had been established, and, since none of the children observed the removal of a piece from the transformed object, both trained and natural conservers predicted that conservation of weight would obtain when the two objects would be placed on the scale. Upon seeing the disparity in weight registered by the scales, all of the eleven trained observers reverted to nonconservation responses. Furthermore, they typically evidenced no surprise and offered perceptually grounded explanations for their statements of nonconservation. In contrast, six of the natural conservers did not accept what the scale indicated. They assumed conservation and, therefore, sought rational explanations for what they saw on the scale. For example, they suggested that the experimenter had removed some from the lighter piece or that some had fallen to the floor. Seven of the natural conservers did, however, revert to nonconservation. Considering how young these children were and that conservation of weight is not generally found until several years later, it is likely that those natural conservers who had reverted were only on the threshold of a new found competence and, therefore, more vulnerable to extinction. In concluding his report, Smedslund highlights the fact that the outcome of the investigation could not have been predicted on the basis of explanations for conservation judgments provided prior to the extinction procedures since children from both groups made the same type of statements. Hence, the durability and functional character of conservation cannot be inferred from verbal behavior.

The interested reader may wish to consult Hall and Kingsley (1968) and Peill (1975) for some contemporary critical research and commentary on Smedslund's extinction position. A perspective meriting attention has recently been cited by Rubin (1976) whose report is in the mainstream of current trends toward life span developmental research. He tested groups with populations ranging from grades two, five and seven, through various major developmental phases of life to elderly subjects, both institutionalized and noninstitutionalized. The focus of the study was resistance to conservation of quantity extinction in both continuous and discontinuous areas. Rubin concluded that there exists a curvilinear pattern regarding resistance judgments and explanations. There is an increase in the first part of life, but a decline after young adulthood. He notes, "... resistance was less likely to occur among elderly and institutionalized elderly than among young adults, and less likely among the latter elderly group than among middle-aged adults" (p. 54). He does not, however, readily accept the interpretation that a weakened resistance to extinction is necessarily based upon neurological deterioration and an accompanying dissolution of cognitive structures. He suggests that the underlying structures may be present, hence the competence for conservation is maintained, but that certain factors may be inhibiting performance. In conclusion, Rubin urges that further research in this area is needed.

Another article in the early Smedslund series (1961E) involves attempting to facilitate the acquisition of substance conservation in children ranging from five and one half years of age to six and one half years of age. The procedure was to induce cognitive conflict without providing any external reinforcement. Smedslund pitted the addition/substraction schema against the deformation schema. For example, he would simultaneously elongate a piece of clay while at the same time visibly removing a section of it. The subjects, being nonconservers, were inclined to think that there would be a greater amount as a result of elongation. On the other hand, they realized that removing a piece should lead to a lesser amount. Smedslund hypothesized, "Since the addition/subtraction schema presumably has greater clarity, simplicity, and consistency, it will gradually or suddenly begin to dominate, whereas the deformation schema with its high degree of ambiguity, complexity and internal contradiction will be weakened and will eventually disappear completely even in pure deformation situations without addition/subtraction" (p. 157). Five of the thirteen subjects disregarded the deformation and were guided by the addition/subtraction schema throughout all three practice sessions. Four of the five also shifted to offering symbolic-logical explanations at a posttest, even though they had demonstrated no conservation at the pretest. Eight of the thirteen subjects consistently adhered to the deformation schema, showing no change from pretest to posttest. Given the relative infrequency with which Smedslund had previously been successful in stimulating the acquisition of conservation (five out of over one hundred) through other methods, he concluded that the cognitive conflict approach could be justifiably considered effective. Smedslund views the result of this experiment as supporting Piaget's theory of equilibration, in which disequilibrium leads to a reorganization of cognitive structures at a higher and more adaptive level.

The Geneva School has concentrated its research efforts upon the investigation of developmental stages, the invarying sequence of these stages, the underlying nature of newly constructed cognitive structures, and the organizational pattern of these structures at different levels of development. Inhelder and Sinclair (1969) and Inhelder, Sinclair, and Bovet (1974), prototypical researchers in the Genevan tradition, have recently presented their advanced theoretical and empirical work which goes beyond focusing upon the structural features of the varying stages. Their study is largely in the nature of the transition through these stages and in the mechanisms that facilitate the transition with resultant acquisition of new knowledge. The authors reaffirm their radical constructivist position, rejecting both the nativist and behaviorist approach to knowledge. Knowing is based neither on hereditary structure nor upon complex associations comprised in additive fashion of more simple ones. In brief, knowledge is neither built into human organisms through hereditary structures nor is it a copy or reflection of reality. It is the result of a continuous process of construction and autoregulation in which disturbing factors, both internal and external in origin, can be cancelled out or compensated for. In the introduction to their work, Inhelder, Sinclair, and Bovet (1974) state, "All regulations that take place during biological growth and psychological development are constructive processes and not just a means of preserving an already attained equilibrium; and all constructive processes imply compensating activities that counteract disturbances in equilibrium" (p. 10). They are particularly illuminating with regard to the respectful stance which the Genevan School adopts toward the child's level of development at any given stage. Their message is that early uncoordinated schemas should not be viewed as errors or as providing inaccurate information. The child who states that liquid poured from one vessel to a higher and narrower one increases in quantity is utilizing a preoperatory mode of reasoning, which equates a higher liquid level with greater quantity. It is a natural stage of development for the child, and he should not be coerced into changing his way of thinking. Nevertheless, these uncoordinated schemas do not offer a full comprehension of reality, although they do serve as the basis for more coordinated structures leading to more intelligent or adaptive functioning.

In their training experiments, Inhelder, Sinclair, and Bovet stress the active role of the child, believing that more successful learning will ensue from the child's own activity. It should be remembered, however, that activity in the Piagetian framework may be of a mental nature and need not refer to the overt manipulation of materials and objects. An attempt was made in the experiments to induce a conflict between different schemas in the child's mind in order to precipitate a reorganization of the schemas which would produce a higher level of a cognitive integration and more effective strategies for the resolution of various problems. The work by Inhelder, Sinclair, and Bovet, presently under consideration is quite extensive and detailed. A brief outline which illustrates two of their many conservation training studies will appear below, accompanied by the results obtained and their general comments.

In the first experiment there was one group of nonconserving children and a second group of children at an intermediate stage. Some children in the second group were virtually at the threshold of conservation acquisition. In accord with the authors' beliefs about development, the children were accorded an active role in carrying out the procedures involved. The children were requested to make predictions about what would be likely to occur upon initiating certain actions and then to compare their predictions to actual outcome. The authors' assumed that this experiment, involving liquid levels and conservation of quantities, would lead the participants to make accurate inferences upon observing the discrepancies between prediction and outcome. An effort was made in the experiment to direct the attention of the subjects toward the kinetic and transformational aspects of pouring liquid from a jar of one size to that of another size, as well as to deter the subjects from focusing exclusively on end states (liquid levels). There are several phases and permutations to the experiment and what follows is a simplified version as presented by Inhelder and Sinclair (1969).

Three pairs of vessels are vertically aligned. Thus A and A' comprise the top row. Below them are B and B'. Below B and B' are C and C'. Vessels in the first two rows have outlet taps which permit the child to manipulate the taps in order to allow the liquid to flow from a higher vessel into one directly below it. Five of the vessels are the same size. A sixth, B', is thinner than all of the others. At the outset, there is an equal amount of liquid in A and A'. The child is asked to allow an equal amount to flow into B and B'. The nonconserving child proceeds to fill B and B' until the liquid levels are equal. Since B' is thinner than B, there is now actually more liquid in B than in B', although the subject does not realize this. There is also some liquid remaining in A', since to have allowed it to flow into B' would have meant destroying the perceptual equality of liquid levels between B and B'. The next step entails opening the taps again to allow the liquid in B and B' to flow respectively into C and C'. The nonconserving subjects expect to find that equal liquid levels will be maintained after carrying out this action. However, what happens is that there is now a higher liquid level in C. The subjects observe not only a discrepancy between prediction and outcome, but also they note that the amount absent in C' has been retained in A'. None of the preoperational children progressed to the point of being able to use operational thinking to resolve conservation problems. The majority (87.5 percent) made no substantial advance at all. A minority (12.5 percent) did advance to an intermediary stage in which they demonstrate oscillation at a posttest between conservation and nonconservation responses. However, it is reported that 75 percent of those who began in the intermediary phase did evidence progress based on the training experiment. Advances were characterized by stability with the subjects employing explanations based primarily upon identity and compensation.

In the work by Inhelder, Sinclair, and Bovet (1974), in which the above experiment appears in greater detail, it is emphasized that the preoperational child does not benefit from the experiment because, despite having his attention drawn to certain salient empirical features in the experiment, he lacks the structures to properly assimilate them. Significantly, they state, "The discrepancy between observation and prediction does create a certain unease in the child's mind, but at this developmental level he is not yet capable of organizing the successive observations into a coherent system of schemes" (p. 54). The authors conclude that the noteworthy progress of the intermediary subjects is attributable to their developmental level at the start of the experiment. They argue that their findings would lead to a rejection of a stimulus-response learning theory, which would ignore the subjects' developmental level and would emphasize the environmental aspects of the experiment. In fact, it was not the important observable aspects of the situation to which the subjects' attention was drawn that made the difference, but rather it was the subjects' internal readiness to make use of those aspects which proved to be critical.

The above report was based upon a training study in which progress was sought in conservation by initiating efforts directly related to tasks in that area. A varying series of studies by Inhelder, Sinclair, and Bovet (1974) sought to determine whether the acquisition of a competency could be accelerated by training in a structurally different competency which, however, derived from the same system of operations. Specifically, an attempt was made to accelerate the acquisition of conservation by training in class inclusion and, conversely, to accelerate the acquisition of class inclusion by training in conservation. Competency in class inclusion requires that the child grasp the relationship between part and whole. He must recognize that $A + A' = B$ and also be able to negate this mental action, such as $B - A' = A$. He deduces that B is larger than either A or A' and that, reciprocally A or A' is smaller than B. Children under eight or nine years of age generally center on either a part or upon the whole class and one of its subsets. Consequently, asked whether there are more roses or flowers in a collection of eight roses and two daisies, they will be inclined to say there are more roses because there are only two daisies. In effect, the two subsets are compared rather than subset and whole class. The child does not comprehend the phenomenon of two different levels of classes being simultaneously compared. The authors point out that conservation and class inclusion differ in basic ways even though both are manifestations of mental operations. In the conservation of matter there is a causal and temporal aspect as a transformation from one state to another state is undergone through time. Contrasted to this is class inclusion in which the necessary information is present from the outset without the passage of time being involved. Conservation is more physical in nature and deals more with objects than class inclusion problems which are essentially logical in character.

The details of the experiments in which attempts were made to accelerate cognitive competencies indirectly will not be recounted here. In general, however, the results unequivocally indicated that training in class inclusion accelerated development in both that area as well as in conservation. The authors believe that the concept formation which took place in the two areas was based upon the invention of new structures. Conversely, there was a much less evident impact upon class inclusion to be observed from the training in conservation tasks directly. Although acceleration of development in conservation itself took place, there occurred only infrequent and partial acceleration in class inclusion through direct training in conservation. It appears that there is a wider transfer of gain when the focus of training is directly upon the more logical field than when it is upon a less purely logical and more physical area. There was also a repetition of the finding reported in the previous experiment, which is that rate of progress for any particular child is largely influenced by the developmental stage he is at when he embarks upon the training. His present structural level must be adequately developed for him to assimilate what is being offered as a stimulus to growth.

Kohlberg (1971a) has made a careful review of training studies on conservation in which he concludes that conservation responses are not readily promoted by training and that, when they appear to be, they often prove to be unstable. However, he has found that genuine acceleration of the invariance concept does occur under certain circumstances. He states as follows:

> In the first place, successful induction of conservation is contingent upon the match in the sense that the child must already be near the level of attainment of conservation in terms of chronological and mental age. In the second place, some successful induction of conservation is achieved through stimulation of the development of the logical prerequisites of conservation defined by Piaget (e.g., the ability to make double classifications or to consider two dimensions simultaneously . . . or the stimulation of imaginative reversal . . .) In the third place, some successful induction of conservation results from creation of experience in which nonconserving expectations lead to certain conditions of conflict . . . (pp. 114-115).

It is clear that Kohlberg's survey of the literature has led him to conclusions that are congenial to the most recent findings of the Geneva School.

4

THE PRIORITY OF COGNITIVE STRUCTURES OVER LANGUAGE

A sound comprehension of Piaget's position on the relationship between language and cognition will contribute greatly to a complete appreciation of his epistemology. The traditional approach has maintained that, as the child gains linguistic ability, he uses his language to order and understand the world in which he lives. The radical constructivist psychology of Piaget has inverted this sequence. The construction and existence of cognitive structures will determine language acquisition and what can be known about reality. A child who does not have the appropriate structures may use certain words, but it can be demonstrated that he does not truly understand what he is talking about. It can be further demonstrated that certain language characteristics invariably emerge only after the corresponding cognitive structures have developed. Piaget's contention essentially is that language is not necessary or sufficient for intellectual development to occur. Studies in language acquisition (Bloom 1970, 1973) strongly support Piaget on this important point, as does work by Furth (1966, 1973) on deaf children. Training studies by Sinclair-de-Zwart (1969) lend even further weight to his position. In brief, Piaget challenges the orthodox position in psychology which has held that thought is dependent upon language. An understanding of the rationale underlying Piaget's challenge will illuminate the nature of thought in his system.

INTENTIONAL BEHAVIOR PRECEDES LANGUAGE

The first major argument of the Geneva School for its position on language and thought is predicated upon infant studies revealing that cognitive development precedes the acquisition of any language. To support this contention, an exposition on the early progression of intentional behavior as observed during the sensorimotor period will be presented. The reader should bear in mind that this is one aspect of total development during this period, which also includes major isomorphic gains in areas of space, time, causality, object permanence, imitation, and play. As intentional or means-end behavior is often cited as a primary characteristic of intelligence, it has been selected for special consideration in this section.

Upon entering life the infant has no innate cognitive structures other than such basic reflexes as sucking, grasping, and looking. He has no sense of a self and, hence, cannot differentiate between self and external world. It further follows that objects beyond the boundaries of his own body are not recognized as such and have no existence for him beyond his own perception and activity with them. In interaction, objects are experienced only as an extension of his own body and as intrinsically a part of the activity he performs upon them. The reflexes, as with more complex structures to follow, provide the meaning system through which the infant comes to know the world. For example, the rattle comes to be known as something to suck, see, or be grasped. Assimilation is cited by Piaget (1936/1963) as the basic fact of psychic life, by which he means that, from the outset, the infant construes or takes in the world in terms of the reflex structures. The cognitive structure or schema, as it is called during the sensorimotor period, has an intrinsic motivation to function. Objects in the environment and even parts of the infant's own body serve as aliment or nourishment for the schema which seeks to function. As Piaget states, ". . . the principal motive power of intellectual activity thus becoming the need to incorporate things into the subjects' schemata" (p. 46). The schema, needing to function, engages in continuous attempts to repeat its own activity. The repetitive acts, however, are not confined to complete rigidity, but instead generalize to varying objects in the environment. This varying of the objects acted upon forces the schema to differentiate according to the characteristic properties of the object. Hence, there comes into being a motor recognition, or recognitory assimilation. In more tangible terms, as the infant generalizes from sucking the nipple, to his fingers, to the rattle, the sucking schema itself must become less simple in its structure and more highly differentiated in order that the infant may adapt to the varying and specific demands of the objects he sucks. As each encounter with novelty in the environment occurs, this assimilating schema itself is slightly modified to accommodate the new. It is this ongoing process of assimilation and accommodation which constitutes adaptation and leads to intellectual development. There is also contained in this activity the nucleus for the infant's eventual ability to recognize external objects as existing apart from his own body and simultaneously in the process to develop a separate sense of self.

While the first stage of intentional development is characterized by the pure functioning of the reflex when triggered off by chance, the second stage ushers in deliberate attempts to coordinate activities so that the reflex may function. For example, in the second stage the child will not only suck when its thumb encounters the mouth by chance, but will make concentrated efforts to bring thumb and mouth together. As Piaget points out, while sucking is one of the few hereditary structures, coordination of hand and mouth is not hereditary. Instead, it is an example of the first acquired adaptation. The essential defining aspect of the second stage is the primary circular reaction. A circular reaction begins with a chance event which the infant then seeks to repetitively reinstate. Since the series of actions is triggered by a chance occurrence, it is not considered essentially intentional, although it is an advance over pure reflex activity. There are three types of circular reactions—primary, secondary, and tertiary —which appear in the second, third, and fifth stages respectively. The primary circular reaction of the second stage centers upon

activities involving the infant's own body. To illustrate how the
present discussion pertains to the second stage of the sensorimotor
period, the following is an observation made by Piaget (1936/
1963) of one of his own children.

> . . . . the chance contact of hand and mouth set in motion the
> directing of the latter toward the former and . . . then (but only
> then), the hand tries to return to the mouth (p. 52).

Later in the same day Piaget brings the infant's hand to his
mouth and observes:

> After a moment, the hand lost the contact but rediscovered it. It
> is no longer the mouth that seeks the hand, but the hand which
> reaches for the mouth. Thirteen times in succession I have been
> able to observe the hand go back into the mouth. There is no
> longer any doubt that coordination exists. The mouth may be
> seen opening and the hand directing itself toward it simultane-
> ously (p. 52).

With meticulous detail, Piaget reports the increasing coordination of various schemas such as looking and grasping or
hearing and seeing. The coordinated activity is designated reciprocal assimilation. In one intriguing example, Piaget comments
upon the child turning to the face of a person who has just spoken.
The child does not yet have a concept of the face as a separate
object possessing the capacity to speak. Instead, the child is
merely stimulated visually by the auditory stimulus. In turning to
look, it is as if he seeks to assimilate the sound to the visual
schema and the face to the hearing schema. The visual schema is
especially fertile in its capacity to extend the infant's applicability
of reciprocal assimilations across a wide range of interactions
with the environment. No longer looking only to provide exercise
for the visual schema, the infant will now look at an object as
a thing to be swung or grasped, hence coordinating it with the
appropriate schemas. Reciprocally, the infant may initiate the
grasping schema not simply to give expression to the intrinsic
motivation for grasping, but to coordinate that schema with the
visual schema. As the reader may well have guessed, these

coordinated activities do not occur fully developed, and we find that there are many substages leading to their full fruition, although these will not be documented here. There exist varying gradations of intentionality in the course of sensorimotor development. However, Piaget makes clear that the acquired adaptations of the second stage, even when an infant may grasp an object to look at it, do not qualify as intentional behavior. The criteria for such behavior will be introduced at a later point in this section.

The focal point of the primary circular reaction has been the infant's own body during the second stage. In the third stage there is an extension toward the external world in the rhythmic activity of secondary circular reactions. The infant now attempts to repeat chance events involving objects in the environment. There still does not exist a goal at the outset of behavior. For example, the child may accidentally pull a string attached to a rattle, which in turn will produce a pleasant sound. The child will repeat the action which, in turn, produces a pleasant sound, which leads to a repetition of pulling the string and, thus, a continuation of the circular reaction. Although the action of the secondary circular reaction is externally oriented, it should be noted that the pulling of the string and the hearing of the sound constitute a primitive differentiation between means and end behavior. The string, after the first chance contact, is pulled to reproduce and maintain the sound or effect. Nevertheless, the initial action of pulling in itself implies the end or effect. True, it is an advance over previous behavior, but the means-end arrangement is not a very differentiated or complex one.

The means-end behavior of the secondary circular reaction constitutes a single act or "self-enclosed totality," as Piaget calls it, rather than a progression through time of a serial arrangement of means-end behavior. Piaget asserts that while pulling a string to hear the sound of the shaking rattle to which it is attached is an advance over simply grasping an object when it is seen, the secondary circular reaction is still not yet truly intelligent behavior. Another feature of the third stage is the tendency of the infant to assimilate even relatively new objects into preexisting schemas. He may pause to observe the novelty, but will then proceed to initiate activities that entail assimilation over accommodation. Younger infants tend to disregard novelty in objects they encounter, while older ones demonstrate a greater effort at accommodation to that which is novel, even eventually inventing new structures for dealing with the novelty. At this third stage the infant can even be observed attempting to act upon objects at a distance in order to preserve an interesting spectacle. Wishing to reinstate the shaking of an object he cannot come in spatial contact with, the infant may initiate the procedure of swinging his hand or leg, ignoring the role of the string which he normally pulls to produce the spectacle.

The fourth stage emerges at about eight to nine months and is defined as the first appearance of decisively intentional behavior. There is no longer a limitation of merely seeking to reproduce interesting effects. The infant at the fourth stage can actually coordinate two separate schemas in a serial fashion through time, utilizing one as a means and the other as an end. There takes place a major breakthrough in the decline of radical egocentrism in this manner, as Piaget (1936/1963) states, " . . . . in proportion as the action becomes complicated through coordination of schemata, the universe becomes objectified and is detached from the self" (p. 211). The infant is capable of constructing a new schema, the means-end schema, based upon the coordination of two preexisting schemas. An essential difference from the secondary circular reaction is that the end to be achieved is obstructed by intermediary obstacles. The end cannot be immediately achieved in the way that pulling a string which is attached to a rattle will immediately produce a sound. As an example, an experimenter may place his hand between the child and an object the child wishes to grasp. The child gropes with his environment to rediscover the familiar means of "striking aside" which he applies to the experimenter's hand and subsequently grasps the desired object. Hence, two familiar schemas, striking and grasping, are coordinated serially to obtain the goal. The means is subordinated to the end. Piaget has gone so far as to suggest that this attainment marks the prototype of logical reasoning in which premise is subordinate as a means to reaching the conclusion or end of an argument. In the circular reactions examined so far there is simply an attempt to reproduce an effect encountered by chance. Now we find the infant intentionally setting out to achieve an end which it had not just experienced. The goal is in mind from the outset even though groping with the environment to hit upon the means may take place. In Piaget's own words:

> In the secondary circular reaction, the means utilized were discovered fortuitously and were applied just beforehand; hence it is only a question of rediscovering them. In the behavior patterns now under study, on the other hand, it is necessary to improvise means and remove obstacles which separate the intention from its final result (1936/1963, p. 228).

Piaget points out that inhering in the means-end schema is the beginning of a significant sense of a system of relationships. For example, to remove an obstacle in attaining a goal the infant is demonstrating a behavioral recognition of spatial and time relations. He now understands on the level of practical intelligence that the obstacle is "in front of" the goal and that its removal is necessary "before" the desired object can be picked up. Piaget is insistent, of course, that in referring to practical intelligence we are not speaking of the conceptual level to appear later, but of a demonstrated pattern of intelligent behavioral actions. In fact, it is precisely this point that Piaget has in mind when he contends that the origins of intelligence are in action and that later intelligence is internalized action. According to Piaget, at the sensorimotor period *success* and not *truth* must serve as the criterion for verification.

The fifth stage marks the appearance of the tertiary circular reaction and the discovery of new means through the growing infant's own active explorations within his environment. The reader will recall, having left the secondary circular reactions at the third stage, that circular reactions are triggered by chance which the infant repetitively seeks to reproduce. However, in the tertiary circular reaction, the child no longer seeks to rigidly reproduce previous effects, but he modifies his behavior as he experiments to innovate new effects. He is now seeking to introduce novelty into his own environment. The child has become genuinely interested in the nature of external reality. He is intent upon exploring objects from the standpoint of their own properties and capabilities. Piaget tells of the child who engages in "the experiment to see" as he drops objects being sure to vary their position, to watch how they fall, and even to observe their final resting place. There is a transition from the day before when the focal point was upon the act of letting go rather than the more externalized and independent character of the objects. It is the deliberate variation of the manner in which he drops the objects with the aim of altering the effects for study which is expressive of one of the major features of the fifth stage. The child searches for novelty and does so to acquire understanding.

A direct outgrowth of the experiment to see in the fifth stage is the distinctive activity of "the discovery of new means by experimentation." Recall that in the fourth stage there did not occur the construction of new means in problem-solving, but rather an application of old means to new situations. The striking schema had already existed; it had simply not been employed previously to strike aside an obstacle in order to grasp an object. However, in the fifth stage there occurs the virtual invention or construction of a new schema or means for achieving an end. Piaget elaborates upon a particularly interesting example known as the behavior of the support. It involves bringing an object which is out of reach closer by pulling the support upon which it rests. In the fourth stage the infant has no schema offering him an understanding of the relation Piaget calls "placed upon." He is referring here, of course, to the fact that when an object is placed upon a support, such as a cushion, it can be attained by first drawing the cushion to oneself. The infant virtually invents a schema of "placed upon" that enables him to understand the appropriate relation by engaging in a process similar to the experiment to see, when he enters the fifth stage. The infant may possibly draw a support with a desired object upon it toward himself during the fourth stage, but this is not in itself proof that he has constructed the schema of "placed upon" as yet. The test is that at this time the same child can also be observed pulling a support toward himself even when the clearly desired object is behind, beside, or being held above the support. In other words, the behavioral criterion of success will not be met, even though in drawing the support to him the child expects it to be. He does not yet recognize that the object must be placed upon the support and not simply in proximity to it, for success to occur. Disconfirmation leads to a series of concentrated efforts in which the child intently studies the connections between support and object, eventuating in the fifth stage with the invention of the schema "placed upon."

Another significant advance in the same vein, discovering new means through actively experimenting, involves a pattern of behavior using a stick. There is a very gradual build-up of a behavioral recognition that the stick can be utilized to bring to the child an object he desires, but which is out of his reach. Even after the child knows that he can displace an object by hitting it with a stick, he must still experiment with a series of cumulative accommodations to effectively bring the particular object sought to him. Therefore, he undergoes a series of random or groping acts as he hits the object repeatedly with the stick. In accord with the fifth stage search for novelty, he varies the way he hits the object to see what will happen. However, unlike the tertiary circular reaction or search for novelty, his movements are much less random as they are guided by a specific goal rather than simply a desire to see what happens in general. In connection with this development, Piaget makes an especially interesting observation about the role of chance. What if the infant hits an object purely by chance and in so doing displaces it? The event is of very little value without the intelligence to undergo a series of coordinated assimilatory and accommodatory actions moving the child progressively closer toward achievement of the goal. In a bold comparison Piaget (1936/1963) states.

> Chance, therefore, in the accommodation peculiar to sensorimotor intelligence, plays the same role as in scientific discovery. It is only useful to the genius and its revelations remain meaningless to the unskilled. In other words, it presupposes a directed search and is incapable of orienting it by itself (p. 303).

What now remains to be accomplished in the sixth stage? It is at this stage that the shift to representation in thought is made. The child need not rely any longer upon behavioral trial and error or guided groping in the environment to achieve his goal. He continues to invent new means, but the action is now literally interiorized. Piaget refers to this new activity as "invention through deduction or mental activity," cautioning that the old behavioral repertoire is not discontinued, but that this new ability becomes the highest level of intellectual achievement to appear so far. In one such instance, Piaget tells of his daughter attempting to kneel down, beginning to do so by leaning against a stool on the floor. As she leans upon the stool, she pushes it away from her. She then stands up, places the stool against a firmly resting sofa, and proceeds once again to kneel by leaning against it. There is no intermediary phase of directed empirical groping necessary. Instead, the child was able to internally deduce a solution to the problem which she executed flawlessly without hesitation. Piaget introduces several examples of this type, some manifesting transitional substages, but all basically predicated upon the principle of internal instant invention of a new means.

In another particularly illuminating example, the child seeks to obtain a chain which is contained in a matchbox that is left slightly open. The slit is not sufficient for the child's fingers to directly enter the matchbox. She attempts this, but does not succeed. She has had no previous experience with the opening and closing nature of a matchbox. Yet now she is observed pausing, while successively opening and closing her mouth. Piaget believes that she has thought out the situation. The opening and closing of her mouth is a transitional phase in which the symbolic behavior is in the process of being interiorized. Transitionally there occurs an overt imitation of the solution which is once removed from empirical groping. Following the pause and expressed imitative behavior, the child goes to the matchbox, opens it wider, and retrieves the chain. In so doing, she does not perform any unnecessary actions. Later, the thinking activity is entirely interiorized without benefit of the observed imitation. The child has invented a new means through mental representation. Piaget emphasizes that the problem is clarified for the child when her first attempt at securing the chain fails. Her initial hypothesis is disconfirmed. She assimilates the situation to previous schemas of experience in which she has opened and closed boxes. Piaget (1936/1963) comments, "Those are the schemata which confer a meaning on the present situation and which at the same time direct the search" (p. 744). Invention is the accommodation of those schemas to the particularized features of the matchbox with its narrow slit. Despite its *roots* in the individual, invention is unmistakably a *creative* act in Piaget's view.

The above account of intentional behavior is a highly abstracted version of Piaget's original work. Nevertheless, some of the most salient aspects are contained in it and, it is hoped that, they will convey a sense of the majestic achievements which evolve during the intellectual development of the sensorimotor period. All this occurs without benefit of language. In a very real and significant way, Piaget justifiably asserts that ontogenetically, intelligence precedes language.

THE SYMBOLIC FUNCTION

Central to understanding the role of language in the Piagetian system is a recognition of its relationship to the generic concept of the symbolic function (Piaget 1946/1962). Prior to the sixth stage of the sensorimotor period, which virtually ushers in the first phase of the preoperational period, the child cannot mentally represent objects to himself. There are, of course, early precursors to representation. Primary among these are the signal and the index, which are in some way part of the object. For example, the footsteps of the mother coming from another room signal her approach. The tracks of a bird walking on the sand or the exposed tip of an object otherwise concealed by something over it are indices of their presence. The child is also capable of perception prior to the sixth stage, but a percept by its very nature requires the presence of the object perceived. Representation, appearing as it does at the sixth stage, frees the child from the constraints of the immediate presence of objects. He can now re-present to himself objects which are no longer present. He does this through the use of either symbol or sign. These are distinct from an index or percept in that they are differentiated from that which they stand for. The symbol differs from the sign in that the former is personal and resembles that which it represents, whereas the latter is social and bears no necessary resemblance to that which it represents. That which is represented may be referred to as the signified and the representation itself is called the signifier. The significate is the actual meaning ascribed to the representation and this is determined by the level of schematic development to which the representation is assimilated.

The symbolic function, more recently called semiotic function, is comprised of symbols and signs, and is distinguished by the capacity to evoke, on a symbolic plane, objects that are absent from the immediate environment. Signs specifically refer to language, which eventually becomes public and is socially shared. However, with the advent of the symbolic function, it is not language which the child as yet has the most mastery over. The beginning use of language has private meanings attached to it, is limited by the child's structural development, and retains facets of the action-laden sensorimotor period. It is the symbol, as opposed to the sign or language, which the child demonstrates the most facility with at first. The major symbols are play, imitation, and image. Progressively more complex playful behavior can be observed in the infant during the sensorimotor period. But it is not until the symbolic function develops that the child begins to play with objects that represent absent objects. The child may play symbolically with a stick that represents a rifle or use a crumpled piece of cloth to represent a pillow as he pretends to sleep. The real nature of the objects used are distorted or assimilated by the child to take on the symbolic meaning he ascribes to it.

Another example of the ludic symbol given by Piaget (1946/ 1962) is a cardboard box and a shell manipulated by a child such that they symbolize a cat walking along a wall. Imitation becomes symbolic when, in the sixth stage, the child can be observed for the first time engaging in deferred imitation. As with play, imitative behavior becomes increasingly more complex throughout the sensorimotor period, but it is not until the symbolic function emerges that the child is able to imitate behavior which he has previously observed, but which is not being observed at the time of the imitative behavior. Piaget (1946/1962) offers the example of his daughter who one day observed for the first time a child having a temper tantrum. Twelve hours later she had her own first temper tantrum in which she distinctly emulated the sounds and movements of the other child. She was sixteen months old at the time. Just as assimilation predominates in play, it is accommodation that predominates in imitation.

The image, a third type of symbol, is actually the interiorization of imitation. It is not, as some have maintained, a faint memory trace of a previous perception, but an active reconstruction. Through an attempt at internalized imitation the child now tries to accommodate the contours of the signified. Hence, an image is personal or specific to the individual constructing it and is based on material or sensorial properties of the object, even though the object is no longer present. The reader may recall the child who opened and closed her mouth in a fashion analogous to the matchbox. Piaget suggests that this transitional act witnesses the gradual interiorization of imitation which leads to the image. It can be seen that through the use of play, imitation, and image the child may disengage from the immediate context to which the sensorimotor child is limited and thereby vastly enlarge upon the scope of his universe. But where does language fit into this scheme of things? Piaget (1964/1968) states:

> As language is only a particular form of the symbolic function and as the individual symbol is certainly simpler than the collective sign, it is permissible to conclude that thought precedes language and that language confines itself to profoundly transforming thought by helping it to attain its forms of equilibrium by means of a more advanced schematization and a more mobile abstraction (pp. 91-92).

It should be apparent from the above comment that, while Piaget subordinates language to thought in development, he does not slight its highly facilitative role.

FIGURATIVE AND OPERATIVE KNOWING

Piaget posits two aspects to cognition—the figurative and the operative. Furth (1970) has elaborated upon these in an effort to deepen the understanding of the role of language in thought. Figurative knowing is the static configuration of things and stresses the sensorial component. Operative knowing is an act of transformation through which incoming data are understood. Figurative and operative knowing are not two totally separate ways of knowing but are two aspects under which things are known. There is a potential for confusing operative and operational which should be avoided at the outset. Operational thought refers specifically to the two last periods of development starting with the concrete operations of age six or seven and extending to the formal operations beginning at approximately age eleven or twelve. Operative knowing, however, is a broader concept which encompasses all of cognitive-structural development from birth onward. The meaning imposed upon the figurative element is derived from the particular level of operative development. Furth uses an example involving the White House to demonstrate these concepts. Figurative knowing refers to the perception or image which provides a static configuration. This sensory input is then subject to a transformation determined by the operative or structural level of the knower. It may come to be known as simply a house where people live, a place where politicians work, or possibly the building where representatives of the people make laws that govern the country. The last of these can itself be understood in terms of varying levels of maturity, depending upon such structures as classification, justice, and ratio, to cite only a few. The point is that the knowing derived from the figurative component cannot go beyond the operative level of development. Therefore, as Furth (1969) has pointed out elsewhere:

> It is the operative component, present in any perceptual or sym-
> bolic behavior, which primarily determines the level of under-
> standing reality. Thus neither symbolic nor figurative functioning

can explain intelligence since these cognitive aspects are fully tied to and dependent on the level of operative thinking (p. 104).

Furth (1969, 1970) stresses that a symbol does not possess an intrinsic meaning as the meaning is derived from the operative level, which itself changes as it is restructured in development. He points out that the figurative aspect of the symbol is an internalization of that which is external to the child. In other words, the static configuration of an image is based upon an internal accommodation of an object which, although not present, resides in the real environment, or at least did so at some time. However, the object as it exists outside the knower does not provide the *meaning* to him, for this is derived from an assimilation to the operative structure of the image. To elucidate this Furth (1970) states, "An operative structure in itself has no figurative component and does not represent the known event but *is* the known event and the prerequisite for its symbolic representation" (p. 249).

In further interpreting Piaget's theory, Furth (1970) distinguishes between operative activity as the *form* which is abstracted from the specific situation or content and the figurative aspect as derived from the *matter* of the specific situation. A child playing with six cubes may *by* his actions with them invent an operative structure which provides knowledge that the sum total of the cubes remains the same regardless of how they are combined. That is $4+2=6$ just as $2+4=6$ and $5+1=6$. The order or clustering has no bearing on the outcome. The knowledge gained is not based upon any properties of the objects, but is derived from an abstraction of one's actions upon the objects, from which an operative structure is constructed. This is logico-mathematical knowledge as opposed to physical knowledge which deals directly with the particular properties of objects.

Furth (1970) insists that in comprehending Piaget's position on language and thought, it is vital to distinguish between the child's repertoire of language symbols and how he is able to employ them in areas involving logical thought. A preoperational child may have a fairly wide range of linguistic symbols available to him, but is delimited in his use of them by the operative structures of that period. Thus, the lack of reversible thought structures will lead to inaccurate verbal responses in such tasks as classification and conservation. The child who says that there are more yellow primulas than there are flowers in a bunch of ten yellow primulas and two red roses does so not because he does not have the vocabulary to give the proper response, but because he lacks the operative structures to promote his understanding of the logical requirements of the task. His use of the language cannot go beyond his preoperational understanding of classification. Similarly, a child who can count a row of ten pennies and a second row of ten buttons situated below in a one-to-one correspondence will say that there is the same amount of objects in each row. Judging from his verbal response, it would appear that he understands something about counting and number. Yet if one of the two rows is condensed, he will say that there is more in the unchanged or longer row. He will persist in this even after he has recounted the two rows. The child has not yet developed conservation structures and, thus, his use of language cannot go beyond his level of operative development. Both Furth (1970) and Piaget (1964/1968) have pointed out that, even when in the concrete operational period, the child must apply his logical structures on actual objects or their representations. While he is now capable of dealing with classification, seriation, and transitivity on a concrete level, hypothetical questions in these areas which would require a purely verbal response will prove beyond his ken until the formal operational period, at which time language takes on the greatest relevancy as an instrumentality in thought.

There is a fine question that should be examined in this context—does language have a figurative aspect as do perception, imitation, and image? Furth (1969) indicates that Piaget de-emphasizes the figural aspect of language and likens them more to general schemas. Furth would prefer to emphasize the figural aspect of language in the developing child. He points out that although it does not resemble the signified in the way that perception, imitation, and image do, the auditory and vocal features of language are figural. Furthermore, the young child's language is highly egocentric and embedded in specific, private meanings. The early use of linguistic symbols bears the mark of their sensorimotor heritage. A single word such as "momma" may not simply stand for the mother as such, but may convey an entire range of actions. It may be a request for the mother to bring food or engage in comforting or helpful activities of various kinds. Furth (1970) compares a young child gesturing as if throwing a ball to his exclaiming "ball" to convey knowledge of a ball as something to be thrown. In both instances, the motoric activity and its vocalized alternative, there are figurative aspects to the representations which attempt to accommodate to the action of a ball as a thing for throwing. Furth (1969) is clear on his position regarding this question. He comments, . . . "it would seem to me more appropriate to include the language of the growing child in the category of figurative instruments to the same extent as mental images" (p. 141).

PRELINGUISTIC ROOTS OF CONCRETE OPERATIONS

Piaget maintains that intelligence is action. Through his own actions upon objects, the child comes to abstract and construct knowledge of the world. He combines and dissociates objects, he orders and reorders them, he engages in a multitude of motor activities as he acts upon and interacts with the things in his world. Conceptual knowledge is internalized action and as he masters it, sooner or later, the child begins to show an ability to put it into language. At about six or seven years of age the child begins to give correct verbal responses to tasks involving classification, seriation, conservation, and transitivity . . . . , when the objects in the task are present and can be directly manipulated by him or the experimenter. However, Piaget (1964/1968) has underscored the fact that conceptual mastery of these tasks has its roots in the sensorimotor period on the behavioral plane. In other words, the genesis of concrete operations is prelinguistic. We have already seen how intentional behavior progresses without benefit of language, although it is certainly the case that later the child will engage in much self-aware problem-solving activity that will be formulated in words. One does not have to stretch the imagination to recognize the development of object permanence as the prototype of conservation. Recognitory assimilation during the sensorimotor period is, indeed, an early prelinguistic form of classification. The infant who, when hungry, rejects nonnutriment-providing objects and chooses to suck only on the nipple of a breast or bottle has engaged in an act of primitive classification on a purely behavioral level. Piaget (1936/1963) observes his infant daughter seriously, effortlessly, and briefly shake her leg upon spying a toy doll which she has often swung. He interprets this as a prelinguistic act of classification. Through recognitory assimilation the child ascribes the meaning of the doll as being a thing to be swung. She has no recourse to language, as yet, and so relies on a behavioral mode of expression. Prototypical examples of relations or seriation can also be found in infancy. Observing his son at four months and twenty-one days of age, Piaget (1936/1963) states, ". . . when he strikes with his hand the toys hanging from his bassinet . . . he visibly gradates his movements as function of the result: at first he strikes gently and then continues more and more strongly, etc" (p. 185). Here we see an illustration of a prelinguistic sense of quantity and of ordering things in relation to one another.

Piaget (1964/1968) has also pointed out that, although the child can handle concrete operational tasks from about six or seven years on, he cannot handle the tasks on a purely verbal level if the objects involved are not within his perceptual range, until he enters the period of formal operations. He has the structures which enable him to properly combine and dissociate concrete objects which he can personally manipulate, but if asked questions in the abstract about universal classes he will not succeed until early adolescence. Piaget's emphasis is that, even though the concrete operational child can coordinate actions in a logical and systematic way in the real world, he still has not yet mastered these operations on a purely linguistic level, where he would have to operate with abstractions and universals. Therefore, it follows that language cannot account for the development of logical structures of the concrete operational period.

A final prelinguistic example, with sensorimotor roots, which Piaget offers deals with transitivity. Transitivity involves drawing a conclusion between two elements by comparing them with an intermediary element, but not directly with each other. If A is greater than B and B is greater than C, it must follow that A is greater than C. The concrete operational child can perform this task on a concrete level by first comparing sticks A and B and then sticks B and C. Having done so, he can conclude that stick A is greater than stick C. However, if asked to solve the following problem on purely verbal level, he cannot do so until he arrives at the formal operational period. "Edith is fairer than Susan and darker than Lily; who is the darkest of the three?" Here, of course, we have another example of the preceding argument in which a concept can be handled structurally at the concrete level by manually handling the objects, but is not yet mastered linguistically. However, let us also trace this back to the level of practical intelligence. Piaget has set up a task in which a child toward the end of the sensorimotor period can observe an object being placed under a blanket. What he does not see is that under the blanket is a hat under which the experimenter actually places the object. In seeking to retrieve the object, the older infant will lift the blanket and when he finds the hat he will then remove it, fully expecting to find the object. Piaget suggests that this is a seminal illustration on the behavioral plane of transitivity relations. In effect, the child grasps on a behavioral level that, if the object is under the hat and the hat is under the blanket, the object is under the blanket. He contends that this is the functional equivalent of not only transitivity on a representational plane, but also of class inclusion, both of which are first mastered at the concrete operational period.

The role of language in formal operational thought will not be elaborated upon at length. Because of the hypothetical and propositional nature of such thinking it would appear that language is a necessary element in formal reasoning. However, it should be obvious that the mere presence of language does not assure a formal operational capacity. If it did, all people who normally speak a language, the vast majority by far, would be at the formal operational period. Research and common observation, however, tend to disprove any such conclusion. In fact, Cromer (1974) suggests that there appears to be little difference between the language of the formal reasoning person and the nonformal reasoning person, except in the sphere of linguistic structures. As at all previous levels this is determined by operative level of development.

LANGUAGE AND COGNITION IN THE DEAF

Furth (1964, 1966, 1971, 1973) is a foremost contributor to our knowledge about the cognitive development of deaf people. A study of the deaf provides a natural opportunity to explore intellectual development in the absence of language. Furth maintains that, while a deaf child is not without symbols, he does not possess a conventional linguistic system. He discards as insignificant the relatively few words acquired by the deaf child by the time he is five years old, because, in contrast to the hearing child, his vocabulary is not informed by the rules of linguistics. Furth regards the gestures of deaf people which are used in communication as a human language; however, he points out that the vast majority of young children who grow up deaf are not exposed to American sign language. Further, he points out that, even until recently, the official educational position was not to teach or encourage deaf school children to learn the conventional sign language used by deaf adults. Generally it has not been until after ten years of age that deaf children have begun to learn American sign language. Gestures utilized in communication prior to that time tend to be spontaneous and are not grounded systematically in linguistic rules. American sign language, which is eventually learned, is predicated upon linguistic rules and is described by Furth as a human language without speech. However, the significant aspect for our discussion is the fact that almost all deaf children have been growing up during their first decade without a language, whereas their hearing counterparts have been learning a formal conventional language during comparable years. In other words, the young deaf child has been deprived not only of speech, but also of language— the former being an act of nature and the latter of neglect and official policy. Furth defines intelligence as an ability to success- fully perform learning tasks of a complex nature and he maintains that a distinction between language and intelligence is conceptual- ly sound. To define intelligence in a manner that makes language intrinsic to it is to beg the question.

It should be obvious that by studying the ability of deaf children to handle complex learning tasks and by comparing them to hearing children, we may learn something of the relationship between language and cognition. Furth has been engaged in con- ducting and reviewing such research over the past several years. His general observations and results will be summarized here. The research covers memory, perception, and conceptual develop- ment. Many of the tasks utilized Piagetian problems and all of Furth's theoretical observations are couched within the framework of Piaget's developmental psychology. Based on his research, Furth has drawn a fundamental distinction between symbol discovery and symbol use. In experiments involving the discovery of a symbol, Furth found that deaf subjects, most notably the younger ones, performed in a manner inferior to the hearing subjects. However, once the deaf subjects understood the symbol, they were able to use it as well as those who could hear. Furth (1966) succinctly states, " . . . on a task using a discovery principle the deaf lagged behind, but on a task requiring comprehension and use of a principle they were equal to the hearing" (p. 147). Furth adopts the position that, where deaf children are found to be markedly deficient in a cognitive comparison to hearing children, it is not due directly to their language deficiency but to their social environment. Because of the way society has related to deaf children, Furth finds that they have not been encouraged to develop a spirit of curiosity or inquiry nor to actively reason about their world. He emphasizes that it is precisely in areas where initiative and challenge are called into play that deaf children prove inferior to hearing children. In comprehension and use of concepts they do not exhibit the same retardation. Hence, where intellectual motivation to explore and raise questions is called into play the deaf children do not fare well because of their impoverished social milieu. Nevertheless, this is to be distinguished from their basic intellectual capacity, involving the understanding and application of concepts, at which they perform well.

In further support of his position, Furth cites a study by Furth and Youniss (1965) in which a rural group of children were given tests on the symbolic discovery and symbolic use tasks. The rural children were drastically different from the deaf children in that they possessed a basic linguistic competence and, hence, were similar in this aspect to the original control group used with the deaf children. At the same time they came from a culturally deprived environment which lacked much of the stimulating enrichment the control group enjoyed. In this respect, they bore a greater resemblance to the deaf children. Strikingly, they performed poorly on the symbol discovery tasks and were equal to the average on the symbol use tasks. In brief, they exhibited capacities comparable to the deaf group rather than the hearing group. Language, per se, did not seem to be the significant variable, but certain aspects of the intellectual environment did seem to be significant. In general, across the range of all the various cognitive tasks utilized, deaf children did as well as hearing children or at the most lagged one to two years behind, as in some conservation tasks. The one exception was in symbol discovery tasks. Tasks which relied heavily on verbal comprehension, of course, did not find the deaf children faring well. The deaf children did manifest a lack of basic information usually found to be in the repertoire of hearing children. Although the deaf children did not do well at unstructured situations (symbol discovery), exhibiting traits of rigidity or passivity, much of this limitation was no longer present by adulthood. In a conclusion to his classic book, *Thinking Without Language,* Furth (1966) states:

Apart from these listed effects, the basic development and structure of the intelligence of the deaf in comparison with the hearing is remarkably unaffected by the absence of verbal language. One can reasonably assume that the major area in which the deaf appear to be different from the hearing is in variables related to personality, motivation, and values. If substantial differences are found, they will likely be due to experiential and social factors of home, school and the deaf community (p. 227).

Furth does not view the impoverished learning climate of the deaf child as inevitable and he urges formal systematic nonverbal communication instruction for the very young child. Recognizing that verbal language is not a necessary condition to thinking should accelerate the development of practices and policies in this endeavor.

A final comparison of some interest is that between deaf children and blind children (Sinclair-De-Zwart 1969). As Sinclair-De-Zwart points out, although deaf children lack linguistic competence, their normal interaction with the environment during infancy lays the foundation of sensorimotor structures. In the case of blind children, however, while they normally acquire linguistic facility, their restricted environmental exchanges delimit the development of significant sensorimotor schemes. Consequently, deaf children manifest at most only a slight lag in development compared to normal children on tasks involving concept comprehension and use, whereas blind children are observed to be an average of four years behind normals developmentally on the same tests. Sinclair-De-Zwartz emphasizes that the language ability of the blind children is insufficient to counter the schematic retardation derived from their limited actions upon the environment during infancy and early childhood. It should be noted, however, that the gap in cognitive development is eliminated in time

RESEARCH FROM THE GENEVA SCHOOL

Sinclair-De-Zwart (1969), Inhelder and Sinclair (1969), and Sinclair (1971) have conducted research on the relationship between language and cognition which offers compelling evidence of the ontogenetic priority of the latter over the former. Their primary aim was to discover whether the emergence of concrete operations is accompanied by a parallel change in language. In addition, they sought to determine whether verbal training of those lacking the operations in the linguistic devices utilized by those possessing them would, in fact, lead to the acquisition of the operations. A vital distinction between vocabulary or content and syntax or form is made. Children could be divided according to this distinction into two groups. All of the children had the appropriate vocabulary at their command, but there were two distinct ways of utilizing it in evidence. In describing pencils placed before them, preoperational children would string adjectives together serially rather than cross multiply them. They would make such comments as "This pencil is long, this one is short; this one is thin, this one is fat." In contrast, children who had already shown an ability to conserve, would say "This one is longer and thinner (than the other one)." Inhelder and Sinclair (1969) draw attention to the fact that this phraseology demonstrates the conservers linguistic capacity to coordinate the descriptive terms and to integrate the comparative judgment into one syntactical arrangement. The preoperational children, while they had the particular words needed within their repertoire, failed to employ such a grammatically economical approach. The linguistic method of the concrete operational children was determined by their operative development, which permitted them to employ compensation in conserving. For example, the conserver will often respond to a conservation task in which one of two equal balls of clay is elongated by saying that the amount remains the same because while it is longer it is also thinner. In other words, a structural advance in the concrete operations enables the child to simultaneously coordinate two dimensions. The structural change is reflected in a parallel linguistic modification. An attempt was then made to train children who were preoperational to adopt the syntax utilized by the concrete operational children to see if this would lead to conservation. It proved quite difficult to inculcate the more advanced linguistic expressions, and, when they were acquired, there was not any appreciable shift to conservation. The trained children began to convey the dimensions in their verbal responses and yet still continued to draw non-conservation conclusions. It is once again apparent that language facility can be misleading and that without cognitive structural development there is no genuine conceptual understanding.

CONCLUSION

Language has been introduced as one of several symbolic functions which come into being as the capacity for representation develops at the threshold of the preoperational period. A distinction was made between figurative and operative knowing, in which the first of these is tied to sensorial content, while the second is freed of material aspects and is based on a mental act of transformation. Figurative and operative elements are not totally separate, but are two aspects of cognition. The genesis of advanced reasoning which can be rendered into sophisticated syntactical arrangements is found in the sensorimotor period in such domains as intentionality, object permanence, primitive classification, relations, and transitivity. At the concrete operational period systematically logical structures are brought into play with materials that can be manipulated in the environment, but the linguistic ability to deal with these tasks on an abstract level is not present until the development of the formal operations. A comparative study of deaf children with a normal group indicated that with minimal lag, and in some cases none, there was comparable reasoning capacity. Reasoning on complex intellectual tasks without benefit of language was established. It was seen that operative development is paralleled by appropriate syntax, but that linguistic training when successful is not accompanied by operative understanding. The weight of evidence supporting Piaget's position on the language-cognition controversy is succinctly stated by Sinclair-De-Zwart (1969) when she asserts, ". . . Language is not the source of logic, but is on the contrary structured by logic" (p. 325).

5

TOWARD AUTONOMY
IN MORAL JUDGMENT

INTRODUCTION

Piaget's fifth book (1932/1965) is a major treatise on moral development, albeit the only work he ever devoted exclusively to that subject. He presented it as a foundation upon which others would build, believing strongly that an understanding of moral development in the child would illuminate the nature of adult morality. Presently we shall focus upon Piaget's own work, from which most of the following exposition is taken, but it should be noted that he had been influenced by the earlier writings of Baldwin and Bovet. The reader should be cautioned that the studies we are about to examine emphasize moral judgment and not behavior. The cognitive-developmental approach states that cognitive structures must develop to enable the individual to eventually grasp universal principles of justice, but that there is no assurance that the presence of the structures (i.e., the ability to make the right judgment) will inevitably lead to moral action. The structures may be viewed as a necessary, but not sufficient, condition to moral behavior.

There are two basic epochal developments in moral judgment—the morality of constraint and the morality of cooperation. The former involves the imposition by an outside authority of specific rules which are to be followed by the individual. This is known as the period of heteronomy, as opposed to the autonomy to follow, and is characterized by duty and submission to authority. The command of recognized authority determines what is right, and this is the accepted criterion regardless of circumstances. In a morality of constraint, credence is given to unilateral respect, moral realism, and objective responsibility, each of which will be examined in detail below. Gradually there develops a morality of cooperation in which a bond of solidarity with others supplants external authority. Personal motives and subjective responsibility are taken into account when making moral judgments. The growing child moves in the direction of equality with adults and unilateral respect declines. Mutual respect and autonomy of conscience undergird the morality of cooperation. In the period of autonomy, the good is founded upon a sum of relations between individuals and is not imposed from without. The good is no longer equated with the existing rule or command, but is dissociated from it, allowing the individual to pursue what ought to be rather than merely what is.

As cognitive development progresses, the child increasingly acquires a capacity for reciprocity of relations. The dissolution of preoperational egocentrism promotes his ability to take the point of view of another and, as he decenters, his judgment regarding the right of others can take into account multiple perspectives. Piaget stresses that, while individuals placing themselves in reciprocal relationships with one another do acquire a more objective picture of reality, they do not eliminate their own points of view. He draws an analogy to a number of travellers climbing a mountain, citing the fact that individual perspectives are inadequate to a full and true representation of the total picture. A more accurate representation could be drawn by coordinating the multiple perspectives of strategically placed mountaineers. In so doing, however, the validity of any one climber's point of view would not be vitiated, even though it is limited. To acquire this role-taking ability, it is necessary to engage in social activity. The child left to himself would remain egocentric and, indeed, would not be able to recognize his own thoughts and feelings as distinguished from those of others. Piaget emphasizes that an awareness of one's own self is forged from repeated comparisons between self and other people. The differentiation between self and external world has its roots in a behavioral level in the sensorimotor period. It is seen during the preoperational period as the child differentiates his own psychic contents from natural phenomena. However, its greatest significance in the realm of morality is derived from the child's progressive development of reciprocity, the ability to take the point of view of another. The young child does not recognize the need in social life to verify his thoughts and to subject them to rational disputation. Similarly, his feelings are accepted as having universal validity, and it is not until he encounters the "judgments and evaluations of others that this intellectual and affective anomy will gradually yield to the pressure of collective logic and moral laws" (Piaget 1932/ 1965, p. 401). The child left to himself egocentrically accepts everything his mind entertains and when subject to his parents without question adopts what they say as ultimate law. If significant progress is to take place, rational criticism must occur and the medium for this is peer-level discussion, for which cooperation is necessary. Piaget insists that mere behavioral conformity to the social norm does not reflect genuine moral conduct; the mind must tend toward an autonomous goal and recognize the inherent value of rules, when such obtain. However, when the value of rules proposed by the adult authority is not evident when subject to the scrutiny of reason, the child who has progressed beyond heteronomy will rely on his own judgment. Bear in mind, that relying upon one's own rational judgment is not the same as egocentrically adopting one's own point of view without question. The independent moral judgment is based upon a recognition of the rights of others which, in turn, is founded upon mutuality or a reciprocity of relations.

The general formulation above is largely an outgrowth of Piaget's studies of moral judgment in the developing child. We shall now turn our attention to those studies and the theoretical amplifications provided by Piaget.

PLAYING BY THE RULES

The section of Piaget's book on moral judgment devoted to rules concentrates upon a comparison between the child's practice in the game of marbles as opposed to his consciousness of the rules. Methodologically, Piaget first thoroughly familiarized himself with the game as played in the locality where the child lived. He then proceeded to adopt a naive stance and began to play with children, asking them all sorts of questions. These questions included whether rules could be invented and what their origin might be. Essentially he sought to ascertain whether the children believed rules could be appropriately modified and whether the rules were construed as fair on the basis of accepted custom or because of an inherent and immutable value attached to them. Piaget cautions, as with the child's conception of the world, that the child does not have preconceptions about rules, but rather the answers he formulates to questions reflect a basic attitude.

Piaget discovered that in practicing the game, the youngest children are at a purely motor or individual stage and play with the marbles at the whim of their desire and motor habits. In the second or egocentric stage, from three to six years, the child is exposed to the codified rules of the game and makes an attempt to follow them in his playing. Nevertheless, he actually plays in an idiosyncratic manner, violating the rules at every turn. Although intending to play by the rules handed down to him, the child assimilates them to his private schemas, failing to accommodate to their true character. Thus, even children playing "together" at this stage are really playing on their own and each can wind up winning. At approximately six or seven years of age there is ushered in a stage of incipient cooperation. Although children now play to win and attempt to unify the rules, upon questioning they reveal highly differing and sometimes even antithetical conceptions of them. The fourth and last stage, appearing between eleven and twelve years, is the codification of rules. During this phase children are surprisingly well informed and in agreement about the rules of the game; they strive to adhere to them in a literal fashion to a remarkable degree.

For a time the rule is considered sacred. This timespan extends from the latter part of the egocentric period to the first half of the cooperative stage. It is held to be immutable, perennial, and the product of adults, who are viewed as omniscient and incapable of error. Such an outlook reflects a form of moral realism in which the rule is seen as an external object, somewhat in the manner that the child substantiates dreams and names. Piaget points out the child's tendency to violate the commands of parents and teachers, while at the same time revering, with great mental subservience, those commands. He suggests that this derives from the same set of attitudes which leads to the unstable adherence to rules in playing marbles, while at the same time holding a conception of rules as inviolate. Although the child acquiesces to the externally imposed rule in his intention to follow it, he does not put it into practice because it is imposed from without and has not become a part of his own conscience. Not until a rule is interiorized and its value grasped will it effect the child's conduct. As he progresses toward a morality of autonomy he will come to realize the social nature of rules which are derived from interpersonal exchanges borne out of mutual cooperation with peers. During the time of moral realism, however, the child's conception of rules is influenced by the unilateral respect he holds towards parents and authority figures generally, including the older children in his milieu.

Piaget raises the question of whether the behavioral rites and symbols which characterize the young child during the individual stage can fully explain the rules of games. Although he cites them as a necessary condition to the development of rules in the ordinary sense he rejects them as offering a fully adequate explanation. They are not a sufficient condition. Ritualistic acts are those which are not engaged in for their adaptive capacity, but are performed with regularity for their mere pleasure. This can be observed in the infant as early as eight to ten months. Toward the end of the first year we see the ritualistic behavior take on a pretend quality, as in a case of the infant pretending to be asleep with a knowing smile on its face. This is an early form of the symbol which is being "played out." The consciousness of regularity in this behavior links it to the rule, but it is not yet such because it is not characterized by a sense of obligation. Obedience to a rule becomes a factor in which there are two or more people involved, whether the other be an authority or a peer. The practice of a pure rite does not contain this submissive component.

In the second, or egocentric, stage we find a form of behavior that is transitional between individual and socialized behavior. There exist many instances in which the rule is modified and used by the child as a rite, even though he is aware of a set of rules and sincerely believes he is playing in conformity with them. The egocentrism which locks him into his own point of view does not permit him to play with others on a level of mutuality and cooperation, nor does it even allow him to be aware of his own social isolation. The child does not conceive of winning the game in terms of defeating the other players, but rather in terms of playing independently even though within a social context. Children in this stage do not pursue the game with a competitive spirit and do not submit to a common set of rules, although they think they are doing so. The child does not take into account what the other players are doing and, hence, there is not coordination of action in accord with the rules. Nevertheless, the child at this stage genuinely desires to imitate the older children and, therefore, to play the game correctly. It is this dual nature of disregarding the rules, while at the same time wishing to play correctly as the elders do, which best describes the egocentric stage.

In the third stage of the practice of rules there emerges, at about ages seven to eight, an impulse to understand the nature of the game within the social matrix. Winning is no longer viewed as an individual act such as knocking a marble out of the square, but is recognized as getting the best of the other players, such as in acquiring more marbles than the others. The child is not now simply eager to imitate the older boys in some vague and general way, but is directly and immediately related to his game partners while trying to play by an accepted set of rules. Pleasure is no longer motoric or egocentric but is genuinely social. However, the cooperation which prevails during the third stage is more in its intent than actuality. The rules are still not known in detail from about ages seven to ten. It is not until the fourth stage that the rules as a system regulating behavior are truly mastered. Children then even thrive on disputes which may lead to judicial dialogue of principle or procedure. During the third stage much of the reasoning about rules takes place as the children play, but there is still little evidence of legislating or generalizing their resolutions to all possible cases, regardless of time and place. In referring to the third stage and anticipating what will come to characterize the fourth, Piaget (1932/1965) states, "But something is still lacking if deduction is to be generalized and made completely rational: the child must be able to reason formally, i.e., he must have a conscious realization of the rules of reasoning which will enable him to apply them to any case whatsoever, including purely hypothetical cases (mere assumptions)" (p. 47). In other words, it is during the concrete operational period that the child is in the third stage of rule practicing and, hence, his reasoning is concentrated upon what is known to him in the environment. It is at about eleven to twelve years of age, when the formal operational period emerges, that the child becomes interested in matters of principle and in anticipating all possibilities to cover every contingency in all games, not only the one he is immediately involved in.

The focus of this discussion will now shift from the practice of rules to the child's own consciousness of them. Piaget speculates that, even when the child first comes across marbles, he has some conviction that rules apply to them. The speculation is based on the observation that the children's lives have already exposed them to considerable variety of rules and regulations and of permissible actions and forbidden ones. The second stage, as mentioned above, is initiated when the child seeks to initiate the rules imposed from without, even though he practices in egocentric fashion. In a most rigid fashion, from the beginning of this stage, rules are conceived of as sacred and unalterable. It is considered wrong to change a rule even if done by consensus of all involved. If the child should appear to accept a change of rule, it is only because he grasps that a modification has actually been effected. In his view, rules originate from either his father, government officials, or a divinity. They are eternal and immutable. Ironically, at the same time that rules are so regarded, we find young children of this egocentric stage practicing the game with little or no compliance to them. However, it is important not to view this childish egocentrism as completely asocial. It is, in fact, social to the extent that it is welded to adult constraint, which is founded upon unilateral respect, that is upon the authority and prestige of the adult. The genuine cooperation of equals, an even more highly socialized arrangement, is not achieved during the egocentric stage.

As indicated earlier, it is the sense of an imposition of external rules, however prestigious in origin, which largely accounts for its lack of effect or practice. It is cooperation between equals which produces change leading to actually playing by the rules. Cooperation also eventually eliminates the "mystical feeling" the child holds toward authority. Although there are four stages in the practice of the game, there are only three stages in the areas of consciousness toward rules. The incipient stage of co-operation, starting at about age seven or eight, continues with a reverence of the rule as sacred until its midpoint is reached. At about age ten, starting with the second half of the cooperative stage, the rule is no longer conceived as external or sacred. The prestige of adult authority and tradition ceases to hold sway. Consensus upon the rule is acknowledged as sufficient to modify, invent, and adopt. Any opinion may now be advanced as long as its proponents seek acceptance by legal procedures. Rules that make winning easy are rejected and those which heighten the interest by placing emphasis upon skill are sought. Collective opinion, not the established order, determines whether the rule is to be accepted or not. The child comes to recognize that there had been no external and externally imposed rules about the game of marbles, but that rules of the game come from the children's own discussions around their play. It is at this juncture that autonomy supersedes heteronomy; that cooperation supersedes constraint; that mutual respect supersedes unilateral respect. Piaget (1932/1965) states, "It is from the moment that it replaces the rule of constraint that the rule of cooperation becomes an effective moral law" (p. 70). It is at precisely this point of a new development of consciousness toward rules (age ten or eleven) that one begins to observe a greater applicability of rules in game playing during the third stage, the stage of cooperation, in the four stages of practice.

The rule is no longer imposed externally but is interiorized in the mind of each participant, and compliance becomes self-willed. Reciprocity in human relations is promoted by cooperation and this is said by Piaget to lead to moral universality and to a greater degree of generosity demonstrated by the child in his friendships. It is recognized now by the child that the rule itself carries the function of generating agreement and facilitating fair play. The children are seen by about twelve or thirteen years of age to embrace a democratic process in which any proposal may be advanced for discussion and rational analysis with the under- standing that its fate in the actual practice of the game is subject to majority vote. Piaget emphasizes that custom and tradition, when accepted without question, are enslaving, whereas the laws of cooperation and reciprocity impose only a method of "intellectual or moral interchange." In Piaget's view, the cognitive- ly mature young adolescent has discovered democracy. As a sobering thought, however, it might be said that, while the method works well in game playing, democratic societies have not yet resolved the dilemma of the tyranny of the majority.

Despite the clarity of stage sequence formulated by Piaget in the area of morality, he cautions us against viewing the features of each stage as being purely successive. He points out that, for example, in the realm of behavior things simultaneously involve motor (individual), egocentric, and cooperative elements. The critical issue is the proportionate degree of each element in relation to the others. There is also a time-lag in development between thought and action, in which a rule executed on a practical plane may not yet have entered consciousness. Also, the stage of autonomy may have been attained in connection with certain rules, even though the child's relation to other, perhaps more complex rules, may still be at the level of heteronomy. Therefore, global generalizations about the child being in one or another stage of moral development are not appropriate.

MORAL REALISM

A concept central to understanding Piaget's theory of moral development is moral realism, which has already been alluded to in its specific application to rules. A general definition, as formulated by Piaget (1932/1965) is as follows: "We shall therefore call moral realism the tendency which the child has to regard duty and the value attaching to it as self-subsistent and independent of the mind, as imposing itself regardless of the circumstances in which the individual may find himself" (p. 111). There are three main elements characterizing it. First, heteronomy is the foundation of duty. The good is defined by obedience to the external rule or adult command. Second, only a literal application of the law is permitted in moral realism. Any attempt to obey the spirit, rather than the letter, of the law would be a movement toward reason and subjectivity. Third, intentionality is not considered in making moral judgments. Responsibility is assessed on a purely objective level in which acts are viewed from the standpoint of rigid compliance with predetermined rules.

Piaget stresses that from a very young age all children are subject to certain externally imposed rules of necessity. He comments as follows:

> All these rules are naturally placed by the child on the same plane as actual physical phenomena. One must eat after going for a walk, go to bed at night, have a bath before going to bed, etc., exactly as the sun shines by day and the moon by night, or as pebbles sink while boats remain afloat. All these things are and must be so: they are as the World-Order decrees that they should be, and there must be a reason for it all. But none of it is felt from within as an impulse of sympathy or of pity is felt (Piaget 1932/1965, p. 191).

OBJECTIVE RESPONSIBILITY

In exploring the moral judgment of the child, Piaget and his collaborators formulated a wide variety of anecdotal materials which were then presented to children of various ages. The children were questioned about these stories and their answers recorded. Piaget reminds us that the method is verbal and not practical or experiential. He advances the hypothesis that the verbal responses of the children reflect the concrete and practical judgments which governed the child in his actions during the years immediately preceding the clinical interview. Hence, a time-lag between practical and conceptual intelligence exists in the moral sphere, as is to be found in intellectual realms not dealing with moral issues.

In one series of studies, children were asked to compare stories involving two kinds of clumsiness. One type involved a child who precipitated a great deal of material damage, but who did so by chance and, in some instances, was even well-intentioned. The other type was distinguished by a child who produced minimal damage, but who was not motivated by good intentions. In either case, the damage was accidental. For example, in one story a boy was called to the dinner table. He did not know that behind the door to the dining room there was a tray of fifteen cups. In complying with the request to come to dinner, he accidentally pushed the door into the tray with the result that all the cups were broken. In the complementary story, a boy took advantage of his mother's absence to try to get some jam from the cupboard. In so doing, he accidentally knocked over one cup which broke. Children in the Piagetian study were asked which child was naughtier and whether they should be punished the same. Similar procedures were followed with repsect to stealing. Acts of stealing that were well-intentioned were presented for comparison with acts of stealing that were selfishly motivated. For example, one boy stole a roll from a bakery for a hungry friend in contrast to a child who stole a pretty ribbon in a shop because she thought it would make a nice adornment on her dress. Children in the study were asked whether each child was equally guilty. They were asked further which was the naughtiest and why. In all of these interviews, the children's responses were pursued and the children were asked to amplify their answers.

In reviewing the findings, it was discovered that, until the age of ten, a single child tended to give two distinct types of answers. In the one, emphasis was given to the objective result irrespective of the actor's motive. In the other, only the intentions of the actors determined the child's answers. As a result Piaget observes that two separate and sequential stages cannot be posited. However, there is observed an unmistakable trend in which objective responsibility diminishes as children grow older. There were no clear instances of it to be found after ten years of age. An analysis of the answers given by children under ten led to the conclusion that the average for a preponderance of objective responsibility is seven, and the average age for subjective responsibility is nine. These findings are interpreted as developmental trends in each child and not merely as statements about two different types of children or of the influence of family education. If this were not the case, the two average ages should be the same. It is noteworthy that even young children whose answers are predominantly characterized by objective responsibility will invoke subjective responsibility when commenting on personal recollections involving their own behavior. This can readily be explained since they are privy to their own motives on both a conceptual and affective level, but may not as yet have developed very refined role-taking capacities, which would limit their ability for reciprocity. Nevertheless, in children under six or seven, guilt is generated in proportion to the material damage rather than the degree of intentionality of their behavior.

Piaget is quite convinced that the child's view of objective responsibility is a product of adult constraint. However, he notes that instances of clumsiness and stealing are influenced in the child's mind not only by the external nature of the adult command, but often by the actual behavioral model of an adult who also evaluates the culpability of the act by the objective damage. For example, many housewives would blame a well-intentioned child more for breaking fifteen cups accidentally, than the self-seeking child who accidentally broke only one cup. The same consideration, however, does not apply in the case of lying, to be examined shortly. Piaget hastens to add that, although many adults scold on the basis of actual material damage, they do not hold the clumsy, but well-intentioned, child to be morally culpable. The child fails to make this distinction, believing that an act can be wrong in itself, regardless of the psychological matrix. Circumstances have no bearing on judging the morality of the actor for such a child. Piaget allows that one may, of course, hold stealing to be wrong despite the object sought, but he emphasizes the curious element involved in children adopting a strictly objective criterion in such an example as cited above, where one child steals for food for a hungry friend while the other steals for pleasure.

Piaget raises the question of how subjective responsibility may supplant objective responsibility in the area he has been discussing. He suggests that children can be led to place greater emphasis upon intentions if parents will encourage them to act with the point of view of others in mind, which will result in their acting to please and not simply to obey. Cooperation and mutual respect precede assessing motives in moral judgment. If the parent will stress to the child the parent's own needs, obligations, and shortcomings, the child will develop a sense of mutual respect within a social matrix, where it is understood that everyone has certain obligations. (Obviously what the parent reveals should be done in a discriminate and relevant fashion.) Parents who fail to do this will have submissive children for a time, but eventually the recognition of injustice will lead to opposition by the child. Eventually, in his interactions with siblings and peers the child will develop mutual sympathy and cooperation. A morality of reciprocity emerges to replace compliance and it serves as the bedrock from which consideration of intentions and subjective responsibility flow.

Piaget considers studies of lies as more vital to our understanding of moral development in children then are the areas of clumsiness and occasional stealing. Lying is a natural universal tendency, directly reflective of egocentrism, which is uninfluenced by adult modeling. The most primitive definition of a lie is found in young children who think of it as being a naughty word. Yet these same children recognize lies in the conventional sense as well. Piaget theorizes that whether the child tells a lie or speaks a naughty word, he is soundly reproached by adults. Consequently, he distinguishes only between that which may be spoken and that which may not be. In the latter category are indecent words and statements that are untrue, both of which he calls lies. A more advanced definition is one in which the child conceives of lies as simply statements which are not true. However, children between five and seven deemphasize the distinction between an intended mistake and a deliberate untruth, classifying both as lies. For example, such a child may believe that a boy who said two plus two equals five has made a mistake, but will go on to say he has lied. Young children do seem to have the capacity to distinguish between intention and involuntary error, as well as between mistakes and lies conventionally defined. Nevertheless, these distinctions are not taken into account when making moral judgments on a purely reflective level. Piaget once again proposes a time-lag, suggesting that on a practical level the child may be differentiating these elements. In any event, by about age eight the child dissociates lies and mistakes, as well as the ideas of the intentional and the involuntary on a reflective level. It is not until around ten to eleven that the child evidences a clear definition of a lie as that which is intentionally untrue.

In one series of stories, each pair contained, first an unintentional inaccuracy which was marked by a sharp break from fact and, second, a falsehood about a likely possibility conveyed with a deceptive intention. Many of the young children interviewed disregarded intentions and focused upon the credibility of the statement to adults. The more likely the lie is to be believed, the less naughty is the person telling the lie. Objective responsibility predominates in the younger children, despite recognition of intentions. This is particularly significant because, unlike the stories on clumsiness and stealing where physical damage was prominent, such material consequences are minimal or eliminated in the stories on lying. Yet objective responsibility still reigns. For example, in one pair of stories we have a little boy who is frightened in the street by a dog and runs home to tell his mother he had seen a dog as big as a cow. We also have for comparison a child who tells his mother that his teacher has given him good grades when in fact he had not received any. The mother rewards him. The younger children insist that the boy in the first story is naughtier because of the improbability of the story and the unlikelihood that the boy's mother would believe he had seen a dog as big as a cow. Also, it is clear from the Children's responses that they understand the difference in motivation between the two main characters. The intentions of the actor simply do not seem of importance from a moral standpoint. Once again, Piaget points out that we are not dealing with two successive stages. Objective and subjective responsibility are found in mixed proportions in any one child. However, the former is frequently found among young children and its importance seems to decline as children grow older. Generally at age seven, the objective type of response predominates, while by an average of age ten the subjective type of response prevails. These figures are based on studies of children ranging from age six to twelve.

An examination of the responses of older children in whom subjective responsibility is more frequently cited is striking because they virtually reverse the argument of those adopting objective responsibility. For these children, if an untrue statement is obviously improbable, exaggeration or error may be involved, but not the intent to deceive. It is the lie which does not appear to be one that is reprehensible.

The child below seven or eight is not successful in consistently communicating truthfully. Although he may not intend to be deceptive, his desires lead to a distortion of reality. Drawing from early writings of Stern, Piaget suggests that statements made by children before seven or eight should not be looked upon as true or false so much as expressions of feelings. The need to speak and pursue truth is derived from one's participation as a social member in cooperation with others. It is, therefore, predicated upon mutual respect and reciprocity. Truth holds no value to the egocentric mind, which is more likely to assimilate reality to the end of achieving its own satisfaction. Veracity and verification take on value as the child's mind interacts with those of others in a genuinely social manner. When still in an egocentric state, truth is not valued and fact will be subservient to whim and desire. It is Piaget's position that the structure of the young child's thought, therefore, makes lying inevitable. Despite this tendency which prevails up to seven or eight years of age, the child experiences a sense of obligation not to lie derived from a sense of duty toward the adult. The rule not to lie, while regarded as sacred and a violation as naughty, cannot be adequately applied while the child's thought is egocentric. The rule not to lie is imposed externally and the child cannot yet value the inherent basis for making truthfulness both necessary and desirable in social relations. Hence, intentions remain unimportant until the child develops to the point of connecting not only with the letter of the rule, but the spirit of it as well. Until then, objective responsibility is predictable and is a product of unilateral respect. Movement toward mutual respect is illuminated by a consideration of why one should not lie. The younger children hold that one should not lie because he will be punished if he does. Asked questions about lies some children will state that, if one is not punished, the untrue statement is not a lie. They will reason further that the lie for which one is punished is naughtier than the untruth for which one is not punished. At a later point in development a lie is considered intrinsically wrong regardless of whether one is punished for it or not. The rule is dissociated from its origin, the adult, and embellished by the child's own reason which elevates it to a universal status. Piaget maintains, however, that heteronomy still characterizes the rule because it continues to be construed as a command which has not yet been interiorized and made a part of the child's own mind. It is when children reach the ages of ten to twelve that reciprocity and mutual agreement are seen as prerequisites to social relations. It is the destruction of trust and affection brought about by lying which makes it intolerable. Piaget hypothesizes that it is the cooperative endeavor which leads to the interiorization of the spirit of the rule not to lie.

THE CONCEPT OF JUSTICE

Autonomy is a necessary prerequisite to justice, which precludes authority as a source of it. In the exercise of adult authority duty is supreme, whereas justice is derived from reciprocity and equality, which in turn requires the consent of the actor. Little children mistake prescriptive law, held before them by adult authority, for justice. Piaget draws attention to the fact that many adults have themselves failed to achieve autonomy of conscience and, therefore, act solely upon social prejudice and encoded law rather than from a sense of justice. It is only through cooperation between children and eventually between child and adult, as adolescence nears, that a sense of justice develops. Young children submit to the dictates of adults and older children. Their behavior is egocentric and impersonal. As children grow older, however, a bond of solidarity with the group is forged. A taboo is voluntarily placed upon threats to that solidarity, such as lying and cheating. Rational analysis and exchange of ideas increase and mere mutual imitation declines. As genuine justice ascends in the area of retribution, we find that children from about eleven to twelve years of age no longer advocate applying the same punishment to all, but instead take circumstances into account. Similarly, in distributive justice the law is no longer seen as being indiscriminately applicable, but rather such considerations as age and health are given attention.

Piaget rejects the notion that justice and love are incompatible. It is only when a stark equality or mathematical equivalence is meted out as justice that this would seem to be the case. Indeed, children before eleven or twelve seem to evidence only this "blow for a blow" mentality. However, children who develop beyond this stage forego revenge as short-sighted, going on to become more charitable and forgiving. Crude equality is transformed into equity, a more mature form of reciprocity predicated upon the maxim, "Do as you would be done by." Equity takes into account personal and surrounding circumstances and, in effect, is equalitarianism elevated toward relativity. In the following sections we shall continue to examine Piaget's work on moral development in the hope of achieving a deepening understanding of the concept of justice.

PUNISHMENT AND RETRIBUTION

The two realms of justice are distributive and retributive. The former deals with equality, the latter with the correlation between act and punishment. There are two kinds of punishment. First there is expiation which is related to heteronomy or constraint and authority. Expiation predominates in younger children, but is gradually replaced by reciprocity as they grow older. Nevertheless, it is true that, for many adults, the transition has never taken place and their morality is governed by expiatory thinking, which is linked to an excessive reverence for the written law. Younger children tend to view punishment as a moral necessity and they advocate more severity than older children. In contrast, older children are content to convey to the violator that the bond of solidarity has been ruptured and to generate a sense of the need for restoration of the balance that was upset by the transgression. The criterion for a sound punishment is its efficacy in prevention and not the harm or pain it imposes. Older children believe that an appropriate explanation may serve as a better deterrent to future transgressions than mere punishment. They emphasize an explanation of the natural consequences of the act in question.

Piaget distinguishes between vengeance originating in primitive sympathy for a victim or antipathy toward an offender and punishment based on justice. The first of these has its roots in infancy and is both personal and arbitrary. The moral action, however rudimentary, must stem from rules which enable the actor to apprehend that his act is intended to punish the guilty and defend the innocent. Indeed, these rules can be possessed at a quite early age. These rules are derived, of course, from adults. Further, Piaget (1932/1965) states, "When the adult is angry because the laws he has laid down are not observed, this anger is held to be just, because of the unilateral respect of which older people are the object and because of the sacred character of the law laid down" (p. 231). Therefore, although expiatory punishment is likened to revenge, it has a disinterested character for the child because it flows from the creators of the law and seeks to avenge the law itself. As unilateral respect declines, attitudes regarding expiatory punishment weaken and, instead, it becomes more important to facilitate the offender's awareness that, in running counter to the ethics of cooperation, his act is wrong.

There are six classifications of punishment by reciprocity and Piaget cites them in descending order of severity. These are as follows: 1) The punisher breaks the social bond by refusing to engage in further activity. Exclusion may be permanent or temporary. 2) Experiencing the natural consequence of one's own transgression. For example, a boy who refuses to go to the store to buy bread for dinner is not allowed to share in the insufficient amount remaining at dinnertime. 3) Discontinuing to allow a transgressor to have access to that which he abuses. 4) The most obvious form of reciprocity, which is performing upon the transgressor exactly what it is he has done. For example, help is refused a child who has formerly refrained from responding to a request for help. 5) The transgressor is expected to offer restitution by restoring whatever it is that his act deprived another of. Censure is not essential to this form of punishment. 6) Censure only with the intent of explaining the natural consequences of the act, emphasizing that the bond of solidarity was broken.

COLLECTIVE PUNISHMENT

In customary fashion, Piaget devised a series of stories designed, in this case, to determine children's attitudes toward group punishment in which several innocent members are present. In one story an adult punishes a group of children with no attempt to ascertain who is guilty and who is innocent. Sixty subjects ranging from age six to fourteen were examined. No one exhibited a belief that it would be just to punish the entire group under the circumstances. All voiced a belief that an individual should be punished only for what he has done. This is all the more striking since ordinarily children under seven are not critical of adult behavior which they regard as fair.

In another type of story the adult seeks to identify the offender who remains silent. The innocent members join him in his silence. Should all members be punished? Piaget points out that in addition to natural solidarity there is now another element of self-willed solidarity. Answers both for and against punishment were to be found among children of every age from six to twelve. However, of those favoring punishment there appeared two main types: 1) The younger children who favored punishment felt that each was individually guilty for not doing his duty by telling the adult who the offender was. 2) The older children who favored punishment felt that punishment was appropriate because each member of the group, by his silence, made a commitment to group solidarity. A third type of response rejected the notion of punishment precisely because the offender was unknown to the adult and it would be wrong for group members to expose him. This answer predominated among children of intermediate age.

A third type of story revealed clear and unequivocal results. It involved the propriety of punishing a group when the offender will not speak up and the other members of the group are unaware of who he is. The younger children advocate punishment simply because they do believe in the inevitability of punishment in the face of wrong-doing. However, their answers do not reflect that they believe the group to be responsible. The older children emphatically bar punishment because this would perpetrate the injustice of penalizing the innocent which is more serious than permitting a guilty person to go without punishment.

Piaget compares these findings to the notion of collective responsibility in the classical sense of the term as found in primitive tribes. He concludes that in none of the cases is this found to characterize the moral thought of the children he studied. To be so characterized, it would have been necessary to find instances of children favoring punishment based on two conditions: 1) moral constraint and accompanying attitudes of expiation, with its emphasis upon inevitable punishment and 2) a voluntary commitment to group solidarity. However, unlike primitive societies, unilateral respect declined as cooperation ascends among children studied and, hence, the two conditions were never found together.

IMMANENT JUSTICE

Expiation has been characterized by Piaget as obligatory in the eyes of young children. Piaget reasoned further that the very young would even believe that things themselves could be a source of automatic punishment and he set out to study this. The stories posed involved situations in which a child transgresses a rule and subsequently is subject to a mishap. For example, in one story a child who had stolen an apple in an orchard eludes a police officer, but on his way home he attempts to cross a river on a rotten bridge. The bridge collapses and he falls into the river. The subjects in the study are asked whether the boy would have fallen into the water if he had not stolen the apple. A response is classified as revealing a belief in immanent justice if the child answers that the boy would not have fallen had he not stolen. There was an obvious decline in immanent justice among older children. The statistics were as follows: 86 percent among children age six, 73 percent among children ages seven to eight, 54 percent among children ages nine to ten, 34 percent among children ages eleven to twelve. In a class of backward children who were thirteen to fourteen years old there was a frequency of 54 percent, reflecting once again that a belief in immanent justice is in inverse proportion to mental age.

Piaget raises the question of whether some children assert an intermediary connection between the offense and the punishment. He pays little attention to such comments as "God did it" feeling that this glib remark is probably due to parental influence. It is Piaget's belief that children really occupy themselves very little with the "how" of the matter. It is not surprising that children believe in automatic punishment as their egocentric world is permeated by life and purpose. Objects are governed by moral law and not chance occurrences. In the absence of an adult, it is only natural that such law would take on an authoritarian role and execute the punishment. It is only if a line of questioning imposes a further account from him that the child might come up with a further interpretation of either an artificialistic or animistic type. Piaget firmly believes that the child has a spontaneous tendency of mind, which, because of the habit of punishment, adult constraint, leads him to anticipate that nature in its own right will inflict punishment at times. He states, "Belief in immanent justice originates therefore in a transference to things of feelings acquired under the influence of adult constraint" (p. 261).

The decline of immanent justice is largely attributable to the child's eventual realization that punishment meted out by parent or teacher is not always fair. The belief in automatic justice does not sustain itself in the face of receiving unjust treatment by adults.

DISTRIBUTIVE JUSTICE

Retributive and distributive justice may come into conflict and Piaget studied children's responses to stories presenting such situations. Distributive justice concerns equality of distribution of objects and favors across a population. In one story a mother was described as favoring the obedient one of two children, giving her more cake, while giving less to the disobedient one. Younger children do not even bring equality into the picture, instead urging that punishment is necessary. The older children tend to opt for equal amounts of cake despite the disobedience of one child. Hence, distributive justice outweighs retribution. Both answers will appear at all ages studied from six to fourteen and the varying proportions found are attributed to differences in family practices. Nevertheless, there appears an undeniable progression toward favoring distributive justice as the children get older, with age nine identified as the major transitional point. It is cited as of significance that those adopting distributive justice appear sensitive to psychological subtleties, such as the possibility of making the disobedient child jealous if equal portions of cake are not given out. One ten-year-old child proclaiming the mother in the story wrong, even suggested that with proper love and kindness the disobedient one may change. The judgments of the younger children tend to be stereotyped and subject to moral constraint while the older children, elevating equality over punishment, are guided by mutual respect.

Piaget pursues this analysis further with additional stories. A mother takes her children for a walk by a river. Each child is given a roll to eat, but the youngest is careless and his roll falls into the river. The children in the study must deal with such concerns as the mother's behavior, whether the child should be given another roll, and the reaction of his siblings to whatever course of action is taken. Basically, three kinds of answers enter into the findings. One is essentially a form of punishment, the children recommending that the boy in the story not be given another roll, accompanied by accusations about his carelessness. Another recommendation is to give him a second roll to assure that all of the siblings have one. This is equality. Lastly, some children urged that the boy be given another roll, offering as explanation the fact that he is a small boy. This is equity, which takes into account the circumstances of a situation. The statistical results on this particular story administered to 167 children are strikingly indicative. Although there was a preponderance of 48 percent punishment type answers and only 17 percent of equity answers among children from six to nine, by ages thirteen to fourteen there were 0 percent punishment answers and 95 percent equity. Piaget offers further variations which confirm all that has preceded. However, a significant clarification is that children who provide equity type answers distinguish between pure justice and being kind. It is recognized that giving a careless child a second roll is not as much justice, since he has already had his share, as it is kindness.

We are reminded once again of a time-lag, indicating that even the child of seven who makes a moral judgment choosing retributive justice or punishment over equity may very well behave quite differently in an actual situation with his friends. Recall that the infant conquers many areas such as causality, conservation of the object, and problem-solving strategies on a behavioral level only to be faced with the necessity of conquering these same areas at more advanced periods on conceptual levels.

EQUALITY AND AUTHORITY

Piaget generalizes three stages of distributive justice in connection with the authority of adult persons. In the first of these retributive justice outweighs distributive justice. The "just" is conceived of as the adult's command. Any rudimentary feelings of reciprocity will find expression only when it is not in opposition to adult authority; otherwise it is suppressed. In the second stage equalitarianism emerges fully and distributive justice is supreme. Punishment and obedience no longer hold sway. Subordination to authority declines in favor of autonomy of moral thought. The developing child has come to experience injustices at the hands of adults and has observed them breaking their own rules. He dissociates the "just" from adult command and simultaneously is developing mutual respect among peers. A third stage evolves from the previous one and Piaget (1932/1965) comments upon it as follows:

> Equalitarianism makes way for a more subtle conception of justice which we may call "equity," and which consists in never defining equality without taking account of the way in which each individual is situated. In the domain of retributive justice, equity consists in determining what are the attenuating circumstances, and we have seen that this consideration enters very late into children's judgments. In the domain of distributive justice, equity consists in taking account of age, of previous services rendered, etc.; in short, in establishing shades of equality (p. 285).

To illustrate equity in relation to an authority, Piaget discusses a story in which each member in a group of boy scouts is assigned a task. The boy who is expected to do the shopping is not around and so the scoutmaster asks another boy, one who has already completed his task, to do the shopping. The child responding must tell what the boy scout chose to do, what he thought, and whether it was fair to expect him to go. This particular lad in the study, age twelve, states that the scout must go as his scoutmaster needs help. He elaborates that, had the scout been forced to go it would not have been fair, but since he accepts to go in order to help out, it is fair. Piaget (1932/1965) observes:

> One could not formulate better the principle of autonomy which characterizes the attitude we are speaking of: if you are forced to do something against equality, it is unjust, but if you accept to do a service, you are doing something superior to strict justice, and you are behaving with equity towards your chief (p. 283).

Remember that, in this section Piaget had been discussing equality specifically in relation to authority. The section closes with a review of situations of conflict between authority and a sense of justice related to bonds of solidarity. The younger children advocate breaking the bonds by betraying their peers and telling the authority of such violations as cheating in an examination. The older children advocate opposing the adult authority to protect peers and even support lying to do so if necessary. Yet these same children, who have obviously taken into account the intention of the lie, report that lying to protect themselves would be naughty.

PEER LEVEL JUSTICE

In his analysis of notions of justice among children Piaget observes that punishment, since authority has no role in peer relations, does not contain the element of expiation. In nearly all instances reciprocity is the critical component. A lad who insists on rendering "a blow for a blow" is seeking to return an exact mathematical equivalent and is careful not to give more than he received. One child, age ten, representatively proclaims that while it is fair to hit back an equal number of times, one should not seek revenge. It is not revenge, but justice and equality, that the children who advocate hitting back in the appropriate stories are seeking. Reciprocity is the keynote. An arbitrary punishment not related to the act is deemed inappropriate. Among younger children there is found a preponderance of responses against hitting back at all, but these children look to the adult to step in and offer protection. The younger children will also announce that vengeance is wrong, but the basis of their position is that it is forbidden by adults and, hence, naughty. In the older children vengeance is eliminated by their sense of fair play and justice.

In a structured game, where rules are violated, Piaget observed only nonexpiatory punishments. A violator may be asked to restore what he acquired illegitimately or an offender excluded from the game, to signify the breach of solidarity, for a period proportionate to his offense.

Piaget does allow for the exception where a grave violation by a child offends the collective consciousness of the group members. He explores a traditional example of ducking a "sneak" in the cold waters of a lake. The punishment is excessive and not in the spirit of reciprocity. However, this particular punishment has its roots in the customs of previous generations. It is Piaget's contention that, "In the rare cases where punishments between children are truly expiatory, a factor of authority, of unilateral respect, of the constraint of one generation upon another has been introduced" (Piaget 1932/1965 p. 297).

Piaget cites the query of why one should not cheat at games as evoking responses which reveal information of children's shift from retributive justice, as described above, to distributive justice in their relations with one another. The answers given are basically of four types. In one type there is simply an emphasis upon the naughtiness of such behavior. It is forbidden. A second type stresses that to cheat is to run counter to the rules of the game. Such responses predominate in the children between ages six to nine. A third type of response cites cooperation indicating that cheating is deceptive, it makes the other players angry, and the game becomes impossible to play. The fourth response stresses equality, pointing out that it is not fair, that the others do not cheat, and, therefore, the violator has no right to do so, and it is unjust to others. These last two types of responses prevail among children from ten to twelve. There also exist many intermediate stages among these four types of responses. Essentially, however, it can be seen that, for the older children, attitudes toward cheating derive not from unilateral respect, but from the autonomous group, founded upon equalitarianism.

In the final section dealing with moral relations among children, Piaget turns to a consideration of distributive justice. The stories administered did not involve adult authority. In all cases the responses indicated an advocacy of the equal distribution of task assignments and goods. It is only when the issue of adult authority intervenes that the younger children, from six to nine, will defer to authority command over equality. A complication is introduced, however, in a story involving a big child and a little child who find while on a walk in the mountains that there is not enough food in their bags for each to have a full lunch. The children in the study are asked how this dilemma should be resolved. It is interesting to note that, although some answers favored strict equality in both the younger and the older groups of children, the prevailing answer among the former urged giving more to the bigger boy in the story (unilateral respect), whereas the prevailing answer among the latter advocated giving more to the little boy (equity).

CONCLUSION

In broad terms, moral judgment has been observed to develop from a morality of constraint, founded upon unilateral respect and egocentrism, to a morality of cooperation, founded upon mutual respect and reciprocity. Although Piaget cautions against viewing the two major stages as purely distinct, the developmental trend as age advances seems unmistakable. The stage of equity which goes beyond the strict equality of early cooperation introduces a consideration of individual circumstances. In the realm of justice it would seem that altruism becomes an element in morality elevating equity above pure equality. The decline of egocentrism in the young child promotes an increasing capacity to decenter and, therefore, to take into account not only his own viewpoint, but other perspectives as well. It is as central to moral development that the child acquire this ability as it is to his comprehension of reality in the physical world.

6

POST-PIAGETIAN THEORY
AND RESEARCH ON
MORAL DEVELOPMENT

CRITIQUE AND RESEARCH

Since the time of its first publication in 1932, Piaget's only major work on moral development has stimulated an enormous amount of replicated and related studies. The weight of evidence largely supports the early Piagetian findings, although this is certainly not the case in every detail. A review of the research can be found in Kohlberg (1963a). The reader who wishes to pursue an extensive survey of the literature may find it helpful to consult Hoffman (1970), Graham (1972) and Modgil (1974). Breger (1974) offers a broad summary of the findings indicating that the heteronomous characterization by Piaget has been validated, including such elements as expiative punishment, objective responsibility, immanent justice, and the sanctity of authority. Autonomous morality, however, is later in arriving, develops over a longer period of time, and is constituted by more stages than originally postulated. Peer group interaction, although important to the decline of egocentrism, does not exercise a significant role in moral development until midadolescence and early youth. Lickona (1969) has written an informative and sympathetic rebuttal to many criticisms of Piaget's theories on moral development. He bases his arguments on the contention that Piaget's position has been greatly misunderstood and that, therefore, the interpretations of many researchers are false and misleading. Nevertheless, he concedes that the research warrants certain reformulations.

The present chapter will not attempt an exhaustive survey of research on moral development. Instead, a review of selected research and of some of the limitations inherent in Piaget's own work will be presented. In selecting the material, the author has attempted to assist the reader to develop a perspective on cognitive-developmental research in the moral domain, highlighting significant content and methodological issues, and pointing up the diversity of activity in the field.

A major delimiting aspect of Piaget's work is the age range of his population, which extends from six to twelve years, with few exceptions. Considerably more attention has been given to moral development during adolescence and youth in more recent years with an outcome suggesting that genuine autonomy does not emerge until late adolescence. Perhaps more disturbing are the indications that relatively few people really do progress to a level of morality in which equity and forgiveness acquire the status of being founded upon stable and predominant structures. In fact, of course, Piaget recognizes that many people would not fully evolve to the highest level of moral attainment. Another limitation is the lack of full attention to sex and class variables. Piaget is not unmindful of these components, however, and he does mention that his studies have been performed mainly with children of low socioeconomic background. Also, Piaget's work has been criticized for its disregard of emotional aspects. In the larger corpus of his work he repeatedly stresses that affect and cognition are indissociable, so there can be little question of his recognition of this area, even though he chooses not to dwell upon it. In a more recent work Piaget (1964/1968) does refer to affect in relation to his comments on will. He identifies will as a regulator of energy and compares it to the operation in cognition. Emotions becoming organized have will as their ultimate form of equilibrium. Will comes into play to resolve tension, such as when pleasure and duty conflict. If, for example, pleasure is the stronger but inferior component, will exerts a force on behalf of duty as the weaker but superior element. In general, Piaget (1964/1968) comments, "Thus, affectivity from seven to twelve years is characterized by the appearance of new moral feelings and, above all, by an organization of will, which culminates in a better integration of the self and a more effective regulation of affective life" (p. 55).

Piaget has been further criticized for deemphasizing the positive role of adult figures in the moral development of the child, as he focuses primarily on their constraining influence. In this connection, although it does not vitiate the criticism, it should be noted that he does delineate a model of behavior for parents to adopt, which would minimize their authoritative stance and introduce a much more beneficial influence. Although the results of recent research place less emphasis upon peer interaction as critical to moral development than Piaget has given it; nevertheless, many believe that he has highlighted a previously neglected area of importance.

Johnson (1962) reviewed three early studies, Barnes (1894, 1902) and Schallenberger (1894) which were conducted nearly forty years before Piaget's work. They utilized large populations of children ranging from six to sixteen years of age. They uncovered such phenomena as moral realism, increasing concern for intentions as age advanced, expiation and belief in the justice of adult punishment, and more severe penalties advocated by the younger children. Johnson comments that these studies would seem to add support to Piaget's conclusions.

In addition to these studies, Johnson (1962) and Goldman (1964) are in general agreement with Piaget on reciprocity and distributive justice. However, it might be more interesting and informative to review some of the findings of Durkin (1959a, 1959b, 1959c, 1960, 1961) which are often cited as deviating from Piaget's work. Durkin (1959a) observed that strict reciprocity in the sense of "a blow for a blow" increased from seven to eleven years of age. Subsequently, and as late as fourteen years of age, the subjects in her research were found to be abandoning strict reciprocity in favor of appealing to an authority for resolution of conflict, much as the seven year olds were found to do. However, the older children who had recourse to authority clearly grasped the complexities of the situation in a way that the younger ones behaving similarly did not. Children who engaged in strict reciprocity interpreted their statements as Piaget's subjects had, rejecting arbitrary punishment not related to the consequences of the act. Durkin concluded that Piaget's assertion that children grow through the years in their conviction that it is strictly fair to reciprocate with a response which is exact in kind to the one received is invalid. Regarding the lack of progressive reciprocity with age, Durkin points out that older children are willing to turn to an authority for help in achieving a just resolution because they have experienced too often what happens when fighting continues amid aggression. She suggests that Piaget might have found the same results if his own subjects had been over age twelve. Graham (1972) offers the explanation that older children are more likely to realize that "a blow for a blow" may lead to a bigger fight in which one may even lose altogether. He further cited that there is, in fact, more pressure against older children not to resort to physical aggression as increasingly more verbal modes of resolution are expected of them. Lastly, he emphasizes that very young children may state that physical retaliation is naughty and may even seek arbitrary adult intervention, whereas older children who appeal to authority may consciously do so because they expect a just determination and, in fact, would not go to an adult from whom an unjust response would be anticipated. Lickona (1969) analyzes Durkin's report on decreasing reciprocity at a time when one might expect it to increase if predicting from Piaget's theory. He maintains that her position is based on a misinterpretation of what Piaget means by reciprocity. She adopts a static view of it rather than seeing it as an evolving concept as Piaget intended. Lickona stresses that, after approximately twelve years of age, rigid equalitarianism or strict reciprocity yields to the rule of equity, in which forgiveness and understanding become more prominent. The finding that strict reciprocity decreases with age after approximately eleven years supports Piaget's position, despite Durkin's interpretation to the contrary. Lickona does comment, however, that, based on group solidarity, one would not expect the child to go to an authority. The present author would suggest that perhaps the child is more likely to break the bond of solidarity by exposing a peer to an adult, if he is the direct recipient of the peer's offense, than if he is not. In any event, Lee (1971) is in general agreement with Lickona, for he indicates that strict reciprocity in the Piagetian view would be expected to increase only up to approximately ten years of age, but that, with the emergence of formal operations, one would anticipate a decrease of exact reciprocity type responses. In fact, in another study by Durkin (1959c) it was found that while exact reciprocity or equality was not found to predominate among teenage children, there was an increase of equity, taking into account the circumstances of a situation, among the children studied, as age increased. The children ranged in age from eight to seventeen years.

The purpose of citing Durkin's research was to provide the reader with some sense of the ongoing dialogue that may be stimulated by studies which do not result in exact duplication of Piaget's findings. Equally instructive, because of the variation of stories utilized, is a study on intention versus objective responsibility by Armsby (1971). One of the limitations of Piaget's book is the manner in which the stories are composed. Many researchers to follow recognized this and recomposed the stories to see what effect this might have upon the outcome. Armsby observed that in Piaget's original version, the stories testing for intentionality did not differentiate between accidental and purposive behavior. For example, both boys, the one who broke fifteen cups and the one who broke a single cup, did so accidentally even though their motives differed. Armsby, therefore, reconstructed new stories in which accidental and purposive behavior were contrasted. He also used written versions of the stories, indicating that children have short memories and when taxed would tend to remember the amount of damage as most significant. Armsby was able to conclude that children were capable of intentionality judgments or subjective responsibility in dealing with moral dilemmas at an age prior to the time Piaget and others had reported. There did exist an age progression, as reported by Piaget, but in general there was a higher percentage of intentionality responses noted. Among six-year-old children, Armsby reported as many as 75 percent responses based on subjective responsibility, with 95 percent of those children from eight to ten years of age responding with intentionality. Armsby further varied the stories to test the effect of severity of damage upon intentionality. He discovered that as high as 90 percent of six-year-old children would make a response of intentionality if the disparity between the consequences of the accidental and purposive acts was minimized. When the severity of the accidental act was made more severe, however, there was a reduction to 60 percent. Similar results were found among children eight years old. On the other hand, Piaget came up with few responses of intentionality among six- and seven-year-old children, and he states that, in most instances, children under nine to ten years of age will give answers predicated upon objective responsibility. Armsby makes the point that, despite the effect of varying the stories, the young children he studied had not yet fully incorporated intentionality, as many of them reverted back to objective responsibility when the consequences of the accidental act were made much more severe than those of the purposive act.

Although we will not examine them in any detail, McKechnie (1971) conducted two studies specifically constructed to account for the effects of story structure and the context of the situation upon moral judgments. He reasoned, based on his findings, that Piaget's stories did cloak the developmental occurrences that were taking place between the two extremes of subjective and objective responsibility.

Medinnus (1959) published an incisive review of the literature on immanent justice. Although citing some deviations, he concluded, "In sum, a number of investigators have sought to verify and extend Piaget's findings concerning changes with age in children's belief in immanent justice. Those studies have supported Piaget's data regarding a decrease in belief in immanent justice with age" (p. 257). The focus here will be upon Medinnus's contribution toward understanding immanent justice reported in the same article. Curiously, Medinnus concluded that his own research did not offer an unqualified corroboration that there is a decided decrease of belief in immanent justice with age. His analysis led him to comment that the child will adopt a point of view which is dependent on the particular type of story he is told. The analysis is based on a comparison of responses to two types of stories. In story I there is no inherent explanation for the child being hurt. It is merely stated that in disobedience of his mother, he took a scissors and began to cut some paper. In doing so he cut his finger. Medinnus found that 62 percent ($N=37$) of a total of sixty children at age six gave an answer lacking in a belief in immanent justice. Judging from the reasons why the boy cut himself offered by the 62 percent, Medinnus states that they were able to draw from their own personal experiences and, hence, did not need to invoke a supernatural force, but could provide a rational explanation. Story II is the familiar one of the boy who steals an apple and falls into the river while crossing a rotten bridge. At each age level examined (six, eight, ten, and twelve), there are even fewer responses relying on immanent justice for Story II than Story I. Medinnus explains this by pointing out that, while no rational reason for the harm which befalls the boy is evidenced in Story I, in Story II it is clearly stated that the bridge is rotten. Therefore, in responding to Story II, the children can utilize information provided in the story itself which reduces the need for some to resort to supernatural explanations. Despite these observations, it should not be overlooked that a good many children did make use of a belief in immanent justice in their responses. In fact, while sixteen of sixty children who were six years of age did so, twenty-three of sixty children did so at age twelve when responding to Story II. This is not what one would predict from Piaget's early work. In summary, Medinnus writes, "It was concluded that a child's expressed belief in immanent justice is dependent on such factors as the meaningfulness of the story described, the presence or absence of rational alternative explanations, and the range of the child's experiences" (p. 261). A similar study building on this research was subsequently conducted by Jensen and Rytting (1971) confirming the expectation that immanent justice type responses could be influenced by varying the relatedness of the story to the child's life and the information provided within it.

In an interesting and atypical piece of research, Stuart (1967) sought to determine whether there was a correlation between the ability to decenter and superior achievement in exercising moral and causal judgment. The process of decentration is identified as the ability to shift perspectives and is said to be the mechanism advanced by Piaget to explain the transition from one stage to the next. Stuart states, "Thus it is decentration that enables children to move from subjective to objective causal judgments, and from objective to subjective moral judgments" (p. 60). Stuart hypothesized that, if decentrating is a necessary condition for advanced moral judgment, then while not all decentrating youngsters will evidence mature moral reasoning, all those who do will be decentraters. It was further hypothesized that decentration alone would account for high level moral judgment after age would be controlled for. The areas in moral judgment dealt with were immanent justice, expiation, and objective responsibility. Decentration was tested for on both social and perceptual planes. The subjects were dichotomized into high and low decentraters. Decentration was also tested for with age and intelligence controlled. Stuart concluded that there is a positive correlation between the ability to decenter, especially in the sphere of social relations, and the capacity for making mature causal and moral judgments. He further comments that this relationship is most evident among the older, more intelligent children and suggests that decentration may prove to be a general competency which ranges across many domains of cognitive activity. Finally, Stuart speculates that training efforts may enable children to move more rapidly along the cognitive developmental scale. In a related study, Rubin and Schnider (1973) sought to determine whether there was a positive relationship between decentration, frequency of altruism, and moral judgment. Using measures of communicative egocentrism to test for decentration, they concluded that the evidence was unequivocally supportive of a positive relationship among their sample of seven-year-old children. They believe the child's increasing capacity to decenter is a significant variable accounting partially for the increase in altruism with advancing age.

An issue of central importance to the present topic is the role of cognition in moral development. In an interesting assertion,

Piaget contends that, while logic is the morality of thought, we may view morality as the logic of action. In a less cryptic vein, Piaget maintains that the rate of moral development depends on the rate of cognitive development. Lee (1971) offers a comprehensive report exploring the theoretical aspects of this subject and presents the result of his own research. He states explicitly that adult constraint and peer group influences will be directly influenced by the evolving cognitive structures of the child. Despite the centrality of this point, there has been little research into the area. Previous studies have sought correlations between the child's IQ and moral development. However, this bears only indirectly on Piaget's position, since the standard conception of intelligence and that offered by the cognitive developmental approach differ essentially. Lee observes that there have been no efforts designed specifically to test the relationship between moral development and the simultaneous development of cognitive structures, which is what Piaget's theory is founded upon. Although age has proved to be the most effective predictor of moral development, Lee points out that cognitive structures are also correlated with age and, hence, may in themselves prove to be the more significant variable. Lee used 195 boys as subjects, ranging from five to seventeen years of age. Each child was tested with a battery of six Piagetian cognitive tasks with the aim of ascertaining level of cognitive competency. The level indicated by these tasks became a basis for predicting where each child would appear on a scale of moral judgment. Moral judgment, in turn, was determined by the level revealed in response to nine situations each characterized by a morally conflicting story. The stories were designed to highlight whether the subject centered on authority, peer cooperation, or acts of humanitarianism. In conducting the experiment, social class, sibling position, and IQ were held constant. A progressive sequence was predicted in which authority-oriented responses would be predominantly present at the preoperational period, while cooperation and reciprocity responses would prevail during the concrete operational period. It was anticipated that progression to the period of formal operational thought would reveal moral judgment based on ideological and idealistic considerations. Lee's analysis has led him to a confirmation of the hypotheses he tested. In his own words:

> The findings of this investigation supported Piaget's contention that cognitive development and moral judgment do, indeed, covary according to the different modes of conceptualization within the two dimensions of thought. Thus, it has been shown that children functioning in the preoperational mode of thought adhere to authority modes of moral conceptualization, while children functioning within the concrete operational mode of thought mostly utilize the reciprocity mode of moral conceptualization. With the attainment of formal operational mode of thought, children tend to relate to the higher societal realities or ideals as bases for moral conceptualization (p. 137).

Despite the rigor of his design and the sanguine results, Lee concedes that the experiment does not rule out the possibility of considering age as the primary variable. He cautions, however, against ascribing too much weight to the ubiquitous variable of age in developmental studies because doing so can detract from the search for other variables which focusing on age may mask. Lee recommends that a future investigator may wish to concentrate on an age group as such to determine the relationship between cognitive ability and moral reasoning to be found in each child of the same age.

THE MORAL WORLD OF KOHLBERG

Kohlberg's stage theory of moral development is within the cognitive-developmental school. It is founded upon Piaget's early work on moral judgment, but represents a considerable extension and refinement. Kohlberg posits six stages of moral development. It appears that the first four are characterized to varying degrees by the morality of heteronomy and stages 2 to 6 are characterized to varying degrees by the morality of autonomy (Breger 1974). Like Piaget, Kohlberg rejects a maturational explanation, believing that the evidence does not support a view of the stages automatically unfolding as neurological structures appear. He believes that social interaction within the matrix of institutional

Pathway to Piaget

arrangements, such as family and school, promotes role-taking activities, which in turn stimulate moral development. New cognitive structures are necessary for advanced moral judgment and behavior, although their appearance does not assure a higher morality. The six stages of moral development identified by Kohlberg are said to emerge in an unvarying sequence regardless of class or cultural variables. However, these variables do seem to influence the rate of development and the ultimate level which a given individual will attain. It is not the case that each person will go through all of the stages and, in fact, relatively few people ever arrive at stages 5 and 6. Actually, although Kohlberg does acknowledge having identified some stage 6 college students and graduates, he cites as prime examples of this level of development such historical figures as Socrates, Jesus, and Martin Luther King, Jr. The stage theory is not an additive one, but rather each preceding stage is transformed and integrated into the next higher one. Kohlberg assesses level of moral development by the formal character of the judgment rather than the content involved. Emphasis is placed on the mode of reasoning exercised in arriving at a position, as opposed to the specific position actually adopted. There are structural dimensions within the social sphere pertaining to the moral arena in a fashion analogous to the physical dimensions pertaining to the cognitive arena. These dimensions are universal and more important in moral development than the internalization of the particular rules and taboos of any given culture. The preceding remarks will now be amplified upon in the balance of this chapter.

STAGES OF MORAL DEVELOPMENT

In the course of his research over the years, Kohlberg has studied populations in such diverse cultures as those found in the United States, Canada, India, Martinique, Turkey, Taiwan, Mexico, Yucatan, and Israel. He has studied both middle-class and lower-class groups, as well as children from preliterate and semiliterate cultures. In addition, a study has been done of delinquent boys. Initially, his work was presented on a group of seventy-two boys (Kohlberg 1963b) from the suburbs of Chicago. There was a follow-up study reported later on the same boys as they progressed into young adulthood (Kohlberg and Kramer 1969). The original study focused on three age groups: ten, thirteen, and sixteen. They have been followed at intervals of three years up to the age of twenty-five. Half of them were upper-middle class, while the other half were lower to lower-middle class. (Although less frequently cited, Kohlberg also used his testing procedures on a group of twenty-four six-year-old children. A more simplified approach than he ordinarily employs was applied to a group of ninety-six children, ages four, five, and seven.) At the outset of the study, attention focused on the alternative choices that were made when the children were faced with moral dilemmas, but Kohlberg observes that the findings did not necessarily reflect a progressive trend in the direction of taking into account human needs. Instead, a consideration of the reasons for the choices and of the manner in which each youngster construed the situations in the stories presented became of paramount importance. It was on the basis of an analysis of this that Kohlberg postulated six stages in the development of moral judgment and character. Locating a child at a particular stage indicates that approximately 45 percent to 50 percent of his moral judgment is characteristic of that stage, whereas elements from both the preceding and subsequent stages are also to be found.

The method utilized by Kohlberg is similar to Piaget's in that the subjects are expected to give responses to stories told to them. However, Kohlberg's stories were designed in the form of moral dilemmas which tend to be more sophisticated and demanding than those of Piaget. The children are expected to identify which course of action they think is right to follow and explain the grounds for their choice. Conflict inheres in the fact that either one of two choices can be justified, but on differing grounds. For example, it may be regarded as wrong to steal in order to save a life because the stealer will have broken the law and violated the rights of another; on the other hand, one may conclude that the right to life has precedence over law and property rights. In general, Kohlberg used ten story situations in which there were conflicts between obedience to law as opposed to human needs and welfare.

The typology of six stages is derived from thirty different moral dimensions categorized from the children's responses, including motivation, rights, orientation toward punitive justice, and the value of life. Each of these different aspects of moral judgment can be located at any one of the six developmental stages. For example, the subject's conception of the value of human life could be assigned anywhere along the scale from stage 1 to stage 6, depending upon the reasoning brought into play when making a moral judgment. Therefore, there are a total of 180 cells in the total classification instrument (30 aspects × 6 stages for each one). The scoring procedure can be quite complicated and varied, but essentially the ratings within the classification system of 180 cells are computed and presented. This more detailed analysis is sometimes replaced in research reports by a global scoring based only on computation from the assigned stages of responses to stories of moral dilemmas, without recourse to the more complex classification system. The interested reader may obtain additional information on scoring from Kurtines and Grief (1974).

The typology itself consists of three levels, each embracing two stages. The first level is called Preconventional or Pre-moral. At this level children, while responsive to notions of good and bad or right and wrong as prescribed by the culture, make moral judgments based on pleasurable and unpleasurable consequences or according to the rule of those in authority. At the second, or Conventional level, we find conformity and fidelity to what is expected by others and to the social order. Immediate consequences are of less concern than meeting the expectations of one's family, group, and country. Emphasis is placed upon not altering the status quo and even defending it. The third, or Postconventional level, is based upon a principled morality of universal application which transcends the authority and rules prevailing in the individual's physical and interpersonal surroundings.

Stage 1 is founded upon an orientation to punishment and

obedience. Although deference to authority is observed, one complies to avoid personal harm. There is no recognition of, or respect for, an underlying moral order from which punishment and authority stem. Basically, good and bad are determined by the anticipated application of reward or punishment. Although Kohlberg's description of stage 1 coincides with Piaget's heteronomous stage, there is a difference of interpretation, for Kohlberg rejects Piaget's emphasis upon the sacred character of rules and authority in the young child. Stage 2 is viewed as one of naive egoism or individualistic egiosm. Like Piaget, Kohlberg finds the years from six to ten to be ones of reciprocity and mutual exchange. There is evidenced an increase of equalitarianism over authority and an increased awareness of the relativity of values. Elements of autonomy as characterized by Piaget are beginning to appear. Nevertheless, the reciprocity involved in this stage are derived from one's own ego-interests and not from a sense of obligation or respect for individual rights. Mutual respect is not central to it. Asked whether a man is right or wrong to steal a life-saving drug for his dying wife from the local pharmacist who discovered it, but is charging a prohibitive cost, many youngsters at this stage will answer yes. However, when asked to support their position, they will frequently answer that if the wife dies there will be no one to cook the husband's meals. Another characteristic response to stories involving doing something for another is that at some future time help may be needed from that person. The hedonistic and reciprocal nature of such replies are obvious. It should not be overlooked, however, that a good deal of social exchange in adult life does indeed pivot around a stage 2 level of development.

At stages 3 and 4 Kohlberg places special emphasis on the emergence of role-taking abilities. The preadolescent anticipates the way in which others might respond to his behavior and acts in such a way as to win approval and avoid disapproval. Obedience is not carried out merely for the sake of the rule or authority itself, but implies the attempt to attain certain social aims. The feelings of others are taken into account. Being of service to individuals and institutions takes on prominence. Stage

3 is labelled "Good-boy Orientation" by Kohlberg. Interestingly, in more recent years he has added the term "nice-girl" in referring to it. The young person at this stage places great emphasis upon affection and approval on the interpersonal level. The notion of reciprocity exercised is not founded upon strict mathematical equivalence ("A blow for a blow"), but is predicated upon putting oneself in the other person's place to determine what is a just action toward him. In other words, Kohlberg maintains that at stage 3 one begins to demonstrate imaginative reciprocity, involving role-taking, rather than engaging in an exact reciprocal exchange. Equity, taking into account individual circumstances, which Piaget has described is found at this developmental stage. A significant limitation, however, is that the youngster's role-taking ability and concept of justice is confined primarily to the domain of his own concrete personal relationships with friends and family. At stage 4 there is a shift in emphasis from a concept of justice applied mainly between individuals to a focus of justice between the individual and the community or social system. The prevailing notion of justice is grounded in maintaining the social order. Patterns of behavior and relationship should remain within the existing rules and social structure. This law and order orientation has been found to be the dominant one among adults in all societies studied by Kohlberg. He stresses that this stage which emphasizes the maintenance of rules and laws is morally more advanced and based on a higher level of rational attainment than the earlier stage of obedience to rules found at stage 1. Stage 4 is only arrived at after the previous stages are passed through and a capacity for role-taking which goes beyond one's immediate milieu to encompass the community has emerged.

Stages 5 and 6 witness the emergence of principled thinking. Stage 5 is based on the democratic process, has a legalistic character to it, and revolves around the social contract. Although moral judgment recommends working within the confines of the current social order, emphasis is upon engaging in the appropriate legal procedures to change laws when they are unjust. The rights of individuals become of paramount importance. The insistence upon maintaining the social order evidenced in stage 4 ceases to play a dominant role. Laws are conceived of as instruments for promoting individual rights and social welfare. Although laws are not seen as sacred, the stage 5 person will, in the conduct of day-by-day affairs, advocate observing them and will refer to them to define what is right. At the same time, a person at this level will recognize the possibility of conflict between a legal or rational societal right and the right of an individual. Kohlberg illustrates this by citing a typical response to the story involving the husband who steals a drug to save his wife's life. Many youngsters at this stage simultaneously suggest that the husband was wrong from the standpoint of society and the law, but right from a personal standpoint. Even though the act may be "just" from an individual viewpoint, a judge would be legally proper, because of the social contract, to sentence the husband.

At stage 4 the person seems more concerned with protecting the collective or average citizen from law violations. The stage 5 person's concern for individual rights will extend to wanting to assure due process for the criminal, as well as the average citizen. The stage 5 person is interested in the preservation and protection of individual rights, while at the same time he emphasizes the making of laws which would promote and maximize social welfare. The methodology of implementing the democratic process is of greater importance to the stage 5 person than are the concrete rules and their enforcement. The reason is that the principles of democracy are said to be based upon certain natural rights which antecede the specific laws which might be derived from the courts. The notion of justice with respect to adhering to a social contract at stage 5 is defined by a mutuality or reciprocity of consent on the part of the individuals, as in marriage, as opposed to merely obeying to preserve the social order. In succinctly formulating the two defining aspects of stage 5, Kohlberg and Elfenbein (1975) have written, "The stage 5 effort to make more universal judgments can take two forms. One is the principle of utility or welfare maximization. The other is the concept of human rights and the social contract—the idea that individuals have rights that are prior to society, and that the powers of the state are limited to those which are protective of or at least compatible with those rights"

(p. 31). Most people do not arrive at either of the two principled stages, even though the United States was founded upon democratic principles, as Kohlberg remarks. In Kohlberg's view, it is obvious that merely acquiring experiences of responsibility, since most people do eventually have such experiences, is not sufficient to facilitate an advance to stage 5. He states, "In summary, personal experiences of choice involving questioning with commitment, in some sort of integration with stimulation to cognitive-moral reflection, seems required for movement from conventional to principled thoughts" (1973a, p. 41). Significantly, Kohlberg and Elfenbein (1975) claim that a longitudinal study has revealed there are twice as many male adults (ages twenty-six to thirty-four) who have arrived at stage 5 as have their fathers. Although the context from which this statement is drawn does not describe the population involved, it is likely that the sons were college graduates. This inference is based on the author's general familiarity with Kohlberg's work, as well as a position advanced by Kenniston (1970). Kenniston who is familiar with Kohlberg's research, first points out that, both in the United States and in other advanced nations, there is to be found a growing degree of postconventional morality among the college population. His speculations on why this is so are worthy of attention. He notes that the opportunity to question or challenge what is conventionally accepted decreases as one assumes employment and takes on family responsibilities. In contrast to this, the youth who moves on to college undergoes a "disengagement" from adult society which does not carry with it the same risks in challenging the status quo which the married and employed face. Further, the youth who enters college is confronted with a great multiplicity of alternative moral viewpoints coming from professors and peers alike. It is likely that the experiences generated by this situation will create some conflict which, in turn, will lead to resolutions at higher levels of development. As a third catalyst which promotes further moral development, Kenniston cites the discovery of duplicity and corruption, particularly in previously respected authorities who had earlier been instrumental in conveying conventional morality. A recognition, as a result of this discovery, that he is also subject to corruption, may serve to stimulate one further in his own moral development. Certainly it is possible that these three elements can be found outside the college environment, but a successful college climate is likely to introduce high proportions of each.

Stage 6 is presented as the highest level of morality disclosed by Kohlberg's research. Both stages 5 and 6 are based on principles as opposed to rules. The latter offers concrete indications of specific actions to be carried out or refrained from. Principles are absolute, universal, and admit of no exceptions. They take into account the respective claims of all parties involved in a conflict and offer general guides to resolutions. Kohlberg sees a principle not as a rule to action but as a guide to choice; it is what he calls a metarule as opposed to a mere concrete rule. Principled justice according to Kohlberg (1971b) signifies the resolution of diverse and competing claims. It calls for dealing with each person equally in the realm of distributive justice, without taking into consideration the vested interest of individuals. However, he notes that stage 5 morality does not offer an adequate guide to when it is proper to violate the law. The solution is that civil obedience is appropriate in response to an unjust law, one which violates basic human rights, but under no other circumstances. Increasingly as the person moves from stage 5 to stage 6, he takes a perspective outside of society and identifies with the just claims of the individuals involved regardless of specific laws that have been enacted (Kohlberg 1973a). At stage 6 morality is viewed as conscience in the form of self-chosen ethical principles based on a universal and consistent concept of justice. The two main universal principles which Kohlberg proclaims are predicated upon Kant's two moral axioms. The first is to act in such a way that the maxim guiding your own behavior would be willed by you to become a universal law. The second is to treat each person as an end in himself and not as a means to an end.

An important issue arises at this point which we will now deal with. It has already been stated that it is not the content but the line of reasoning behind the choice which determines the level of moral development. Hence, form and content are viewed separately, with emphasis upon the former. Theoretically, there may be six different people against capital punishment, for example, yet each may be at a different stage of moral development, depending upon the reason offered for their position. There is no logical problem posed here. It would also seem that theoretically two people may be at stage 6, one in favor of capital punishment and one against it. However, it is clear from some of Kohlberg's published material that he does not, in fact, draw this conclusion. Kohlberg and Elfenbein (1975) report that generally as one moves toward higher levels of moral development there is a rejection of capital punishment. Based on a longitudinal study they report that in almost all instances the subjects' position on capital punishment correlates with their general level of moral development. There was a difference in only eleven cases out of 105 in which the subject's position regarding the death penality was not founded upon the same level of moral reasoning in other areas. Further, there were almost no exceptions to the finding that subjects at stage 3 and below accepted capital punishment. Subjects at stage 4 tended to favor one or the other position on the issue of the death penalty. There were no exceptions to the finding that all stage 5 subjects rejected capital punishment. Despite the distinction between content and form or structure, Kohlberg and Elfenbein maintain that there exists what they call a "probabilistic tendency" for specific attitudes to be derived from specific structures. They use this term because they acknowledge that there are variables other than moral stages influencing judgment. The stage 5 respondents based only part of their reasoning on a rejection of retaliation. In part, their position was also based on an acceptance of data which suggest that the death penalty is not a deterrent. Nevertheless, Kohlberg and Elfenbein define more adequate modes of reasoning as those levels which tend toward agreement and, citing their own data, they state, "The higher the stage, the greater the likelihood that individuals at that stage will agree not only in their mode of moral reasoning but in the content of their moral judgments as well" (1975, pp. 629-30). The general universality of a principle implies the greater likelihood of achieving consensus from people at the higher levels. For Kohlberg and Elfenbein moral principles are characterized as inadequate if they yield disagreement. Although they view stage 5 reasoning on capital punishment as more adequate than stage 4, they believe it is inadequate in contrast to stage 6 because an agreement could shift in favor of the death penalty if data supported the deterrence theory. The stage 5 line of reasoning would then emphasize that on balance many individual lives would be saved and, hence, the general welfare promoted. However, the stage 6 morality is not at all relativistic and is based purely on a universal ethic. The Kantian axiom that no individual is to be used as a means to an end is at a high level of abstraction and does not yield to statistical data. Stage 5 reasoning allows for a contradiction between its dual emphasis on the individual's right being protected by the social contract and the utilitarian principle of promoting the social welfare. In the case of capital punishment, for example, as long as one accepts that it is not a deterrent, the potential for contradiction is not apparent. Once one adopts a position that it is a deterrent, however, a conflict is revealed between the individual rights of the offender and the general welfare. In the view of Kohlberg and Elfenbein, the stage 6 line of moral reasoning resolves this conflict. It is their contention that moral development is not simply a matter of applying one's cognitive structures, but also structures of role-taking and justice. At this juncture, Kohlberg and Elfenbein introduce the concept of the "original position" advanced by Rawls (1971). A concept of justice is arrived at by imaginatively contemplating a hypothetical society in which one's own role(s) is unknown. In this manner, Rawls suggests a "veil of ignorance" precludes a judgment from being based upon vested interests. Applying this approach to the area of corrections, it is contended by Kohlberg and Elfenbein (1975) that a just penal system would be one that is predicated upon the "original position." They argue that a person unaware of the role he is to assume in a future society would not opt for retribution in the form of capital punishment for he could very well turn out to be a criminal in that society. If he were not operating under a "veil of ignorance" and knew that he would be a criminal, he would probably opt for no punishment at all.

Since he does not know his role, he may appear in the society as an ordinary citizen or perhaps even an innocent victim. Therefore, he would certainly maintain that some form of punishment be required within the society. Protecting himself as a potentially nonaggressive citizen, yet entertaining the possibility that he could alternately be a criminal, the person in the original position would advance as just retribution that action which would be minimally necessary for effective deterrence. It might be argued, for example, that life imprisonment rather than death would protect the free citizen from a murderer, while stopping short of unnecessarily depriving the criminal of his life. The point is that all people who engage in this contemplative exercise, which involves a role-taking structure, would on grounds of logic and justice arrive at the same conclusion. A fair solution will stand the test of this role-taking task, so that as one moves from one person's subjective view to another's, a coordinated solution that is just and equitable emerges, under the prevailing circumstances of the situation. The stage 6 person doing this in relation to capital punishment will acknowledge the need for some kind of restraint, but will rule out the death penalty as unnecessary. Actually this presentation is an attenuated version of Kohlberg's and Elfenbein's more subtle and complex formulation. The reader is reminded that the author's purpose here is not to compel assent, but merely to clarify that, despite his frequently cited distinction between content and structure, Kohlberg does believe that at the highest level of moral development one is more likely to find agreement on content, as well as the same mode of reasoning.

REGRESSION AND REVISION

In a follow-up study by Kohlberg and Kramer (1969) of the original sample that had been studied longitudinally, it was reported that there were no moral stages to be found in adulthood that had not already appeared by the time of adolescence. The notion of a seventh stage was, therefore, rejected. The researchers maintained that, by the end of high school, stage 5 had reached its peak with little evidence suggesting any advance from then to age twenty-five. There was only a minimal, but nonsignificant, increase in stage 6 reasoning. There was a trend, however, for individuals who had been below stage 4 to develop toward it between the ages of sixteen to twenty-four. There was a pronounced tendency for the stabilization of the more advance stages, especially at stage 4, with a clear diminution of the lower modes of moral reasoning. In fact, Kohlberg and Kramer reported this stabilization at stage 4 to be the primary fact of moral development after high school.

A curious finding discovered by Kohlberg and Kramer was that, in contrast to the tendency of moving toward the increasing use of one's highest potential, 20 percent of the middle-class sample regressed from a higher level of maturity to stage 2. This occurred when they were high school seniors or in the first half of their college career. Before the regression they had all been classified as evidencing a mix of stages 4 and 5, hence straddling conventional and principled stages of morality. Although characterizing the students as being hedonistic relativists, the researchers do note that their responses were couched in a vocabulary reflecting philosophical and political overtones. There was also evidence that none of the retrogressers had lost their former capacity to grasp stages 4 and 5 moral reasoning even though they did not utilize those stages in expressing their own beliefs. Despite these observations, it was discovered that 100 percent of the regressed members had recovered their formal level of moral maturity by the age of twenty-five and, in fact, demonstrated more of stage 5 than of stage 4 when compared to their initial high school responses. At the time Kohlberg and Kramer originally reported these findings, they accounted for the structural regression as a functional advance arguing that it was a preliminary step in which ego development was enhanced as the subjects were striving for a personal integration which would facilitate their use of the higher moral structural level. In elaborating their position, acknowledgment was given to the fact that they were borrowing Erikson's model of "moratorium, identity crisis, and renewed commitment."

Kohlberg (1973b) has since "revisited" his own research and

revised his findings, as well as the interpretations initially employed in construing them. He bases his shift on an intensive considera- tion of the nature of stage theory in relation to any possible regression, a reworking of his scoring system so that it would more accurately detect structure over content, and continued longitudinal study with the same subjects.

The conclusion drawn by Kohlberg once reworking his theory and research, is that adulthood stages do exist, despite an earlier disclaimer. The alleged retrogression from stage 5 thinking, he now believes, bears evidence that genuine principled thinking had not actually been achieved. In redefining the phenomenon of apparent "regression," Kohlberg concedes that he had mistaken a shift in content for a slip backward in structure. He now views the phenomenon as a loosening of the conventional level as the transition process toward principled moral reasoning was embarked upon. The seeming regression to stage 2 is now seen as an advance to stage 4B, a midpoint between conventional and principled levels of moral development. Although still viewing morality as conventional, the students in transition are seen as beginning to challenge the legitimacy of such a position. A higher level of abstraction and philosophizing than had preceded is set in operation. The purpose and utility of the rules and laws embraced by conventional morality are being called into question, even though the student at stage 4B has not as yet given up the conventional level or achieved the principled level. Following subtle and detailed theoretical analysis, Kohlberg revises his original contention to state that genuine stage 5 moral reasoning is not to be found before the age of twenty-three among his subjects. Furthermore, with the more refined analysis at his command, Kohlberg observes that not even by the age of thirty can stage 6 be found to dominate among his subjects.

Kohlberg concludes his revision with some speculative thoughts about the possibility of a seventh stage, acknowledging that his comments are philosophical and not empirical. Such questions as "Why be moral?" "Why live?" and "How to face death?" are all admittedly not resolved on rational grounds, but encompassed in a stage 7 outlook. In Kohlberg's view, the humanistic perspective of stage 6 is transcended and a cosmic perspective in which the stage 7 individual identifies with all of life is adopted. It is with considerable anticipation that we may await further reports from this fertile and creative thinker as he advances along his own developmental scale.

The reader who is interested in pursuing two challenging and promising works which are congenial to Piaget's theory of moral development, but which enter realms other than those we have been pursuing, may wish to review Rawls (1971) and Boszormenyi-Nagy and Spark (1973). Rawls is a Harvard philosophy professor who has written a major book formulating a theory of justice, in which he gives a footnote acknowledgment to Piagetian influences and draws attention to the similarity between his own work and Kohlberg's. The book has evoked considerable interest among behavioral scientists and humanists and has been widely reviewed. The book by Boszormenyi-Nagy and Sparks, both family therapists, is a view of family dynamics and therapy based upon concepts of reciprocity and justice within a three-generational framework.

7

THE ONTOGENESIS
OF TAKING
ANOTHER'S PERSPECTIVE

VISUAL PERSPECTIVE-TAKING

Piaget's conception of intelligence is founded upon adaptation. One of the most significant aspects of our world which requires adaptation is the social environment. The capacity to take the perspective of another and to coordinate it with one's own viewpoint is crucial to effective interpersonal relationships. It appears from a burgeoning literature on the subject, that this capacity and the referential communication it facilitates can be traced ontogenetically, as they are developmental phenomena. Piaget's own work on assuming the visual-spatial perspective of another and on role-taking in communication has served as a point of departure for the literature on social cognition which will be examined in this and the following chapters. Therefore, some of his seminal efforts dealing with role-taking, although introduced previously, will be amplified here.

Research by Piaget and Inhelder (1948/1967) provides a starting point for a considerable amount of subsequent attempts by others to explore the child's growing ability to decenter from his own perspective and to see things from another's point of view. In the experiment, they utilized a pasteboard model representing three different colored three-dimensional mountains. The smallest, a green mountain, is situated in the foreground, to the right of the child's original position. A brown and somewhat higher mountain is to the child's left and a trifle to the rear of the lower mountain on his right. The highest of the three mountains, grey and pyramid-shaped, is situated in the background. Each mountain is also distinguished by being topped with a house, a cross, or a snow-covered peak respectively. Also utilized is a collection of ten pictures representing the mountains in their original colors and distinctive features. Lastly, the apparatus includes a miniature doll which is placed by the experimenter in various positions around the simulated landscape. The child is required to decide, through a process of reconstruction and inference, what the perspective of the doll is as it is moved to various positions. Alternately, the child is requested to identify where the doll must be placed to give it a particular view of the landscape. The ten pictures are used to facilitate the choices the child may make in these tasks. In a third task, the child is given three additional pieces of shaped cardboard and asked to first imagine the perspective of the doll from a given position and then to reconstruct with these pieces the type of "snapshot" that would be taken from that angle. The experiment was conducted with one hundred children ranging in age from four to twelve. It is obvious that, in this experiment, it is only the visual perspective of the other which needs to be taken into account. Later we shall examine studies in which it is necessary for the child to make inferences about psychological events or processes which are taking place internally in the other person.

Piaget and Inhelder have observed that children clearly undergo a developmental progression from egocentrism to a complete relativity of perspectives in which their own views are coordinated with the various alternate possibilities. Piaget actually begins his descriptive account of the stages with stage 2, readily dismissing stage 1, for the children at that point do not even understand the questions. Stages 2 and 3 each have substages which shall be briefly depicted here. In substage 2A the child regards his own point of view as the only one possible, failing to realize that varying positions around the landscape will produce alternate perspectives. Children would also sometimes select an arbitrary picture to represent the doll's viewpoint, thereby indicating that any picture would be suitable as long as it contained three mountains. In one instance, a youngster selecting a picture

reflecting his own perspective, when asked to identify the view of
a doll in a different position from his own, proclaimed, "That's
the best one, he sees all three as they really are." The egocentric
character of this remark needs little elaboration. The child's own
singular perspective is not recognized as a limited vision of
reality, but is absolutized into the totality of reality. In substage
2B the child is in transition and seems to have become aware
that there are various points of view, but he has great difficulty
in attempting to relate the separate elements of the landscape.
The child, for example, may reverse the position of an individual
mountain when reconstructing the doll's view with the separate
cardboard pieces, but he does not correctly and systematically
alter all the relations of the parts with respect to left and right,
on the one hand, and foreground and background, on the other.
At this substage a child who is asked to reproduce the view
of a doll opposite him will instead first assemble the supplied
pieces of colored cardboard into an arrangement equivalent to
his own viewpoint and simply reverse the entire landscape so that
the doll opposite him now is facing the child's own view. In doing
this the child has begun to evidence some sense of the relativity
of viewpoints, but he has failed to reconstruct the viewpoint of
the other. In fact, what he does is to place his own viewpoint
in front of the doll which could not realistically be observing this
view from its own position. The internal relations of the mountains in the landscape are not modified at all from the standpoint
of left-right or before-behind when the entire configuration is
simply turned to face another way. Although the child has dimly
perceived that there is a differentiation between his perspective
and that of the doll's opposite him, he cannot yet recognize that,
if the brown mountain is on his left and the green is on his right,
the relation must be reversed to accommodate the perspective
of the doll facing opposite him. Similarly, if the grey mountain
is in the background of his view, it must be in the foreground
from the view of the opposite position. Characterizing this aspect
of substage 2B, Piaget and Inhelder (1948/1967) state, "Thus,
all observers are assumed to see the mountains looking the same
as they do to the child, but from their own viewpoints. This is

indeed a start to relative discrimination of viewpoints, but one which in no way impairs the immutability of the egocentric viewpoint" (p. 226). Another significant characteristic of substage 2B is the child's tendency to exclusively focus on a salient feature in a picture, making the tacit assumption that the remaining internal relations of the configuration all fall into place. The arrangement of the mountain is treated as an immutable whole. For example, in one instance the doll is situated to the left of the child facing a perspective at a 90° angle from the child's. The doll sees (from left to right) grey, green, and brown mountains. From the child's perspective the outstanding aspect of the doll's outlook is that it is close to the grey mountains. Therefore, the child selects a picture reflecting the grey mountain to the foreground as representing the doll's perspective. However, the child has neglected the fact that, in the picture he chose, the grey mountain is to the right and the green one to the left and that the brown is hidden by the green! Hence, the child at substage 2B finds it sufficient to be guided by one dominant feature and proceeds as if the remaining relations, which he fails to take into account, are automatically correct.

During substage 2B the child tends to treat the three mountains as though they are part of an immutable whole. The various relationships among them from the many possible perspectives are simply not grasped. In substage 3A, however, the child comes to realize that the observer's position will determine relations of before-behind and left-right. At the same time, the complexity of the situation is great and the child cannot yet quite be in command of these relations or construct an integrated and coordinated whole. For example, in his attempts to adapt to a different perspective, he may successfully deal with before-behind relations and fail to modify left-right relations. In other words, if he is seated so that the grey mountain is in the background, he discerns that the perspective of the doll opposite him would have the same mountain in the foreground. Nevertheless, he imagines that the brown mountain on his left and the green one on his right will retain those relative positions to the opposite viewer. It is now recognized that relationships internal to the landscape can change according to the observer's position. The total configuration of the mountains is no longer seen as an immutable whole, and the relativity of perspectives is now genuine, although not yet complete. Piaget construes stage 3A as being the midpoint between the egocentrism of stage 2 and the true relativity of stage 3B. He makes clear that there exists complete continuity of development from 3A to 3B. Upon full emergence of substage 3B the child is aware that each position allows for only one given picture or viewpoint. He can now put into operation an anticipatory schema which enables him to simultaneously take into account all the necessary relationships within the landscape to correctly reconstruct a given perspective. At stage 3B he has arrived at the capacity to decenter from his own viewpoint, reconstruct alternate perspectives, and coordinate these various possible perspectives. Fishbein, Lewis, and Keiffer (1972) have identified the coordination of perspectives in its broadest sense as, " . . . The *knowledge* that the appearance of objects is a function of the spatial position from which they are viewed, and to the *ability* to determine what the appearance will be for any specific viewing position" (p. 21). There is a decisive pattern of age-related development with the child generally arriving at substage 3B at approximately ten years of age.

There is considerably more variation and subtlety in the ontogenesis of the child's spatial perspective-taking than is captured here. The interested reader can do no better than to consult this material in the original version by Piaget and Inhelder (Chap. 8). Essential confirmation of the research conducted by Piaget and Inhelder on spatial relations has been reported by Dodwell (1963), Laurendeau and Pinard (1970) and Flavell et al (1968), with some admitted variations. Dodwell found that older children performed better than younger children, but he did not discover any consistent pattern linking performance and a margin of egocentric errors. The research conducted by Laurendeau and Pinard made more stringent demands than the Piagetian methods, with the result that only 28 percent (fourteen) of the sample (fifty) of twelve year olds completely achieved the ability to coordinate perspectives. In an analysis of the cognitive structures required to coordinate perspectives as required by their tasks, Laurendeau and Pinard reject the notion that formal operations are required, but contend that the degree of complexity inherent in the task would require that the subject be in the last period of the concrete operations for mastery. The research of Laurendeau and Pinard has considerable methodological advantage over that of Piaget and Inhelder and the criticism they offer is an example of a genuinely constructive critical spirit. A point of particular interest introduced by Laurendeau and Pinard is their caution against construing egocentrism as being found exclusively in one period followed by its absence. The relative complexity of the tests utilized may invoke egocentrism even at more advanced developmental levels. Fishbein, Lewis, and Keiffer (1972) have also devoted attention to this issue. In a more general statement, they observe, " . . . as task complexity increases children may be led to adopt earlier modes of thinking to solve the experimental problem. Thus children may use concrete operations to solve simple problems, but preoperational thinking to solve complex problems" (p. 23). They found that although performance improved as children grew older, there were more egocentric errors. It should be remembered that an error may be either egocentric or nonegocentric. In the former, the child working on a given task does not evidence that an observer at a different position would have an alternate perspective, while in the latter, the child recognizes that the other would have an alternate perspective, but is mistaken in his prediction of what it consists of. Salatas and Flavell (1976) have offered further confirmation of past studies that egocentric errors increase with task complexity. It would seem reasonable to conclude that a child in a given experiment may provide no egocentric errors on a task of relative simplicity, while providing egocentric errors on a task of greater complexity. Similarly, as a child develops in the natural environment, he is likely to seek contact with stimuli of increasing complexity and may initially revert to egocentrism in such encounters during the initial striving toward mastery.

Using the work of Piaget and Inhelder as a springboard,

Flavell et al (1968) set out to further test children's role-taking capacities involving perceptual tasks. They worked with a sample of 160 subjects of predominantly middle-class background. There were ten subjects of each sex ranging through grades two to eight and eleven in a public school system. Four displays of increasing complexity were presented to each subject in ascending order. At the presentation of each display an experimenter would sit first on the right side of the table in relation to the subject, then opposite the subject. Separate parts replicating the displays were available to the subjects and the task required that they reconstruct the visual perspective of the experimenter in each instance. The results indicated a very high level of consistent increase with age of task mastery. They also confirmed the progressive difficulty in dealing with each of the displays, for each subsequent display was mastered by only approximately one half of the number mastering the previous display. In comparing their own data to those of Piaget and Inhelder's, Flavell et al point out that there was little in the way of egocentric errors as defined by stage 2A to be found in their subjects. This is exactly what they had predicted prior to a careful analysis of the data, for children in stage 2A tend to be between four and six years whereas the youngest subjects studied in the Flavell et al research were seven years of age. Their data also confirm an impression recorded by Piaget and Inhelder to the effect that the right-left variable offers more difficulty for the child than the front-back one in spatial perspective-taking tasks.

In discussing their findings, Flavell et al characterize development in the area under consideration as being more quantitative than qualitative, as if a single skill is being progressively refined. In addition, they ask why they would adopt this view in contrast to Piaget and Inhelder who advanced an interpretation based essentially on developmental stages. It is their suggestion that the Piaget and Inhelder data, rather than being categorized into four basic divisions (stages 2A, 2B, 3A, and 3B), should be classified into two. In the first category would be children who are completely unaware that another observer positioned differently would not share the same perspective. The qualitative shift would be to the second category in which children are at least aware that the other observer would see things differently. Changes within this classification are then more of degree than kind. Since most of the subjects in the research of Flavell et al were already beyond stage 2A, these researchers were more impressed with the quantitative developments than Piaget and Inhelder who emphasized qualitative changes. In any event, there is clearly a compatibility of the findings from the two major experimental studies under consideration thus far in this chapter. Visual perspective of another can be accurately anticipated in a non-egocentric fashion by middle childhood or early adolescence. Nevertheless, task difficulty is a highly significant variable. It should be noted that display 4 utilized by Flavell et al is even more complex than the landscape employed by Piaget and Inhelder. Maximum scores were attained in dealing with display 4 by only eight out of twenty sixteen-year-old adolescents. Borke (1975) has recently addressed herself to the subject of age and egocentrism in relation to task complexity. She argues that the more difficult a task, the more likely it will call forth an egocentric response, an argument now familiar to the reader. She further maintains that even in a complex situation, egocentrism may be minimized by utilizing objects that are discrete and readily differentiated in contrast to the relatively homogenous configuration of the classic three-mountain landscape used by Piaget and Inhelder. Lastly, Borke points out that the method invoked in getting the subject to convey his knowledge of another's perspective is significant to success or failure in completing the task. Success scores increase when the child is provided with an apparatus duplicating the original scene and is asked to rotate the replication to indicate what it is that the other sees. She contends that even four year olds performed better using this method on the three-mountain task than when being required to identify a correct picture or reconstruct a model.

Two related studies (Shantz and Watson 1970, 1971) introduce some interesting insight and questions regarding the development of spatial objectivity and role-taking. Shantz and Watson offer an incisive description of declining egocentrism accompanied by increasing objectivity in attaining spatial objectivity. There is said to be no expectancy by the very young child that the appearance of an object will change as he alters his position spatially. In time this total egocentrism decreases as the child comes to realize that the appearance of objects and the way they are arranged will shift according to his spatial position. He has not as yet, however, developed any specific notion or expectancies with respect to how things will look from a different position. As he progresses, the child develops specific subject-object relations of a discrete nature, without yet organizing them into a comprehensive framework. Ultimately, the differentiated subject-object relations are integrated into a network. Shantz and Watson sought to test the spatial expectancies of young children by adopting the "expectancy violation" principle advanced by Charlesworth (1966). The application of the principle involved allowing a child to review a landscape which is then covered, after which the child is requested to walk to a different position around the landscape. As he does this, the landscape is rotated so that the original scene will be shown to him when it is uncovered. The child who had anticipated a different scene will register either surprise or bewilderment. Approximately half of forty-eight children between the ages of three and five years could unequivocally distinguish between trick and authentic situations. Fourteen of the subjects were also able to correctly account for the expectancy violation. Shantz and Watson hypothesized that the ability of many young children to predict locations as they change position around a scene is positively related to the ability to make accurate spatial predictions about another's perspective. They sampled three groups of children ranging in age from three years eight months to six and one half years. The hypothesis was confirmed. Children who did well in anticipating object location when they moved around tended, to a statistically significant degree, to do well on a modification of Piaget's landscape task. Those who did not do well on the former were much less likely to do well on the latter. The researchers also raised the question of whether a relationship exists between ability to discern trick rotations of the scene and accurately predicting an observer's viewpoint. Reactions of surprise or perplexity were found to be positively related to both taking another's perspective and anticipating object location when the child moves around, It was discovered in general that, when the child moves around, it is relatively easy to predict object location even for three and one half to six and one half year olds, even though predicting another's perspective on a symbolic level is more difficult, as we have seen previously, for children in this age range. Shantz and Watson did not feel that there was sufficient evidence to conclude that the easier of the two tasks was a necessary and/or sufficient condition for the more difficult one despite their finding of a positive correlation. Nevertheless, this research suggests that children can effectively conceptualize spatial relations earlier than would be concluded on the basis of isolated experiments on perspective-taking of another.

    The experiment involving expectancy violation is particularly interesting. Shantz and Watson analyze the differences between the task in which the child moves around the scene and the conventional Piagetian landscape arrangement. One of the major distinguishing characteristics of the former is that the scene is covered during the move. Therefore, one might speculate that the perceptual distraction in the conventional task inhibits the exercise of the necessary cognitive operations, whereas in the less conventional task the masking of the scene frees the operational capacity of the child. In an extensive review on social cognition, Shantz (1975) takes up this issue by introducing the work of Brodzinsky, Jackson, and Overton (1972), Brodzinsky and Jackson (1973), and Shantz, Asarnow, and Berkowitz (1974). In the first of these studies, children age six, eight, and ten were tested under conditions utilizing both screened and unscreened arrays of objects. The screening seemed to have an effect only on the middle group of eight year olds. The researchers suggested that the youngest group lacked the necessary structures altogether, so that relieving them from the distraction of their own viewpoint by masking it could not be useful. Further, the older children had already developed such stable structures that the masking was not necessary to facilitate their performance. However, the middle group was transitional in the development of spatial concepts and the masking served to promote the use of the developing spatial structures available to those children in that group. The findings of the other studies cited above were not completely congruent with this report of the first of them and Shantz indicates that differences in ages and procedures makes it difficult to account for the discrepancies at this time.

Just how young can a child be and still handle problems involving spatial concepts? Fishbein et al (1972) claim that their research supports the position that coordination of perspectives can be successfully executed by children only three and one half years of age if the conditions of the experiment are appropriate. Masangkay et al (1974) conducted research which led them to conclude that some ability at spatial perspective-taking is present in children from two to three years of age. This becomes manifest in the experimental situation when the task is simple enough. However, they acknowledge that the skill involved may be more limited than that required to solve Piaget's landscape problem or even than simpler analogues based on that problem which may utilize only one object. In a review of the contrasting range of research literature on the development of visual perspective-taking, Flavell (1974) asserts the essential correctness of Piaget's formulation, while, at the same time conceding that there are gaps in it. He raises several vital questions bearing on what it is that the two and three year olds in Masangkay's research possess regarding visual experiences and perspective-taking that are not found in sensorimotor youngsters, while at the same time he ponders what it is that they lack in comparison to more highly developed perspective-takers. In an attempt to impose some order upon the diverse spectrum of research findings, he has constructed a model depicting several levels of development. An exposition of that model appears below.

Flavell proceeds by first drawing a sharp distinction between the *existence* of the notion that perspectives vary according to position and the competence to accurately *infer* the other's viewpoint through the employment of cognitive strategies. The model he postulates deemphasizes the inference aspect of development, which has received considerable attention in the past, in order to focus more heavily upon the existence domain. There are four levels to be examined. Level O does not actually attribute any perceptual capacities to the observer and tends to be on a plane similar to the practical intelligence of the sensorimotor period in Piaget's system. The child at this level is related more to the practical knowledge that the object remains constantly available to him than to the appearance that it will evidence from different vantage points. He knows that he can walk around a barrier to retrieve an object, but he does not anticipate that it will appear different to him when on the other side, nor does he represent the visual experience of an observer who is already on the other side of the barrier. The invisible psychological process of perceiving is simply not yet an object of cognition. In the Masangkay et al research, there is a task in which a card depicting one object on side A and a different type of object on side B is shown to a child. The picture is then held vertically so that the child can see what is on side A, but cannot observe side B, which faces the experimenter. If the vocabulary of the child at level O is adequate, he may be able to answer the question, "What is on my side of the card?" when asked by the experimenter. However, he would not be able to answer the question, "What do I see?" In fact, he may repeat the question, "What do I see?" and, thereby use himself as the referent with the result of giving an egocentric response, as Shantz (1975) points out.

The child who arrives at level 1 is able to recognize that the observer seated across from him has a perspective of his own which differs from the child's. Therefore, the child can now respond appropriately to the experimenter's question, "What do I see?" and no longer runs the risk of assimilating it to his own frame of reference. However, although he now comprehends that the observer sees the objects on the other side of a barrier between them, he does not reconstruct any particular perspective of the observer. In other words, he does not grasp *how* the observer sees, but only *what* he sees. Masangkay et al (1974) report that approximately half of the two year olds studied and all of the three olds were at level 1. The child is now able to shift in the use of the pronoun "I" as he realizes that, when he speaks the word, it refers to him and that, when the observer speaks the word, it refers to the observer (Shantz, 1975). A primitive role-taking capacity has emerged.

By the time a child enters level 2 he can manifest a knowledge not only of *what* the observer sees, but also of *how* he sees it. Even when observing the same object, but from different positions, the child realizes that the perspective of the observer is different, and he can reconstruct that perspective with regard to such vital dimensions as left-right and front-behind. Thus, mastery of the three-mountains problem involves level 2. Shantz (1975) emphasizes that preschool and kindergarten children have demonstrated some capacity to operate at level 2 if a single, meaningful object that has readily nameable sides is utilized, as opposed to the much more complex three-mountains problem.

The final phase of this proposed developmental sequence, level 3, requires that the subject be able to reconstruct an exact retinal image of the observer's perspective. For example, in performing such a task, not only would the subject have to deal with relative positions such as front-behind, as in level 2, but he would also have to demonstrate knowledge that on the three-mountains problem, a mountain in his foreground would appear larger to him, but smaller to the observer opposite him. There is presently no research available with this level of perspective replication, which includes the retinal image of the observer in every literal detail with precision. Characterizing his own model, Flavell (1974) comments, ". . . each level seems to reflect a more abstract, internal-percept-oriented versus external-object-oriented, form of knowledge than its predecessors. The higher the level . . . the more clearly and unambiguously one is dealing with inferences about *percepts* rather than *objects*" (p. 100).

Piaget has consistently held that egocentrism declines largely through peer social interaction during childhood. The ongoing confrontation with clashing wills and views forces the developing child to differentiate between his own and other's views with the result that he acquires the ability to assume alternate perspectives. On this basis, Neale (1966) hypothesized that emotionally disturbed children with deficient socialization backgrounds would do poorly on role-taking tasks compared with a control group of normal children. He tested this using Piaget's three-mountain problem with twenty children from a hospital, where they had been sent because of their antisocial behavior in the community, and twenty children from a local public school. Each group was broken into four subgroups of five children each representing ages eight through eleven. Results indicated that at each age group the institutionalized children were more egocentric than the non-institutionalized children. Subsequently, a further analysis was made within the group of emotionally disturbed children. Children who had been placed in various homes through Children's Aid Society (CAS) prior to hospitalization were in one group and children who had come to the hospital directly from their own homes were in the other. It was predicted that CAS children would be significantly more egocentric than the other children because of the even poorer socialization opportunities afforded them by the multiple placements they had had to endure. The prediction was confirmed.

Neale further noted that, although there was an expected correlation between age and egocentrism, an inverse ratio for the noninstitutionalized children, this proved not to be the case for the institutionalized ones. Given the lack of normal social interaction by the hospitalized children and the crucial role played by such interaction according to Piaget, these findings are not at all surprising.

ROLE-TAKING IN PERSPECTIVE

In an extensive survey of the literature on role-taking Shantz (1975) sharply differentiates it from what social psychologists generally mean by role. It does not refer to role enactment in which a subject assumes the posture or gestures of another person, nor does it signify the traits expected to be observed in such designations as occupational or sex role. Rather, it is a set of cognitive skills which enable one person to infer something about another person's thoughts and feelings. It can take place in greater proportion as egocentrism declines, which facilitates the individual's ability not only to take the perspective of another, but to co-ordinate that with his own. As Shantz points out, role-taking capacities are often employed as a means to an end, as in efforts to persuade, playing a game to win, and resolving social conflict. Since both people in an interpersonal dyad have some degree of role-taking abilities, there is a reciprocal and cooperative character to it in operation. Until now we have been concerned with spatial role-taking, but the balance of this chapter will be devoted to examining role-taking activities in nonspatial domains. Especially prominent in the present section will be the work of Feffer, Selman, and Flavell, each of whom forged role-taking developmental models based on their research using Piaget as a starting point.

FEFFER: TOWARD A MODEL OF INTERPERSONAL BEHAVIOR

Feffer (1959) introduced the Role-Taking Task (RTT) which he initially designed on the basis of Schneiderman's Make A Picture Story (MAPS). The test material selected provides a series of common scenes, such as a living room and street corner. Various figures of children, men, and women are placed in the scenes. The subject in a RTT is asked to tell a story utilizing three figures in a given background scene. He is then asked to retell the story, but this time he is requested to vary the version so that it is conveyed through the perspective of each of the three figures.

On a theoretical plane, Feffer attempted to redirect the concept of decentration, so vital in Piaget's view of constructing knowledge in the physical world, to the social dimension. It is Feffer's contention that the RTT tests the subject's capacity to decenter from the perceptual stimuli in the social environment and from his own original viewpoint. The first of these is explored in terms of *level of actor-description,* each level becoming more abstract. Level 1 is designated space-action and refers to actual events in the situation that are tangible. These would include physical descriptions, such as commenting on the color of a person's hair, as well as specific actions that are carried out by the actors. Level 2 consists of comments upon internalized states of the actors in the stories, such as emotions, intentions and thoughts. These, however, are temporal and situational. Level 3 is called characterizations which are comprised of attributes that apply to the present story, but which are more enduring and, therefore, are typical of the actor in a variety of social contexts. Feffer views characterizations as being most reflective of a balanced decentering because of their generalized nature.

The second area of decentration is perspective-taking, in which the subject demonstrates a capacity to relinquish an exclusive focus on his viewpoint in order to refocus on the role of the actors. It is essential to note that the initial story formulated by the subject imposes a structure which must be adhered to as he proceeds to alternately tell the personal versions of each of the actors. In fact, every time he adds an additional perspective from a given actor in the story a new complexity and structure are imposed. Hence, a continual demand for decentration is taking place, while, at the same time, the subject is called upon to maintain an overall continuity of the story. A review of the three classifications involving perspective-taking in the RTT may make the preceding remarks clearer. The first is *simple refocusing.* An example would be describing a mother in one of the stories as being sad, from her viewpoint, but as being pleased from the father's viewpoint. Here we have a refocusing within the story from one perspective to another. The subject does not centrate on only one of them, nor on his own. Nevertheless, it should be noted that there is an inconsistency in the two versions. One would not ordinarily expect that a person feeling sad would be perceived as pleased by another in the environment. A higher level of balanced decentration is to be found in *consistent elaboration,* for in this classification there is continuity maintained from one decentration to the next. For example, the father who "felt lousy" when speaking for himself, is construed from the mother's viewpoint as quiet. Although each vantage point differs, there is a meshing within the framework of the story. Finally, the classification *change of perspective* must include both simple refocusing and consistent elaboration, but must also add a balanced de-centering specific to any given viewpoint. There must be continuity not only across viewpoints, but within any particular one. This can be seen in the example of a father in the story who states that the mother did not seem too pleased to see him, while describing himself as unhappy because of disappointment that a sale he expected to make did not materialize.

Note the internal consistency within the father's viewpoint which the subject attributes to him. The father must describe the mother on the basis of overt relatively superficial aspects. Upon coming home at the end of the day he is not aware that the mother is simply tired because she had been washing the floor all day. However, he is able to utilize more factual and internal information about his own state because he is privy to these personal data. Conversely, the subject offering alternate perspectives in the story may have the mother state that she is feeling tired because she has been washing floors all day. However, because she does not know what has taken place for the father, she merely describes him as morose. Like the father in the story, she has maintained consistency within her own viewpoint.

Methodologically, results from the RTT were scored and compared to independently rated scores on the Rorschach Developmental Indices. The latter were used to assess cognitive maturity of the subjects and are known to be verified measures of developmental level. Feffer concluded that the comparison provided confirmation of his inference that, " . . . adequacy of perspective-taking activity in the RTT is significantly related to level of cognitive development as inferred from the Rorshach Composite Index" (p. 166). A similar inference regarding the level of actor-description was not supported.

In the initial venture reported above of attempting to link decentration as a central concept bridging cognitive development in both physical and social spheres, Feffer used a sample of thirty-five males. Shortly afterward Feffer and Gourevitch (1960) employed the RTT with children in order to invoke a chrono-logical age criterion. Scores on the RTT were compared this time to Piagetian tasks which directly called upon decentering activity for successful completion, which was not the case with the Rorshach responses. Among the problems utilized from the Piagetian repertoire are those involving classification and conservation. Feffer emphasizes that the decrease of reliance on sensory impressions as cognitive development progresses is structurally the same in both conservation tasks, for example, and role-taking tasks. Similarily, just as the more cognitively mature child eventually desists from successfully shifting from length to width and back again, so to does the cognitively advanced child move beyond focusing on successive viewpoints without continuity in his role-taking activities. In later development, conceptual prowess preempts sensory distraction and promotes the organization of experience. The correlation study between children's RTT scores and the Piagetian tasks showed a positive relationship. The positive relationship between the two measures was maintained upon controlling for age and verbal intelligence. Taken independently, both measures indicated a positive relationship between chronological age and balanced decentration. Given the commonality of decentering activity as crucial to both measures, Feffer and Gourevitch conclude that RTT performance can serve as a basis for interpreting cognitive maturity. The sample for this study included sixty-eight boys, categorized in age groupings of six to seven, eight to nine, ten to eleven, and twelve to thirteen years. In particular, the most impressive increase on RTT decentering scores was in the shift from ages eight to ten to ten to eleven.

Feffer and Gourevitch draw their paper to a close with some interesting speculations on the relation of their work to social adaptation. They see their idea of balanced decentration in role-taking as rooted in Piaget's biological paradigm of assimilation and accommodation. As Piaget emphasized these processes in developing his ideas on adaptation in the physical world, Feffer and Gourevitch (1960) construe them as fostering adaptation in the social world. They state, "In successful role-taking, the S has to express change, i.e. decentering, while at the same time observing the structures implied by each previous change, i.e. balance. That is he has to assimilate the new role to the previous perspectives he has taken, while accommodating to the implications engendered by each new perspective" (p. 394).

Continuing to expand upon the preceding work, Feffer and Suchotliff (1966) set out to explore the hypothesis that effective interpersonal behavior derives from an individual's ability to consider multiple perspectives simultaneously with respect to his own behavior. Analyzing Piaget's concept of decentering, it is emphasized that centration leads to distortion and that only a partial correction of the distortion is achieved when the individual engages in decentration of a successive nature, that is, shifting sequentially from one part of the perceptual field to another. It is only in simultaneous decentering, taking into account a number of facets of a situation at one time and in relation to one another, that distortions are more completely corrected.

In a sense, Feffer's own work can be seen as a decentration from the almost exclusive focus of Piaget upon the impersonal world in order to take into account the interpersonal world as well, thereby correcting the "distortion" inherent in the Piagetian system. Individuals who centrate on their own viewpoint sequentially will encounter difficulty in appropriately modifying their responses to suit the interpersonal dynamics of a situation. In effective social interaction, the individual can assess his intended behavior from the standpoint of what he would anticipate the other person's reaction would be to that behavior, were it to be carried out. The skill involved in performing this cognitive act entails keeping one's own perspective in mind while simultaneously taking into account the perspective of the other. In so doing, a distortion that may derive from exclusively centering or focusing upon one's own outlook in a situation can be corrected for by adjusting this in relation to the other's outlook. For example, a young man who has been overlooked at a time of year when pay raises are issued is angered and contemplates storming into the boss's office to demand an explanation. However, upon placing himself in the role of the boss, he anticipates that the boss will counter with even greater anger at this unbridled display of impulsivity and hostility. Therefore, having anticipated an undesirable reaction to his intended behavior, our young man modifies that behavior without having carried it out. Instead, he selects an approach which is more likely to lead to a desirable outcome. Hence, we see that a balanced decentration, in which a correction in made for the maladaptive behavior that would have occurred had he centrated exclusively only on his initially intended behavior, leads to more effective social interaction.

However, the RTT and the preceding example deal with the decentering ability of a single individual. In the present study, Feffer moves his work one step forward by examining the reciprocal decentering capacities of two interacting individuals. A sample of thirty-six students enrolled in an undergraduate psychology course were administered the RTT to determine their decentering abilities in an interpersonal context. Dyadic couples (eighteen) were then formed in which similarity of decentering skill served as the criterion for pairing. Each pair was subsequently tested on a task calling into play cooperative social interaction. The structure of the task involved eighteen index cards placed before each participant. Each card had a word printed on it and was exposed only to one member of every dyad. The donor, or member of the dyad knowing the word, had the task of communicating it indirectly by selecting another word closely associated and telling that one to his partner, as a clue to the original test word. The task of the listener was to guess at the test word on the basis of the association clue. Communication along these lines was permitted to continue until either the test word was identified by the recipient of the association clues or a period of ninety seconds had expired. The number of clues necessary and the length of time required served as criteria for evaluating the degree of effective social interaction. Feffer and Suchotliff suggest that this task is analogous to the decentering situation in an interpersonal matrix described earlier in which one person's intended behavior is modified by his anticipation of how the other person will react. The task requires that the donor, whose goal is to communicate the test word, carefully consider all the many associations he may have to the word from the standpoint of selecting the one that will convey the most informational value to his partner. Hence, the donor's general intended behavior of revealing the test word must be specifically modified by anticipating the listener's response to whatever he might say. On the other hand, the listener or recipient of the clues is required to modify his responses by taking into account past clues and his own past responses as he attempts to accommodate to the task of guessing the test word. Feffer and Suchotliff (1966) characterize the process as follows, "The progressive modification and dove-tailing of responses thus required to communicate and receive the test word appeared to rest importantly upon the relative ability of each participant to attend simultaneously to aspects of his experience from more than one viewpoint" (p. 418). The methodology employed in this research project is quite complex and beyond what has already been reported is designed to rule out variables other than decentration skills and social interaction having an influence on the results. There were basically two conditions under which the "password" or clue was conveyed to the recipient by the donor. The first was called "loud" and it involved a face-to-face situation in which the donor was permitted to hear the recipient's response as he spoke it aloud. In the second or "silent" arrangement, the donor kept his back to the recipient, who wrote down his response without being permitted to speak it aloud. A comparison of these two condition highlights the fact that the former allows a greater amount of social interaction to take place, whereas the latter greatly constrains such a possibility and does not permit reciprocal adjustments to occur. Analysis of the data revealed that those dyads possessed of higher RTT decentering scores achieved greater success in the password task, requiring fewer clues and less time, under the loud condition than was the case with dyads having lower RTT scores. Furthermore, this was only the case under the loud condition, whereas a significant association between RTT scores and successful test performance was not found under the silent condition.

Such a clear dichotomy strongly suggests that the interactive component was the significant variable which allowed those with high RTT scores to bring their balanced decentering abilities into action. Feffer and Suchotliff interpret these findings as confirmation of their hypothesis that, when two individuals are able to simultaneously consider their behavior from alternate viewpoints there is likely to be more effective social interaction between them.

In a related attempt, Chaplin and Keller (1974) reversed the procedure somewhat in that they first identified whether children in their sample were high or low effective social interactors, as determined by their peers, and then sought to test their decentering skills as revealed by RTT scores and the three-mountains problem. They point out that in the study by Feffer and Suchotliff it is social interaction which is seen as the dependent variable, whereas in their own study it is approached as the independent variable. Piaget's early work, it will be remembered, emphasized social interaction as a significant activity which itself facilitates the decline of egocentrism and the increased ability of decentration. The sample consisted of twelve boys and twelve girls each at grades three and six. Based on sociometric-type questions, the responses of peers were used to divide the children from each grade level into evenly distributed groups of good social interactors and poor social interactors. Subsequently, the two tests were administered. Relationships were then sought between a child's rating as a social interactor and his ability to decenter. It was found that sixth graders in general were better able to decenter than third graders when performing on the RTT which involves an interpersonal context. However, it was only at the third grade level where there was observed a significant relationship between social interaction and decentration. Third graders who were rated via their peers as good social interactors evidenced a greater level of developmental maturity in decentration than those rated as poor social interactors. They were not, in fact, inferior to the sixth graders in their performance on the RTT. In explaining the lack of differentiation between good and poor social interactors at the sixth grade level regarding their decentering abilities on the RTT, Chaplin and Keller suggest that they are probably at the level of formal operations. Therefore, while they would be able to decenter in an abstract conceptual situation, it does not necessarily follow that they would be effective social interactors in everyday practice. In brief, high decentering skills may be a necessary, but not sufficient, condition for good social interaction.

Feffer (1970) offers a provocative and incisive, although exceedingly complex, attempt at synthesizing the various elements of cognitive development he had explored previously with Piaget's central concept of equilibration. At the same time, he acknowledges the preliminary empirical state of his interpersonal model building. These speculative efforts will not be elaborated upon here, but suffice it to say that the core of the model rests upon a series of balanced decentrations between two interacting individuals. In Feffer's words:

> The interpersonal event . . . is comprised of interacting participants who occupy such roles and reciprocals as giving-taking, asking-answering, and dominating-submitting. The greater complexity notwithstanding, a stable construction of the interpersonal event depends, as in the impersonal realm, on a reconciliation of these complementary dimensions (p. 208).

Feffer (1967) has attempted to show how primitive social interaction, in contrast to balanced decentrations, can be utilized to explain symptom expression. His analysis of the subject will appear in Chapter 9.

SELMAN: SOCIAL REASONING AND ROLE-TAKING

A fruitful mode of interpersonal perspective taking has been advanced by Selman (1971a, 1971b, 1976) and Selman and Byrne (1974). It is one which Loevinger (1976) finds similar and congenial to the conception of ego development elaborated upon in her latest work. In his own words, Selman has utilized the "Piagetian structuralist-developmental approach" in exploring the ontogenesis of social role-taking. He cautions that one should not look to a social-cognitive analysis to provide causal explanations of behavior. Instead it serves as a means for describing and organizing behavior and in turn leads to strategies of intervention to help the child improve his social reasoning and functioning. The approach in clinical practice derived from a social-cognitive model would not be a "cold-blooded" one, but rather a highly individualized one which makes every attempt to accurately diagnose the child's cognitive level of stage development in order to comprehend how he is construing his social world. For example, it may be discovered that the child who acts hostilely and persists in fighting whenever a peer accidentally bumps into him, may not yet have developed to the stage of differentiating between intentions and objective consequences.

In addition to working in the Piagetian tradition, Selman has also been influenced by Feffer (1959, 1970) and Flavell (1968), both Piagetian derived theorists themselves. Selman has largely focused upon applying his own interpersonal model to the moral sphere and in so doing has drawn heavily upon the Kohlbergian dilemmas while utilizing the clinical method in pursuing children's responses to them.

The stages presented by Selman (1976) range from 0-4. Below is a characterization of those developmental stages. The ages cited are suggestive, based on current research.

Stage 0: Egocentric Role-Taking (Ages Three to Six). The child does differentiate between self and others but fails to do so specifically with respect to their points of view. Emphasis is given to overt appearances as opposed to internal psychological states. No capacity is demonstrated to assess a person's actions on the basis of his underlying reasons. Alternate perspectives of differing participants in a situation cannot be related. As Loveinger (1976) points out in commenting on Selman's stage 0, either physical terms or egocentric wishes are criteria exercised in characterizing interpersonal relations. Hence, a child may construe a friend as a person who lives close to him or as another child who possesses desirable toys.

Stage 1: Social-Informational Role-Taking (Ages Six to Eight). The child views himself and the other as having essentially different points of view about the same social situation. Access to different information is believed to lead to alternate views. People may also be in different situations and, as a result, think or feel differently. Now the child has a grasp of the subjectivity of persons other than himself, but he does not yet realize that another can consider him as a subject. He cannot place himself in the role of the other, while at the same time maintaining his own perspective. There is a shift from stage 0, where others are merely seen as collectors of social data that are visibly manifest, to seeing them as capable of processing information as well. Persons, therefore, are capable of evaluating as well as collecting information. Reasons are now understood to serve as internal mediators which cause behavior.

Stage 2: Self-Reflective Role-Taking (Ages Eight to Ten).

It is now comprehended that each individual has a unique set of values and purposes and that these govern how one thinks and feels. The child's role-taking capacities are still rooted in the dyadic or two-person context, but he has now acquired the ability to take the perspective of another. Furthermore, he grasps that the other person can perform similarly; that is, he realizes the other person can figuratively enter his shoes and this enables the child to reciprocally anticipate how the other will respond to the child's own thoughts and feelings. The sort of recursive thought processes developing here are dealt with at length in Miller, Kessel, and Flavell (1970), who have adopted for their paper the highly indicative title, "Thinking about people thinking about people thinking about . . . : A study of social cognitive development." A striking advance in this stage is the child's awareness that others may be multimotivated and, hence, that either another person or the child himself may be in conflict between altrustic and self-interested concerns or between any two conflicting feelings. Reciprocity of a *quid pro quo* nature is especially characteristic of this stage.

Stage 3: Mutual Role-Taking (Ages Ten to Twelve). At this level of development the child can adopt a disinterested perspective as if he were a spectator overlooking the dyadic situation. He can now adopt a view as taken by a generalized or average member of a group, differentiated from the perspective of his own self. Whereas in stage 2 perspective taking is successive and not simultaneous, the child at stage 3 ". . . discovers that both self and other can consider each party's point of view simultaneously and mutually. Each can put himself in the other's place and view himself from that vantage before deciding how to react (the Golden Rule)" (p. 305). In addition to this simultaneity of role-taking, each child can rotate from participant to participant and assume a perspective from the point of view of a third party, who holds a coordinated and impartial perspective. Friendship at this stage is seen as going beyond mere "reciprocal back scratching" that takes place in the immediate present, but assumes a mutual character of an enduring nature which is not vulnerable to the vicissitudes of temporal quarrels or fleeting ruptures. A friend is no longer simply one who does a favor or acts in a generally benign manner from one's own perspective, as in stage 2. Selman states, "Thus mutuality at Stage 3 is evidenced in both structure (a simultaneous coordination of perspectives) and concept of the person (the understanding that both self and other hold mutual expectations)" (p. 306).

Stage 4: Social and Conventional System Role-Taking (Ages Twelve to Fifteen plus).   At this stage the youngster transcends the dyadic situation. He can not only adopt the viewpoint of a single impartial observer, as in stage 3, but now he conceives of a *generalized other* which is representative of the social system. It is recognized that each self in an interpersonal relationship shares the view of the group or generalized other, representing an integration of the prevailing conventions and mores of the society. There now exists for the youngster a group perspective embodying social custom and laws of the society. He is able to stand outside of himself and adopt that perspective. Loveinger (1976) points out that in adopting the viewpoint of society or the legal system, the youngster at stage 4 has entered a hypothetical or abstract realm. She stresses that at this stage in Selman's model there is a conception of persons and human relationship that is both very deep and complex. The beliefs, attitudes and values of another person are now recognized as being elements that are developing in that person and which comprise a complex intrapsychic matrix. These evolving internal components are now recognized as predictive of an individual's future behavior and instrumental in understanding his past performances.

In relating the stages of his own model to research findings, Selman (1976) suggests that social role-taking skills are necessary, but not sufficient for corresponding moral judgment. He sees role-taking as being at the midpoint between logical and moral thought. Each stage in Kohlberg's developmental scheme requires the appropriate stage in role-taking ability as a necessary condition. Although Selman has only carried his work up to the fourth stage, Byrne (1975) has forged out stages 5 and 6 in an as yet unpublished work. Citing various empirical findings, including his own, Selman underscores the discovery that there usually exists a parallel between stages of role-taking and moral development or that, at the most, in normal populations role-taking ability is only one stage beyond the moral stage. In contrast, the role-taking skills have been found to be two or more stages above those of the moral stages in a group of young adult delinquents. This particular study (Hickey 1972) with delinquents makes it clear that a much higher level of social reasoning than moral thinking can obtain in a single individual. There is clearly a potential danger to others in such circumstances, since it offers fertile grounds for antisocial behavior. In general, of the studies surveyed by Selman, while it was sometimes found to be the case that a subject's role-taking ability was above the corresponding level of moral development, there were no instances in which moral reasoning exceeded social or role-taking reasoning. As he points out, it would seem that in order to have a mature power to reconcile conflicting claims in the moral domain, one must first have ascended the developmental scale of social reasoning. When a child's stages of both moral and social reasoning appear to be lagging significantly, it would seem that the first approach might well be to focus on promoting role-taking skills. If this does not succeed in stimulating the growth of moral reasoning, as it may or may not, training designed to directly effect moral development could be instituted next. Given the prior necessity of role-taking structures in resolving moral dilemmas, this would have merit as the more parsimonious and logical intervention strategy.

However, it is certainly conceivable that attempting to stimulate moral development directly at the outset may lead to a simultaneous surge of both social and moral reasoning.

Selman, who is Director of Boston's Judge Baker Guidance Center school for children with learning and behavioral problems, illustrates diagnosis and intervention based on social reasoning levels with the case of Tommy. Although eight years old, Tommy was at stage 0. He, therefore, was performing on an egocentric basis, which is typical of children at ages four and five. Natural observation of him interacting in the environment with others such as peers, teacher, and diagnostician revealed that he did not differentiate between his own and other's feelings. Grossly deficient in role-taking abilities his relationships were fragmented and temporal, indicating no sense of reciprocity whatever. Good and bad were defined in terms of his own desires. Failure to meet his needs without delay or question meant that the nonrespondent hated him. It is obvious from this description that his relationships must have been dysfunctional and were destined to deteriorate in time. The prescription for treatment was to enroll Tommy in a therapeutic camp in which great emphasis was placed upon explaining constantly to him the reasons for social rules, games, and behavior. The underlying motives of others at the camp, peers and counselors alike, were articulated for him. The normal and reasonable expectations which others would have of him were disclosed continuously. In brief, the therapeutic efforts were geared to assisting Tommy in the task of differentiating his own thoughts and feelings from those of others, learning to seek internal causes of behavior, and to take the role of others so that he would understand their perspective. In the span of eight weeks Tommy shifted from stage 0 to stage 1. He acquired many new friends, despite being extremely disliked at the beginning of the summer, and his notion of friendship evidenced progress. In conclusion, Selman stresses that he is not advocating that traditional diagnostic approaches be replaced by a cognitive-developmental one, but rather that the latter should be added to those already in use.

Shantz (1975) cites the congeniality between Feffer's and

Selman's structural-developmental models. She sees "simple re-focusing" and stage 1 of Selman's sequences as emerging around age six. At about age eight or nine, Feffer's "consistent elabora-tion" and stage 2 become manifest, both characterized by sequen-tial coordination of varying perspectives. Then, as she points out, at about ten years of age the simultaneity and mutuality of per-spectives, represented by Selman's stage 3 and the "simultaneous coordination" of Feffer, are manifest. The reader who is interested in pursuing the subject of social cognition beyond this chapter may wish to consult Shantz's excellent review of the literature.

FLAVELL: THE DEVELOPMENT OF ROLE-TAKING

The most ambitious project in the subject under discussion has been undertaken by Flavell et al (1968). Introduced in this section is a portion of that material dealing explicitly with role-taking. In chapter 8, some of the material bearing on the develop-ment of communication skills will be presented. Essentially, Flavell et al view themselves in their approach to the work reviewed here as developmental naturalists. They sought ontogenetic qualitative patterns as opposed to taking up the question of causation and effect. Causes and variables accounting for individual difference were set aside for future research. It is their position that first mapping out a detailed description of qualitative aspects in development will increase the prospects for more fruitful hypoth-eses to be tested later in the areas of causal and correlation studies. The motivation for role-taking may be either to under-stand the other, as an end in itself, or to utilize this understanding functionally to achieve a goal of some sort in relation to the other. The early theoretical roots guiding the conceptualizations and strategies pursued by Flavell et al (1968) are found in the writings of Piaget, Mead, and Vygotsky.

The studies presently under examination utilize a population of 160 students, generally of middle-class background, drawn from a public school system in a suburb of upstate New York. Grades two through eight and grade eleven were all represented. There were ten subjects of each sex from every grade, thus spanning middle childhood and early adolescence. The researchers anticipated that the greatest changes in role-taking abilities would occur in grades two through eight. The inclusion of grade eleven was to observe whether any significant changes would occur after early adolescence.

In the first study, the subject is engaged in a guessing game with another person. He is requested to state the next move which the other will make in the game and to explain his reasons for the prediction. There are actually two experimenters involved. The game is explained to the child in the presence of both. There are two cups which are turned upside down. Stuck to the bottom of each are one nickel and two nickels respectively. Since the cups are upside down the bottoms face upward and the coins are visible to all. The number of coins displayed signify the amount of money to be found under each cup if it were to be lifted. For example, the cup which has two nickels displayed also has two nickels concealed underneath it. By removing the cup, the nickels can be obtained. It is explained to the subject that one of the experimenters will leave the room. During the time he is out, money will be removed from under one of the cups. When the second experimenter (E2) reenters the room he will be asked to select the cup which still has the money under it. The task of the subject is to outguess E2. That is, he should attempt to predict which cup E2 will select and remove the coins from under that cup in advance. The child is instructed to bear in mind that E2 is aware that the child will be attempting to fool him.

The results reveal a progression of age-related responses characterized by increasingly more subtlety and complexity. There are four strategies, which are designated 0, A, B, and C. Strategy 0 is simply a classification of responses in which the subject either refuses to make a prediction or, if he does, fails to provide an explanation for his choice. In strategies A, B, C all explanations are classified as either involving monetary or nonmonetary factors. Strategy A is a class of responses in which the child fails to take into account the possibility that E2 might have some thoughts about the child's own behavior. The subject's explanations are exclusively focused on the cups and coins. In other words, a child would commonly predict that E2 would choose the cup with two nickels stuck on the upturned bottom because, he would explain, E2 would get more money that way if the coins turn out to be under the cup. A nonmonetary-type explanation might be the selection of a particular type cup on the basis of that cup most often covering the coins on previous trials. In strategy B the subject evidences a rationale for his selection which anticipates that E2 is thinking about what the child is thinking about. The subject may explain that E2 figures the child will try to fool him by removing the coins from the cup with two nickels, since the child would normally expect E2 to select the cup where the most money could be obtained. Therefore, the child predicts that E2 will try to outguess him by selecting the cup with one nickel.

Strategy C adds one more loop to the reasoning process in the role-taking skill depicted for strategy B. In other words, the child will anticipate that E2 figures out all of the above from strategy B and then will carry it a step further by expecting the child to leave the two coins under the cup and remove the one coin from the other cup. The child, therefore, predicts once again that E2 will chose the cup with two nickels under it. However, it should be stressed that, although the subject makes the same selection in strategy C as he has in strategy A, his line of reasoning has gone from a quite simple one to a highly complex one. In effect, the child of strategy B is saying, "I think he thinks that I think he will pick the two-coined cup. Therefore, I predict he will pick the one-coined cup." Whereas, the child of strategy C is saying, "I think that he thinks that I think that he thinks that I think he will pick the one-coined cup. Therefore, I predict he will pick the two-coined cup." If the reader is faltering under the impact of strategy C, be assured that it proved to be a very rare class of response, having appeared only twice at grade six and twice at grade eleven. The most significant developmental data were found in strategies A and B. The first of these generally declined with age and the second increased. At grade two there was only one of twenty responses of strategy B type although by grade eight there were ten of twenty such responses with a gradual increase evident across the various grade levels. Strategy 0 was utilized by some at every grade level, but reflected no appreciable age progression or decline. The researchers enter into a quite complex analysis of development in role-taking after presenting their data. The portion which shall be presented here attempts to extrapolate the essential steps which are posited as necessary in the transition from strategy A to B.

The subject must first come to realize that the other person can have thoughts not only about things external to the subject, but that he can also think about the subject himself. Flavell believes that this step is preceded by the subject recognizing that the other person can have thoughts about other inanimate objects and people in general. The child next advances to a realization that not only may the other person think about him, but that the other person can think about what it is the child is thinking. In other words, the other person has a cognitive domain which can encompass the child both as an object and also as an object with a subjective component, about which the other person makes inferences. These two steps are considered absolutely necessary for the transition from strategy A to B to occur. Despite the considerably greater complexity of strategy B, Flavell stresses that even strategy A is a form of role-taking, for it does entail ascribing centrain attributes or motives to the other person. (i.e., "He'll choose that one because there is more money under it.") In fact, he suggests that a considerable amount of the, ". . . genuine interactions with peers, marked by efforts at cooperation, compromise, real argument, and other characteristics which reflect some awareness of the other's point of view" (p. 54) are predicated upon the "nascent role-taking activity" of strategy A. As the child moves from middle childhood into preadolescence and adolescence an increasing use of strategy B characterizes social interactions. Flavell (1968) refers to Sullivan (1953) in commenting that:

The child is now prone to develop intimate interpersonal relationships with a same-sex chum, relationships in which meticulous

attention is given to the careful gauging of the thoughts and feelings of the other (especially toward oneself), of comparing and
contrasting his perceptions of the world with one's own, and the
like. And this sort of thing certainly continues with a vengeance
during adolescence, to the child's profit and pain, with reference
to others of both sexes: "Does she think I'm good looking?"
"How will they take it if I do such-and-such?" etc. Could scarcely
be called atypical cognitions for this age group (p. 54).

The child who does not undergo the appropriate advances in
developmental strategies of role-taking will certainly suffer the
consequences of arrested interpersonal relationships.

A second research procedure conducted by Flavell et al
(1968), also spanning middle childhood and adolescence, tests
the subject's capacity to transcend his own viewpoint which
contains information the other person would not have, in
order to interpret data accurately from the other's perspective.
The subject is shown a set of seven pictures by the first experimenter and requested to elaborate the story suggested by
them. Three of the pictures are then eliminated and a second
experimenter (E2), who has never seen any of the pictures
previously, is introduced. The four pictures when separated from
the total group suggest a very different story than when they are
all together. The task of the subject is to reconstruct the story as
it would be seen through the eyes of E2 based on only the four
pictures. To perform this task successfully, it is necessary for the
subject to set aside the original story he constructed from viewing
the seven pictures and to place himself in the role of the new-
comer (E2). The first seven pictures clearly depict a story
line involving a boy who is frightened by a vicious dog. He
escapes from the dog by climbing a nearby tree. Once safely
situated in the tree he plucks an apple and begins eating it. The
three pictures which are removed are the only ones in which a
threatening dog appears. Therefore, the four remaining pictures
in isolation convey no element of fear or escape, but merely
that of a boy who climbs a tree to obtain an apple he wishes
to eat. One of the four pictures does still contain a dog, but he is
some distance away, does not appear threatening, and is merely

an onlooker as the boy is eating in the tree. An analysis of the various responses in which the subject is attempting to tell the story from the perspective of E2 reveals four categories. In category 1 the subject accurately assumes the perspective of E2, thereby excluding any interpretation of a fear motive that could only have been derived from observing all seven pictures. At the other end of the range is category 4 providing an interpretation based on the threatening dog and a fear motive for climbing the tree, even though there is no basis for this in the four pictures being presented. Category 3 commonly includes responses which initially leave out motives of any kind, whether derived from the first or second set of pictures. However, immediately upon questioning, these subjects will usually reply that the boy climbed the tree to escape from the dog. Responses in category 2 did not seem to fall into any of the other categories. Whether spontaneously or upon questioning, the subjects generally offer a motive based upon fear; yet at the same time these subjects manage to manifest some grasp of the fact that E2 has access only to the four pictures on display. The child might actually make reference to E2 observing the four pictures. He may suggest that E2 is implying that the boy is afraid of the dog in view of the dog's presence across the street, or he may even make up a fear motive not relying on the dog at all. In each instance, although the subject is inaccurate, he is evidencing a primitive degree of role-taking which places him in a more advanced position developmentally than subjects in either category 4 or 3. In general, category 1, which consist of correct responses, increased in frequency across the grades. At grade two there were eight of twenty such responses; by grade eleven there were fourteen of twenty. (Interestingly, at grade seven there were eighteen of twenty responses in category 1.) Category 3 witnessed a sharp decline as grades increased. Subjects who gave no fear motive spontaneously, but offered an unequivocal fear motive upon inquiry, went from eight of twenty at grade two to none at grade eleven. Categories 2 and 4 were never particularly frequent and did not vary greatly in moving from grade to grade.

As Flavell notes, the magnitude of progression is not large, with the most significant shift occurring from nine to ten years of age as the children go from grades three to four. He makes quite clear that he does not see the apex of role-taking skills arriving at such a relatively early age, acknowledging the possible limitations of the task and the category method utilized in measuring responses. His comments, however, are confined to the parameters of the study which was in fact executed. Flavell observes that it would appear at first that there were hardly any role-taking skills involved at all, for both subject and E2 had the same data, the four pictures, before them. The difficulty, of course, lies in the fact that the child has already seen the pictures in a broader context previously and is now having trouble viewing them in isolation from his own preceding experience. The critical factor that impressed Flavell et al was the degree to which the subject either could or could not separate his original interpretation from future possible interpretations. Subjects having difficulty with the task seemed to ascribe a quality of absolute truth to their initial story. They lacked the capacity to approach the pictures as being ambiguous and relative to context, therefore, being subject to a variety of interpretations. Comparing this observation to Piaget's work, Flavell states, "Piaget, among others, has described this sort of cognitive attitude in many publications and in many different ways: it calls to mind his notions of operations, reversibility, decentration, relativity, centration, intellectual realism, and the like" (p. 76). It follows that the child whose thinking is characterized by realism will view the original story as somehow irrevocably true and inhering in the pictures. He will, therefore, carry forth the initial interpretation to any subsequent situation; centering exclusively upon it. In linking these role-taking aspects to cognitive functioning as described by Piaget, Flavell is seeking to emphasize that the two components are inseparably bound within the matrix of one complex system.

In conducting the present study Flavell took advantage of the available verbal productions to test an incidental aspect of the research, which is worth reporting here briefly. The reader is already acquainted with Piaget's observation that as children grow older they employ increasingly more causal connectives of a "because" nature than is evidenced in their earlier syntax. Flavell et al accordingly predicted that a higher incidence of causal connectives would occur as age advanced and this was confirmed by a content analysis made of subjects' responses to the story task under examination.

CONCLUSION

There has been no attempt in this chapter to present an exhaustive review of the literature on taking another's perspective. Instead, a decision to present the major views and models currently available on the subject was carried out. Both visual perspective taking and role-taking with regard to the other's internal states were examined. The early work of Piaget was cited as a point of departure, with special emphasis given to the subsequent work of Feffer, Selman, and Flavell. The focal point has been the developmental sequences that the child passes through as he moves toward attaining increasingly more complex and subtle role-taking skills. It has been underscored that although there have been some reports of such skills being manifest as early as from two to three years old, their presence seems to be very much determined by the nature and complexity of the task being coped with. To be sure that one is truly dealing with nonegocentric skills and genuine perspective-taking it is vital to rule out the possibility that the child is simply ascribing to another his own feelings or what he might feel if he were to find himself in the same situation as the other. It is specifically the capacity to ascertain another's thoughts or feelings when they differ from one's own which characterizes nonegocentric thought in the Piagetian tradition (Chandler and Greenspan 1972). A spirited and instructive debate on this issue is to be found in the work of Borke (1971, 1972) and Chandler and Greenspan (1972).

As indicated previously, role-taking may serve either as an end in itself or as a means to an end. In the case of the latter, the goal is frequently that of achieving more effective communication. The following chapter will be devoted to this subject.

8

ADAPTIVE COMMUNICATION

PIAGET ON LANGUAGE AND THOUGHT

Speech as we know it is certainly one of the most distinguishing characteristics of human beings. The effectiveness with which it is commanded in interpersonal exchanges will in large measure determine the quality of our personal relationships. The social matrix places constant demands upon us for acts of negotiation, compromise, persuasion, and cooperation. All of these are significantly influenced by communication skills requiring that the sender have the capacity to take the perspective of the listener. The acquisition of language itself, although an epochal achievement, does not assure that the child's verbal productions will effectively convey the intended meaning to the receiver. There is even the question of whether the child's early speech is intended to be communicative. We shall begin by exploring a work by Piaget which has spawned a considerable body of contemporary research in the field of adaptive communication.

The first book written by Piaget (1923/1955) was devoted to the child's developmental shift from egocentric to socialized speech. It has served as a seminal work which has caused a recent surge of effort by many to further explore its implications for adaptive communication. In Chapter 2 of this book, the reader was introduced to some of the essentials of Piaget's first book-length work. What appears here will be an amplification of that introductory exposition.

In discussing the functions of language, Piaget identifies two major categories. The first is egocentric speech, which is so called partly because the child speaks mainly of himself, but primarily because he ". . . does not attempt to place himself at the point of view of his hearer" (p. 32). He is not motivated to convey information nor to persuade the listener of anything. The three classes of egocentric speech are repetition (echolalia), monologue, and dual or collective monologue. In the first of these, the child repeats words and syllables with no communicable intent. He often does not even appear interested in making any sense out of what he says. Whether repeating his own sounds or words he hears from others, he does so for his own pleasure. In a monologue the child does not direct his comments to anyone and he speaks, ". . . as though he were thinking aloud" (p. 32). Although the child may soliloquize in the presence of several others, what he says simply has no social function. Very young children will often act to the accompaniment of words and so it is that they may frequently be observed engaging in a monologue as they perform various actions. A young child asked to jump or to sit down may often be overheard saying the words as he obeys, suggesting a remaining link to the sensorimotor period. In a collective mono- logue, the other person serves as a stimulus to each child's verbal production, but there is no continuity of theme and each speaks only for himself without taking into account the other's interests. In a collective monologue, the response of child A to a remark by child B, will have no necessary relatedness to what child B has just spoken. Instead it will derive from child A's own interest.

Socialized speech is classified into five types. The first of these is adapted information. In such speech the response of one child is appropriately related to what the other has just said. There may be argument or collaboration manifest in the speech utilized, but in either case the intent is social in that an interpersonal exchange is taking place. The child may even be talking about himself as long as he is supplying relevant content to the other for the message to qualify as adapted information. The remaining forms of socialized speech will not be elaborated upon here, but they are as follows: criticism, commands, requests, and threats, questions, and answers.

Piaget draws an interesting distinction between egocentric thought which, although private, cannot be kept secret, and socialized speech which may be secret, despite an ultimate intent

to communicate publicly. Regardless of how privately the adult
may be involved with certain thoughts, he keeps in mind a social
element. Even the solitary scientist who may be conducting research over many long and lonely years will anticipate revealing
his discoveries to the scientific community. And when he does
this, his findings must be so formulated as to conform to socially
agreed upon canons of verification. In brief, the point of view
of others must be borne in mind throughout his lonely pursuits.
He may act in secret, but his actions are socialized. Conversely,
the child up until about seven years of age is egocentric in his
speech even when in the presence of others. He does not seem to
have the adult's ability for containment and his self-related comments are frequent utterances. On the surface, this may seem to
be socialized behavior, but a content analysis of his verbal productions disproves such an interpretation. Piaget believes that at
around age seven or eight children shift significantly in the direction
of seeking greater comprehension of each other and increased
effectiveness in exchanging their thoughts. Before that time the
child's speech is characterized by Piaget in the following manner:

> Although he talks almost incessantly to his neighbors, he rarely
> places himself at their point of view. He speaks to them for the
> most part as if he were alone, and as if he were thinking aloud.
> He speaks, therefore, in a language which disregards the precise
> shade of meaning in things and ignores the particular angle from
> which they are viewed, and which above all is always making
> assertions, even in argument, instead of justifying them (p. 60).

Piaget investigated the question of whether children actually
understand each other when they assemble and talk. Situations
were initiated in which one child was asked to tell another child
certain stories. Attention was paid to how accurately the second
child reproduced the stories upon hearing them from the first
child. Communication was also investigated by explaining a
diagram to one child, which he in turn had to explain to another.
The second child had to reproduce the explanation with the
diagram in front of him. Approximately one hundred different
experiments were conducted with a sample of thirty children.

On the basis of these explorations, Piaget concluded that children do not understand each other any better than they understand adults. To begin with, they do not attempt to adapt the information to the perspectives of the listener. Furthermore, the listener does not attempt to adapt to what he hears, but instead extrapolates from the content what appeals to him most and encodes that material in terms of his preconceptions. Significantly, Piaget observes that a crucial reason why children do not understand one another is precisely that they believe they do. Making the assumption that the other will understand, or perhaps that he already understands, eliminates the necessity of even attempting to communicate with exactitude and clarity. He stresses that children daily have around them adults whose knowledge far exceeds theirs —people who require little effort from the child before understanding his needs and wishes. Specifically, in offering explanations to peers in the studies, the speaker often left out any reference by name to the objects he was talking about. Furthermore, the speaker would tend not to provide adequate reasons for events, and causal links were either omitted or not placed in an order signifying causality. The child, already believing that he would be understood, perceived no need to be concerned with syntactical ordering. Piaget cites excerpts from the protocol of one egocentric speaker in which the words "and then" are repeatedly used to signify neither causal nor logical relations, but merely, ". . . a personal connection between ideas, as they arise in the mind of the explainer" (p. 123).

The deficiency of order in communication is pronounced at six to seven years of age in contrast to seven to eight years of age when it appears infrequently. The egocentric child seems to disregard the "how" of natural and mechanical events when he explains things to others. Unrelated components may be juxtaposed without really explaining "how" the speaker will produce an "effect" in his explanation. Piaget maintains that in thinking to ourselves we do not bother to detail the exactitude of various cause-and-effect phenomena. However, in socialized speech, the personal fantasy that allows us to overlook the "how" of events must yield to the demands of adaptive communication. The egocentric speaker fails to make the necessary shift from the network of his own imagination to meeting the requirements of the listener's informational needs. His expositions are frought with a lack of coherence and a series of juxtaposed sentences bearing no evidence of grasping causal relations. The word "and" may replace "because" and the sequence of thought readily reverses cause and effect to effect and cause. The child might just as well say either "The car will not go and the gas tank is empty" or "The gas tank is empty and the car will not go."

It is striking, that, despite the obscurity of the messages articulated by the speakers in Piaget's investigations, there were rarely any protestations from the listeners. The subjective assurance of being understood on the part of the speaker had its mirror image in the listener whose own egocentrism provided him with the assurance that he, in fact, was understanding. The youngest children seemed the most content in this respect, for it was in the age range of seven to eight where the few objections that were registered originated. In the main, egocentric listeners would simply assimilate what they heard into preexisting schemas without any accompanying effort at accommodation. If there are previous commonalities of schemas between speaker and listener, there may occur some accidental understanding.

Piaget emphasizes that the emergence of a desire to communicate and be understood arises at about seven to eight years of age. It is at this time that the child demonstrates a concern and awareness regarding the objectivity of his statements to others. Prior to this age, children who do not understand what they hear will invent stories or explanations when asked to reproduce the information. They evidence no awareness that their romancing, as Piaget calls it, issues from their own imagination. Children at seven or eight years of age rarely romance and, contrary to younger children, they can distinguish when they are doing it on rare occasions. Primarily, however, they are more concerned with the fidelity to fact of their accounts and they genuinely strive to achieve objective communication. The reader is well acquainted by now with the knowledge that egocentrism is never totally eradicated during development. Nevertheless, that form of it which so limits referential communication sharply declines around the age of seven or eight, when a pattern of socialized speech begins to show increasing prevalence.

Alvy (1968) set out to test Piaget's contention that the child's ability to shift to the other's perspective will promote more cooperative or effective communication. He designed an experiment in which pairs of children had to take another's perspectives in order to succeed at a task which they were asked to share. Alvy's subjects were ninety-six students divided into three groups of ages six, eight, and eleven. Half of those in each group were girls and half were boys, totalling thirty-two in each group. Based on the earlier Piagetian work, it was expected that some cooperative speech would be manifest even in the youngest group of six year olds. It was hypothesized, however, that such speech would become increasingly more evident with age. Conversely, egocentric communication was expected to be most prevalent among the youngest children and least in evidence among the eleven year olds. It was also predicted that the more successful accomplishments with the task would be achieved by those characterized by the least amount of egocentric communications. This was based on the assertion that egocentric communication signifies that the speaker is failing to shift perspectives, whereas the nature of the task was so designed as to require a shift in the speaker's perspective in order for the pair to execute it correctly. Specifically, two children were seated, each at one end of a long table. An opaque screen between them prevented them from seeing one another. Both of them had a set of identical pictures laid out before them on the table. The pictures were of faces reflecting various emotions through the nuances of visual expressions. The speaker was instructed to describe what each feeling being expressed was on each face. The listener's task was to select the corresponding picture in his set based on the speaker's description. If he did not have sufficient information initially, he was free to request more. In the six-year-old group there was a 34 percent rate of successful matching, a 47 percent rate for the eight-year-old group, and a 67 percent rate for the eleven-year-old group. An analysis by sex indicated no statistically significant difference. Data were collected and examined regarding the use of ambiguous language, which was taken as a measure of egocentric speech. A speaker's language was considered ambiguous if he used the same descriptive term for two or more of the pictures, thereby failing to explicitly differentiate the one being described from all others. Among six year olds there was a 98 percent use of ambiguous description, 77 percent for eight year olds, and 52 percent for eleven year olds. As the percentage of matched pictures increased, the percentage of speakers using ambiguous language decreased. In other words, as the subjects became older they adapted to the informational needs of their partners, which in turn led to a higher incidence of successful task completion. What if the speakers were given a second and third trial after being informed about whether or not a picture was matched by the listener in preceding attempts? In fact, the study was designed to allow for this. The issue was to what extent subjects would modify their ambiguous descriptions based on the feedback regarding previous success or failure. An examination of subsequent trials revealed that 91 percent of the six year olds persisted in utilizing ambiguous descriptions, 63 percent of the eight year olds did so, and only 13 percent of the eleven year olds. Success rates in matching, therefore, increase as age progresses, with an accompanying decrease in ambiguous descriptions.

Listener behavior was scored directly by tallying the number of listeners, on all trials combined, who asked for additional information. The data revealed that older subjects requested more descriptive statements than younger ones. Among the six-, eight-, and eleven-year-old groups, the percentages of subjects asking for additional descriptions were 21, 61, and 73 respectively. It is worth noting that subjects were specifically encouraged to ask questions. Also, the very few questions asked by the six year olds were quite limited and were not really constructed to elicit much additional information. It should also be noted that, as age increased, more extended exchanges between listener and speaker occurred, as the former sought additional descriptive information.

Alvy concludes that his study, along with several others by previous researchers, offers confirmation of Piaget's position on the inverse relationship between the decline of egocentrism and the increase of cooperative speech. Interpersonal behavior is seen to be influenced by cognitive development and increasing age, with language serving as a mediator. As one becomes better able to shift perspectives, he becomes sensitized to the needs of the other. In communication this results in an increasingly greater selection of explicit and relevant information for conveyance by the speaker to the listener.

VYGOTSKY AND INNER SPEECH

The work of Vygotsky (1934/1962), a Russian psychologist, is at variance with Piaget's interpretations of egocentric speech and is worth citing in this context. Vygotsky acknowledges the high frequency of egocentric speech in the child under seven years of age, as well as its general decline in overt manifestation. However, unlike Piaget, he does not believe that it merely diminishes gradually in favor of socialized speech. All speech is social in origin for Vygotsky. It then splits off into what he views as egocentric and communicative speech, both forms remaining social although different in what they aim to accomplish. Egocentric speech is construed as instrumental in ". . . seeking and planning the solution of a problem" (p. 16). Vygotsky arranged activities for the children in experimentation in much the same way as Piaget had reported in the 1923 work *Language and Thought in the Child*. However, he then proceeded to introduce various frustrating and difficult circumstances to see if these would affect the production of egocentric speech. For example, a child in one of these experiments would not be able to find a pencil or the color he wished to use. Vygotsky observed that under such conditions the degree of egocentric speech almost doubled in comparison to either the earlier reports of Piaget or the natural observations of Vygotsky's subjects when obstacles were not placed in their way. Hence, he concluded that an impediment in the free flow of a child's activities is an impetus evoking egocentric speech. In one instance a child was drawing a streetcar and the point of his pencil broke spontaneously. He attempted to persist in the drawing, but could no longer produce the lines he needed. He then exclaimed to himself that it was broken and proceeded to draw a broken streetcar with nearby watercolors. Occasionally he would still talk to himself while drawing. Vygotsky's contention, citing the above as merely one of many examples, is that the egocentric exclamation did not simply accompany the action, but was actually instrumental in directly altering it. Hence, the function of egocentric speech is self-guidance. Vygotsky believes that egocentric speech reflects a transitional process in which the speech is going "underground" where it will function as inner speech, but will not disappear. Its instrumental function is retained into adulthood. Inner speech is not structured in the same linear, syntactical manner that communicative speech is. Dale (1976) speaking of Vygotsky's version of egocentric speech states,

> It is a hybrid form: it has the structure and function of inner speech but is vocalized as social speech. Gradually the child's ability to use egocentric speech for self-speech becomes increasingly streamlined and effective for this purpose. The end point of such an abbreviation process is the complete internalization of egocentric speech as inner speech (p. 254).

The young child is seen by Vygotsky as being parasocial in that he does not differentiate between speaking to himself and speaking to another person, but in either case the speech is functional. Kohlberg, Yaeger, and Hjertholm (1968) point out that the abbreviated character of egocentric speech, which they call private speech, is similar to the conversation between two intimates sharing mutual interests and experiences. They may omit many words which leave their overt speech unintelligible to a third listener and yet both comprehend very well what they are saying to one another. In the same fashion, the overt speech of the child, later to become inner speech, which has a self-guided aim is quite intelligible and functional to himself but is not so to anyone else in his presence. Nevertheless, it clearly has a communicative intent in which speaker and listener are one and the same. As Kohlberg, Yaeger, and Hjertholm point out, while Piaget maintains that the egocentric child does not differentiate between himself as the speaker and his listener, Vygotsky claims that the distinction which the child fails to make is that between himself as receiver of the message and the other person as receiver. Hence, self-guided utterances and speech aimed at communicating to others are at first undifferentiated. The distinction is eventually made, of course, and culminates in the former going "underground" to become inner speech. Kohlberg, Yaeger, and Hjertholm (1968) report research which tends to verify that this process does take place, as posited by Vygotsky. Be that as it may, adaptive communication in the social context, as observed by Piaget, is not an innate ability. We shall now examine a current attempt to discover the developmental process in its acquisition.

THE COMMUNICATION STUDIES OF FLAVELL

In this section we will discuss two studies from Flavell et al (1968) which are specifically designed to explore adaptive communication. Following the studies, we will present a delineation of the model on role-taking forged by Flavell and his collaborators on the basis of all their research reported in *The Development of Role-Taking and Communication Skills in Children*.

Flavell finds that, throughout middle childhood and adolescence, the speaker's ability to phrase his message to suit the informational requirements of the listener increases. According to Flavell's theory, unless the speaker invokes a role-taking capacity the message will not go beyond self-coding spoken aloud. The listener may serve only as a stimulus to the speech, but does not automatically make any special attempt to recode the message so that it will be congruent with what the listener needs to hear in order to understand it. However, when the speaker exercises a role-taking capacity, he tunes in to the role attributes of the listener which, in turn, demands that the original self-coded message undergo a modification in the direction of listener needs.

This seemingly simple, but absolutely essential distinction, will be more fully appreciated after reading the following ingenious experiment executed by Flavell et al.

A middle-class sample of 160 children ranging from grades two through eight and grade eleven was employed. The core of the design involved having children provide information to two different types of listeners. One type included listeners who were sighted and, therefore, able to observe the objects and processes about which they were being told. The other listeners were blindfolded and as a result were totally reliant on auditory input to understand the message. It was anticipated that as children became older, there would be a sharper contrast between messages offered to the two groups of listeners, facilitated by the development of the role-taking ability previously discussed. For purposes of the experiment, the researchers invented a game involving a multicolored board, a cube with colors matching those on the board, and a toy pig which is moved to whatever color corresponds to the cube when it is tossed by the player.

Although one side of the cube is colored black, there are no such squares on the board. Thus, a tossed cube registering black signifies that the player is not to move. There are two players, and the winner is the one whose toy pig is the first to move across the board and back. In teaching the game to the children, the first experimenter (E1) does not speak, but merely goes through the actions while making appropriate gestures. The task of the child is to verbally explain the game to the second experimenter (E2), who later enters the room. At each grade level, half of the children participate with a blindfolded experimenter (E2) and the other half with an experimenter (E2) who is not blindfolded. In the second and eighth-grade samples, comprising forty subjects, each child sees a third experimenter (E3), who is always blindfolded. Therefore, twenty of these forty subjects experience a sequence of E2 who is not blindfolded and then E3 who is blindfolded. The remaining twenty undergo a sequence in which both E2 and E3 are blindfolded. In all instances involving the total sample of 160, the children are told that they will be explaining the game to someone who knows absolutely nothing about it. The ground rules of the task preclude the children from touching any object as they explain the game and the experimenter from giving the child any feedback as he talks. The child is permitted to point, however.

A distinctive feature of this research design, as pointed out by Flavell, is that it allows for comparison between the two types of messages as directed toward listeners with different informational needs. The comparisons made are based mainly upon three measures. The first is a scoring of the frequency with which words are varied. A word that is repeated in its identical form could only earn 1 point. A word varied, such as, from "my" to "mine" earns a higher score. The second measure is rooted in the extent to which the speaker explicitly identifies information about the game. For example, does the child state that there is a cube and tell what color each side is? This would refer to materials used in the game. Does he convey information about procedures necessary to playing the game? Lastly, does he provide additional information not classified above, but which would facilitate the listener's understanding of the game? The third criterion for measurement is based on the omission of significant information, which would inhibit the listener's ability to comprehend the game. A lack of specific referent would be an example of this, as when a child speaking to a blindfolded experimenter says, "This side is red." When such a sentence is the first one spoken, it is obvious that the object being referred to is unknown to the listener. Furthermore, if it is the board being referred to rather than the cube, the receiver would also have no way of knowing whether it is his side of the board or the speaker's side which is red, even if he were aware that there is a board between them. Of course, this is not at all obvious to the egocentric speaker, whose speech tends to be marked by precisely this sort of shortcoming.

An analysis of protocols from some second-grade subjects who spoke to E2 who was sighted, followed by E3 who was blindfolded, reveals a considerable similarity between the messages regardless of whether they were directed at E2 or E3. The character of the messages suggests a self-coding which simply fails to take into account listener need, much less to distinguish between the two types of listeners and their differentiated needs. The researchers go so far as to suggest that were the children able to describe the game to and for themselves when alone, they might very well end up with the same verbal production. The messages were virtually that unresponsive to the receiver's needs. It is pointed out that the sighted experimenter does fare somewhat better because he at least is able to supplement verbal limitations with gestures made by these children. The children, however, appear oblivious to the inability of the blindfolded experimenters (E3) to take advantage of the gesturing. They fail to recognize the need that E3 would have for more precise referents in the message.

In striking contrast to the second graders, analysis of the eighth grader's protocols discloses genuine sensitivity to the needs of their listeners. A general comparison between the messages of the second and eighth graders reveals that the latter devise significantly more adequate communications. Beyond that, however, the intrasubject comparison shows that, in shifting from a sighted to a blindfolded experimenter, the eighth graders adapted their communications to the special listening needs of the latter. Putting themselves in the role of E3, they would commonly adopt a communications strategy of identifying verbally each of the various objects utilized in the game and would proceed to carefully tell how they were to be used. Were the youngest children completely devoid of role-taking ability and adaptive communication in the study? No, at the very least most children evidenced a minimal, if only sporadic, attempt at adaptive communication. It is an open question as to how children as young as four to six years of age would respond in a study of this kind. In general, older subjects will use more of a variety of words when addressing a blindfolded experimenter than when speaking to a sighted one. Younger children will tend to show a stronger similarity of word content between the two audiences. Note that this is not simply to be explained by the older children having an enriched vocabulary, for the shift from sighted to unsighted audience can be observed in the same child at the same time. Also, it is the impression of the researchers that even young children who do not significantly modify the content of their message in going from one audience to the other, do have the necessary vocabulary within their repertoire. The modified information provided by the older children in shifting audiences is finely adapted to promoting the understanding of the game by the blindfolded experimenter.

Flavell recognizes fully that there are inherent difficulties in attempting to determine role-taking ability from communication skills. A child's failure to communicate adaptively may be explained in one or more of several ways. True, he may simply lack role-taking capacities. However, even if he recognizes that the audience has special listening needs, he may not realize *what* information is needed. Lastly, he may have a sound appreciation of what is required and yet, for one reason or another, be unable to construct the appropriate message. Flavell suggests that in unadapted communication all three possibilities are intertwined to varying degrees, with the first of these being the most significant explanation among younger children.

A second study carried out by Flavell concerns "persuasibility." By this term, Flavell means the capacity one has to persuade another person of something. Two hypothetical situations are set up in the study and the subject is requested to say everything he can think of to persuade the other person. One situation involves selling a tie to a customer who enters a store and the other involves persuading father to buy a new TV for the subject's room. The findings of this procedure will not be offered in detail here, as the author is more interested in highlighting Flavell's general observations on persuasibility. The study itself is a somewhat limited one and must be appreciated for the groundbreaking attempt it represents, as there appears to be no precedent for research into this characteristic. Essentially, the structure of the design is geared to tapping the frequency and variation of the appeals employed while engaging in the persuasion activity. In general there was an increase in persuasibility with age and the increase is particularly pronounced from ages nine through fourteen. There appears to be a diminution of arguments based on simple pleas and an increase in the frequency with which arguments became more reasoned. Flavell characterized the shift as one from a hard-sell to a soft-sell approach. The age-dependency nature of persuasibility is interpreted by Flavell as being due to the development of role-taking skills. Effective persuasion requires one to discern the characteristics of another that are susceptible to certain lines of reasoning and appeals. Maximum persuasibility is promoted by skill in recognizing the desires, needs, motivations, and goals of other people. Confusion of these with one's own attributes could readily lead to highly ineffective attempts at persuasion. Noteworthy in the study was not only the age trend in persuasibility, but a similar trend in role enactment. That is, the older subjects tended more to actually assume the role of a salesperson and, therefore, a content analysis of their protocols indicated a greater frequency of such phrases as "May I help you?" and "Yes, sir." Flavell speculates that role enactment may facilitate persuasibility because the subject is allowing himself to become immersed in the task. The protocols further reveal "varieties of persuasive subtlety, finesse, and ingenuity" (Flavell 1968, p. 144) which escape the rigidity of the method employed in scoring.

The full weight of significance accorded to persuasibility by Flavell is perhaps best reflected in his own words:

> . . . . the child's ability to persuade others appears to lie at the crossroads of numerous other developing behaviors. It ought therefore to constitute a valuable index of such things as his social perception, his understanding of human motivation and cognition, his role-taking prowess, his social-interactional skills—perhaps his social development as a whole (1968, p. 146).

The two studies by Flavell et al which have been introduced here and those from Chapter 7 do not exhaust the work advanced in their book by this research team. It is hoped, however, that they will signify to the reader something of the scope and promise of their studies.

The research conducted by Flavell et al eventuated in a basic model in which role-taking serves as mediator to achieving a desired goal. That model will now be presented. There are four basic components and they are explicated both in Flavell et al (1968) and at greater length in Flavell (1974).

Existence. Two aspects comprise this primary component which must precede all others. First, the child must become aware that people do experience internal psychological states. Second, he must further become aware that these states differ among people, including himself as opposed to others, even when the same object or event is under consideration by those involved. The absence of this second aspect is exactly what Piaget means by egocentrism.

Need. The child may possess the necessary awareness about the existence of psychological states and even know that another person's may differ from his, while at the same time failing to recognize the need to bring to bear his role-taking ability in a given situation. When the capacity to appreciate the need is not present, the evocation of role-taking does not occur despite the child having the ability. There are many possible reasons why the capability is not called forth, but a sense of need must be present before role-taking will come into play. Elementary school children appear to experience little of this need even though they have some primitive awareness of psychological states and some rudimentary ability to take another's perspective. A child, for example, who has the vocabulary to identify certain objects he is talking about to a blindfolded partner, may omit the appropriate referents and point to the objects. It is not likely that he actually thinks the partner can observe him and the objects; nevertheless, he does not recognize the other's informational need.

Inference. The components of existence and need are generally not given attention or are taken for granted when considering social cognition in adults. It is the area of inference, however, that draws the most attention by those interested in adult social cognition. Initially, Flavell split this into two separate elements. One is prediction, which deals with an analysis of the inferential process through which an individual is actually able to cognize accurately the thoughts, feelings, and perceptions of another person. As we have seen, this takes on levels of complexity with age. The other element is maintenance, which is the ability to adequately block one's own viewpoint on a sustained basis, or whenever necessary, from interfering with the role-taking activity. Concomitantly, it involves keeping in mind that which is grasped about the other's internal state for as long as functionally required to achieve the intended goal.

Application. Conceivably one may wish to engage in inferential activities, role-taking, with no aim other than satisfying one's curiosity to understand another person. However, one may wish to use the knowledge gained as a means to an end, such as adaptive communication. The skills involved in recoding one's private messages so that they are congruent with the listening requirements of the receiver are not necessarily the same as those exercised in inferential activity. Verbal facility, syntactical knowledge, and vocabulary prowess may all come into play during application, but are not essential to the inferential process. Hence, it is possible that even accurate inferences may be made about another's internal state and yet the child may not be able to construct an appropriate application from his role-taking activities.

SUMMARY

A closing quote from Flavell (1974) might clarify his general model of interpersonal inference, pulling together the several components cited above.

> Supposing S is about to play chess with an unknown opponent (O). He is first of all certain to know the general meaning of such psychological properties as "chess skill," and "knowledge of the game," and also that O could conceivably possess these properties to a greater or lesser extent (Existence). He will also be aware that it would be sensible (Need) of him to try to find out (Inference) just how skillful and knowledgeable O is, so that he can adjust his own game accordingly (Application) (p. 72).

Flavell has indicated that he, himself, will operationalize some of the research suggestions he has advanced which were based on the writings we have been examining. The student interested in the development of social cognition will have much to look forward to.

SOCIAL ENVIRONMENT AND COMMUNICATION

In an extensive review of the literature on social-class and referential communication skills, Glucksberg, Krauss, and Higgins (1975) caution that differences obtaining among the members of various groups may be due to factors other than the speaker's competency. For example, members of one group may perform better on a given task than those of another group because the former are more familiar with the materials used. Another explanation could readily be that members of the group performing poorly are more inhibited or intimidated by the experimental setting or possibly even the experimenter himself. However, it is also possible to observe variations among groups in the general outcome of their performance or with regard to the basic skills that contribute to successful outcome which are based upon the presence or absence of intrinsic abilities. Glucksberg et al also highlight the significant point that differences observed in children of various ages, regardless of group membership, may not be derived from the same source as those observed in children of the same age from across diverse social class groups. They suggest that differences that are age-related are likely to pertain to general cognitive development, whereas differences of same age children comprising various social-class groups may be more directly related to abilities pertaining to specific tasks. Glucksberg et al have concluded from their review of the literature that it reflects an unclear picture and that the various disparate findings do not permit a definitive statement on social-class correlates of communication skills. Rather than routinely reviewing a sampling of the research to reflect the contradictory findings of the last decade, this section will present three of the most recent studies which the author believes to be of especial interest.

Alvy (1973) explored the ability of subjects to construct listener adapted communications, which take into account in-

ferences made about the listener's cognitive and/or emotional
states. The three dimensions examined were age, sex, and social
class. It is predicated that adaptation in interpersonal relationships is largely a function of the capacity to make accurate assumptions about the other's internal states and to communicate
accordingly. For example, one does not ordinarily ask for a
raise at a time when the boss is evidently feeling angry or sad.
If it is necessary to do so at a time when the boss is angry or
sad, however, the message may well be worded differently than
it would if he appeared happy. Similarly, a French tutor sensing
that his pupil has not mastered the rudiments of that language
will not persist in teaching at an advanced level, but will modify
his message so that it will be appropriate to the student's level.
Listener-adapted communication may be seen to be reciprocally
functional for it both promotes the listener's understanding and
facilitates the attainment of the speaker's goal. Alvy posits that
both linguistic and person-perception skills foster listener-adapted
communication. He notes that these skills would not only develop
with age, but that they are a product of an ongoing socialization process. In surveying the relevant Piagetian concepts presented
in the opening section of this chapter, Alvy points out that he
uses the term nonlistener-adapted spoken communication as
synonymous with egocentric spoken communications. Alvy makes
references to the considerable body of research that has been
stimulated by Piaget's early work on egocentric and socialized
speech. He notes, however, that the emphasis in the many
studies involves tasks requiring subjects to make assumptions
about the listener's cognitive states, but does not utilize tasks
in which emphasis would be placed on inferences made about
emotional characteristics. Furthermore, although the studies confirm Piaget's contention of age-related differences in development,
they do not supply data on social-class differences. In fact, most
of the studies use middle-class samples. (The disparate findings
on social-class and referential communication reported by Glucksberg et al are not to be confused with explicitly Piagetian-based
research. Referential communication will be examined in the
next section of this chapter.)

Alvy introduces the work of Bernstein (1958, 1959, 1966) as a rationale for predicting that there are differences in communication skills based on social-class variables. Bernstein formulates two types of social relations which result through socialization in two different linguistic codes or speech modalities. In one type there is a predominance of communication from the parent to the child in which authority and status appeal are foremost. The child is expected to do as he is told precisely because it is the parent who has spoken. The roles of the participant shape the speech system rather than the unique attributes of the individual family members. Feedback from the child is not permitted and, therefore, any attempt along these lines does not succeed in altering the parent's or speaker's behavior. According to Bernstein, the child exposed to this form of communication develops a restricted linguistic code. The alternate form of socialization is predicated upon a fine attunement to the individualized characteristics of each family member. Authority and status appeal are deemphasized, explanations are offered by parent to child, and feedback from the child may result in modification of the parent's expectations and responses. An elaborated linguistic code is the product of this form of socialization. Distinguishing features of this code are the use of diverse and accurate grammatical constructions and an extensive vocabulary. The opposite is true for those who possess a restricted code and they tend more toward nonverbal rather than verbal expression. It is Bernstein's contention that the restricted code is associated primarily with the lower-working-class population and that members of that group are not likely to have facility with the elaborated code. The elaborated code is associated with the middle- and upper-class levels, and members of these groups are said to possess both restricted and elaborated speech systems. Alvy speculates that if Bernstein is correct, it would be expected that these two diverse linguistic codes would result in differences in listener-adapted communications between social classes. Lower-class children, it would be anticipated, would utilize less of adapted communications and, when they did use them, the communications

would be qualitatively inferior to those of children from middle-
and upper-class social strata.

The major purpose of Alvy's study was to determine the
possible existence of social class influence through tasks which
would tap the speaker's ability to adapt his messages to the
listener's emotional as opposed to cognitive characteristics.

The study by Alvy had a sample of 180 white children. There
were three age levels involved—six, nine, and twelve years.
At each age there were sixty children. Each of the children at
each level were further divided into groups of lower-, middle-,
and upper-class backgrounds. Each social class had twenty
children at each age level. Alvy invented a communication task
specifically for this study. The child was placed in six hypothetical
tasks with each one having two listeners. The listeners (simulated
full length drawings of people) each had different emotional
features which were potential influences upon how the speakers
might construct their messages. For example, both listeners might
be teachers, one frowning and one smiling. The speaker is about
to approach them with a request for a grade change. The
experimenter draws attention to the appropriate emotional characteristics of the hypothetical listeners. A score is kept of the
extent to which differential as opposed to the same messages are
offered by the speaker. An assessment is made of the type of
change, when it occurs, to determine the quality of the modified
message. Upon completion of all message deliveries, the children
were asked to explain the basis for their statements to each set
of listeners.

Alvy has drawn conclusions from his study based on sex, age,
and social-class variables. In all three classes, girls of ages nine
and twelve were superior in their performance of providing
messages that were more suitable to the emotional states of the
listeners when compared with the boys. Alvy attributes the
difference to the socialization process in the United States in which
females are more sensitized to emotional life with all its variations
and nuances than are males. Social class was not observed to
effect this variable.

Age was found to be significantly related to both quantity and quality of listener-adapted speech. Increases in both domains appeared as age increased. The younger children did not frequently change their communications, regardless of which two in each of the six pairs of listeners they addressed. However, on occasions when they did, it appeared that both their assumptions about the listener and the manner in which they utilized those assumptions were less complex than was the case with the older children. The older children not only adapted their communications more frequently, but they also demonstrated more expertise in the quality of the adaptation. For example, in asking a favor, the younger child would be more likely to simply add "please" when shifting from a smiling to frowning listener. On the other hand, the older child would take pains to reconstruct the message to offset the disadvantage of addressing a person who appeared annoyed or unhappy in order to give himself some additional advantage. In brief, the older child showed greater appreciation of the complexity of the situation and the interpersonal nuances inherent in it, while the younger child was more concretistic.

Alvy has discovered a particularly important distinction in the areas of explanations offered by children for their communications. The older children, as might be expected, provided sounder explanations for their modification of messages. It was noted, however, that the younger children made inferences about listeners' communication-related characteristics which were similar to those made by the older children. What they seemed to lack was the capacity to recognize the bearing the assumption had on the need to tailor their message to the listener. The potential for training children to grasp the relevance of these *assumptions* about listeners to the *need* for communication change is an exciting one to which Alvy draws attention.

Social-class differences were found in this study. Middle- and upper-class children exhibited more frequent and higher quality adaptive communicatsions than did lower-class children. They also provided better explanations in discussing the rationale linking their communications to the emotional state of the listener.

Alvy concludes that these findings on social-class offer confirmation of Bernstein's position that lower-class children are not as likely to employ a "verbal channel of communication," as are children of middle- and upper-class levels. It will be recalled that Bernstein believes this to be the outcome of a socialization process involving a role-oriented parent as opposed to a person-oriented parent. Further confirmation of many of Bernstein's notions can be found in Hess and Shipman (1965). In passing, however, it should be noted that Bernstein's formulation has not gone unchallenged and is rejected in some quarters.

Alvy pursues some of the adverse consequences for lower-class children who do not utilize listener-adapted communications nearly as effectively as other children do. In our society, the capacity to comprehend and linguistically explicate aspects of interpersonal relationships is one upon which a high premium is placed. Many major social institutions beyond the family parameters will dispense rewards to those who are facile with the "verbal channel of communication," but will withhold them from those who are not. Alvy speculates, quite validly, that non-adapted communications may provoke the listener who genuinely wants to understand, but who cannot in the absence of an effort on the part of the speaker. The speaker bound to a restricted code may not be able to be adequately responsive to the listener's needs, but if the listener does not know this he may generate very negative feelings toward the speaker. A reciprocally spiraling effect of negative feelings could, of course, ensue. The individual who is deficient in listener-adapted speech is not the only one who suffers, for the net result could be a profound rift in the entire social fabric of a society. It should be remembered that the capacity to employ listener-adapted communication greatly facilitates the achievement of personal and group goals.

Alvy suggests that the multisituational tasks he constructed for this research project could be utilized as a clinical diagnostic tool. He points out that the hypothetical situations involve the child exercising some influence on the people in his environment. It is possible, for example, that a child who does not modify his message to a more compelling one as he shifts from asking a smiling man for a favor to asking a frowning man for a favor, may feel that he does not have any control over his environment as it becomes complicated by a negativistic person. This inference would be even more likely to be valid if the same child had demonstrated listener-adapted communication in other circumstances.

Information about parental relationships to the child and the family matrix could possibly be garnered from the multi-situational tasks. Alvy suggests that if a child is observed omitting listener-adapted communications whenever he addresses adult females and yet employs such speech with other children and adult males, he may perceive his mother as being not susceptible to persuasion or dialogue. Lastly, the content of a child's attempts may be especially revealing of how communication takes place at home within the family. The child who resorts to threats of physical abuse or makes offers of precious gifts may be signifying something about how communication is harnessed to obtain compliance at home. Alvy ends his report by recommending that the multisituational task may be used as a device to teach children listener-adapted skills, as well as serving as a diagnostic instrument.

Bearison and Cassel (1975) have also adopted the ideas of Bernstein (1972) as helpful in understanding communication within a social context. They subscribe to previously leveled criticism that Piaget has neglected the physical and social environment in his position on cognitive development. Therefore, it is their recommendation that the social context should provide an arena within which cognitive functioning can be studied to further understanding of communication. The by now familiar distinction of Bernstein between person-oriented and role- or position-oriented relationships is made, emphasizing that the latter discourages seeking into the intentions and motives of other people through verbal means. Stressing that coordinating one's own perspective with another's differing perspective is central to effective communications, Bearison and Cassel anticipate that children from families that are basically person-oriented will prove to be more effective communicators than children from role-oriented families.

In the study they conducted the population consisted of thirty-seven children with a mean age of six to seven years. There were twenty males and seventeen females. Communication scores were based upon an adaptation of the Flavell (1968) study in which subjects conveyed messages to both sighted and blindfolded listeners. Scores were derived from five dimensions analyzing the content and form of the messages. Vocabulary scores were also obtained. The mothers of each of the subjects volunteered to participate. Their scores pertaining to person-orientation versus role-orientation were obtained by eliciting their responses to five common situations in which they were asked how they would influence their child's behavior. A content analysis was made and, depending on the nature of the response made with respect to how the mother said she would regulate her child's behavior, each statement was assigned to one of fifteen categories of either person- or role-oriented approaches. A combined score for the mothers on their relative use of these two approaches yielded a social code score.

The results of the study revealed a significant relationship between social code and listener condition in each of the five communication areas scored. (Listener condition refers to whether the listener was sighted or blindfolded.) In the words of Bearison and Cassel (1975), "Children from predominantly person-oriented families showed greater evidence of accommodating their communication to the listener's perspective than children from predominantly position-oriented families" (p. 34). A comparison between two statements, the first to a sighted listener and another to a blindfolded one, demonstrates that the speaker who is from a position-oriented family constructs strikingly similar messages. A comparison of two paired statements by a child from a person-oriented family reflects a contrary finding, namely that the messages are dissimilar; the one addressed to the blindfolded receiver is constructed to take into account the fact that the listener does not share the same visual perspective as the speaker. It appears that while the child from a person-oriented family coordinates perspectives, the one from a position-oriented family does not. By means of several analyses, the possibility that superior verbal facility could explain the correlation, rather than skill in coordinating perspectives, was discounted. Bearison and Cassel do not maintain that children are explicitly instructed by their mothers in the specific facets characterizing the two types of social systems. Instead, they suggest, "The family's social orientation constitutes for the child, continually adapting to that system, the psychological reality by which he initiates and maintains interpersonal relations" (p. 36). In conclusion, the present study by Bearison and Cassel is compatible with, and lends support to, the one by Alvy (1973).

In the tradition of the two preceding studies there is one by Hollos and Cowan (1973) which also focuses on the environmental aspect of Piaget's interactionist position. It is a revealing study of the part played by social isolation in the development of logical operations and role-taking abilities. The primary variable of this study was the degree of verbal interaction across three social settings. Scores on verbal interaction were then examined in relation to performance scores independently arrived at on tasks involving role-taking and logical operations. It was expected that the variable would systematically register a different effect on the two types of cognitive tasks.

Because of the centrality of this study of sociocultural background, it is vital to provide a brief sketch of each setting. All of the children participating in the study came from a rural region in Eastern Norway. They lived either on a farm area, or in a small village or medium-sized town. Despite the geographical variations within the region, the cultures of the people within Eastern Norway are known to be quite similar throughout. No systematic differences were found from setting to setting in any of the major cultural categories of education of parents, religion, ideology, and basic language spoken. All of the children came from whole, working-class families. Differences in social interaction were observed and recorded by one of the two researchers, who lived among the people for sixteen months.

The most salient feature of the descriptive material on the social interaction of the farm children was the relative isolation of their upbringing which severely delimited verbal opportunities.

Before starting school the children remain on their parents' farm. Play is generally solitary. Most interaction, when it occurs, is generally nonverbal, regardless of whether the child is relating to a sibling or an adult. The mother is always available and freely offers help to the farm child, but the interaction in these instances is also mostly nonverbal. The speech system employed in the child's presence, such as at dinner time, tends to be "restricted" as described by Bernstein. The advent of school does not greatly increase the farm child's opportunity for social interaction as he only goes three days weekly and is returned by bus immediately afterward for the first three years. This is in sharp contrast to the village child who is permitted to play with other children when school is over each day. Prior to the time he has to attend school, the village child spends a significant amount of his time playing with other children. He is allowed to leave his home and seek out playmates. There is a considerable amount of group interaction with peers and adults. Hollos and Cowan state that village children are raised in a milieu in which they experience much more verbal interaction than the farm children, but the speech system obtaining in the farm and village environments are basically the same restricted type. For example, although the village children are afforded more opportunity to talk, they ". . . are listened to politely rather than questioned when their accounts are unclear" (p. 633).

The town in the region is host to several major educational facilities including a teacher's college and an adult educational center. There are also many other cultural resources not found in either the farm area or the village. However, the children of the town interact with others in much the same manner as those from the village. They are not tied to their homes and are given the freedom to come and go as they wish. They do, in contrast to the village and farm children, meet more adults and are more accustomed to strangers, as well as to a wider range of settings. It should not be inferred that the town children reflect a shift to the elaborated speech system of Bernstein's sociolinguistic formulation. In fact, despite the increased social interaction facilitated by the town environment, Hollos and Cowan comment,

"The more complex social interaction may lead to a more complex system of communication, but the range and detail of the concepts involved appears to be characteristic of the 'restricted code' " (p. 634).

The sample in this study consisted of 144 children: forty-eight from each of the three environments. Each group of forty-eight was comprised of three subdivisions of sixteen children ages seven, eight, and nine. The youngest were preschoolers, with the two older groups representing first and second grades respectively. In all but one instance the sexes were equally represented.

A total of nine cognitive tasks were administered to measure the developmental level of the children. Six of them tested the children's ability to perform concrete operations in task areas of classification and conservation. The remaining three tested role-taking skills. These are already familiar to the reader. The first was a measure of visual perspective based on a modified version of Piaget's landscape problem. The second assessed the children's ability to accurately communicate a story to another child who is absent from the room when the story is originally relayed by an experimenter. The story and procedure adopted were first introduced by Piaget (1923/1955). The third test was the one introduced by Flavell (1968) in which the child first creates a story based on seven pictures and then must reconstruct a story based on four pictures.

Hollos and Cowan observe that one would predict that there would be an increase in role-taking skills going from farm to village to town. The rationale for this prediction is derived from Kohlberg (1969), who contends that role-taking ability is the product of social interaction. The findings only partially uphold this expectation. As anticipated, children living on farms demonstrated deficient role taking performance in relation to village and town children. Nevertheless, despite having had more experience in social interaction, the town children did not perform any better at role-taking tasks than village subjects. Furthermore, it was discovered that the scores of the farm children on the conservation and classification tasks were equal and in some instances better than children from the other two settings. Hollos and Cowan assert that had a "deprivation hypothesis" been applied uniformly across tasks, it would have been expected that farm children would also have performed relatively poorly in tasks involving logical operations (classification and conservation). Yet this was not the case. Social interaction level apparently had a differential effect on tasks involving either logical operations or role-taking. An analysis of the data reflects that ability in logical operations was largely affected by age and grade level, whereas role-taking skills were primarily influenced by degree of social interaction.

In discussing the findings of their study, Hollos and Cowan emphasize that although the farm children were in settings offering a deficient amount of "social-verbal isolation" they did have a high level of support and stimulation from their readily accessible mothers. Opportunities for imitation and observation were paramount. The environmental structure of the farm children promoted physical interaction with the surroundings involving a high level of manipulating and acting upon objects. The students of Piaget will be well aware that such activity is a source for the invention and development of new cognitive structures. Therefore, it appears that, despite the relative lack of social-verbal stimulation, the farm children were raised on fertile soil for the development of logical operations. Hollos and Cowan urge that the tendency to view whole groups as deprived be applied in an analytic rather than gross manner. Members of a given group may be low in some areas of performance, but high in other areas. It is particularly noteworthy that in the study under consideration, the seven-year-old farm children actually performed better in the concrete operational tasks of conservation and classification than did children of the same age in the village and town. Hence, although school does later have an influence on language and cognitive development, it is not necessary to the construction of logical operations. In general, Hollos and Cowan interpret their findings by advancing a "threshold hypothesis." A level of verbal-social interaction is necessary to development in areas of both logical operations and role-taking. However, the threshold is lower in achieving competency with logical operations and consequently even the preschool farm children were able to perform more than adequately in conservation and classification tasks. The threshold is higher in role-taking tasks and, therefore, the farm children did not perform well in this area. The minimal degree of verbal-social experiences they were exposed to was not sufficient to bring them up to the threshold. In the case of village and town children, members of both groups exceeded the threshold. Beyond that point, additional experience did not seem to produce superior performance. Town and village children did equally well in role-taking tasks, despite the greater exposure to verbal-social interaction experienced by the former.

The present study should draw attention to the influence of the environment in making differential assessments of cognitive developments. It should also sensitize the reader to some of the complexities inherent in attempting to compare various groups with respect to particular variables. It is important to avoid adopting a single standard of evaluation when assessing groups and to bear in mind the relevance and adequacy of development to the ecological demands of the environment, as Hollas and Cowan point out in their concluding remarks.

REFERENTIAL COMMUNICATION

Studies in referential communication are significant to the subject of the present chapter. They tend to emphasize an aspect of adaptive verbal coding and decoding which Piaget does not devote attention to, although they also give full recognition to the need for nonegocentric, listener-adapted communication. Some of the leading work on the subject is that of Rosenberg and Cohen (1966), Glucksberg and Krauss (1967), Krauss and Glucksberg (1969), Cohen and Klein (1968), and Fishbein and Osborne (1971). While these studies will not be discussed in detail here, a general overview of the basic concept involved will be presented. The following comments are a summary from a portion of an excellent literature survey by Glucksberg, Krauss, and Higgins (1975).

Early in their review, the authors assert that communicating effectively depends upon the speaker's ability to utilize words in a referential manner. A distinction is made between denotative and referential meaning. In defining referential meaning the specific context is essential. It pertains to that which is being referred to in particular, as opposed to a generic or abstract meaning regardless of context. An example is given using the words Mars and planet. In a specific communication the speaker can request that the listener either look at Mars or look at the planet up there. In such a context, both Mars and planet may be used interchangeably as a referent for the identical object. Yet in general, on a denotative level, the two words actually have different meanings. Since most words do not have a univocal meaning, there exists grounds for ambiguity and confusion in communication. The task of the speaker is to choose from the total range of his vocabulary, that word or phrase which best conveys what he intends. Words may in fact be much too general, even if utilized correctly, to be of any help in effective communication. Telling a blinddate that you will be wearing clothes when you wait for him or her in front of the opera house, will be accurate but useless information. Unless, of course, you are residents of a nudist colony. In that case, telling the listener that you will be clothed is an excellent referent because it discriminates between how you will appear in contrast to all others present. The essential point is that it provides the listener with the information that is needed to pick you out from among everyone else. The fact is that the use of referential communication, particularly in ambiguous situations, is not innate or the immediate accompaniment of vocabulary accretion. It is a developmental phenomenon which gradually emerges with age and does not match adult levels of attainment until early adolescence. Of equal interest to researchers in this area is the feedback provided to the speakers by the listeners. Focus is placed upon how the feedback influences the speaker's original message. The speaker may offer an entirely different communication in response to feedback, or possibly modify the original message, or simply repeat what he had previously said.

Glucksberg, Krauss, and Higgins collate four fundamental

processes that thread their way through the research on referential communication. The first is "sensitivity to the referent-nonreferent array." It is the ability to accurately select the referent which will distinguish the object or event under discussion from a spectrum of nonreferents which would only confuse the listener. The second is "sensitivity to characteristics of the listener and the listener's situation." In constructing a message it is essential for maximum adaptive communication to take into account both what the listener already knows and what he needs to know. Among other skills, the speaker must be able to discriminate between knowledge which the listener holds in common with him and knowledge which he, the speaker, possesses exclusively, in relation to the listener. The third is "sensitivity to listener's feedback." Very young children are either silent or repetitive when confronted with feedback requesting more information or voicing confusion. Older children and adults will tend to alter the message or reconstruct a new one (Glucksberg and Krauss 1967). The fourth deals with the listener's assessment of the message. A listener may detect the deficiencies in a message, may possibly make these known to the speaker, and he may even go so far as to convey what additional information he requires to comprehend the message.

These four processes identified by Glucksberg, Krauss, and Higgins have been cited here to underscore that even though they are conceptually distinguishable, in the communicative transaction they are actually intertwined.

THE FACILITATION OF COMMUNICATION SKILLS

Adults eventually emerge from childhood and adolescence with highly refined skills in communication. Can the child traversing through the preadult stages of development be assisted to accelerate the acquisition of these skills? Few studies exist which report training attempts at this endeavor. However, the question is an important one in view of the central role played by these skills in interpersonal effectiveness.

Fry (1966, 1969) has reported two training studies with

unimpressive results. These studies are also presented in Flavell
et al (1968). In the first study, subjects instructed listeners in
a task involving the selection of a specific picture from an
assortment of many. Feedback was obtained by observing the
listener at work on the task and receiving comments from him
about the communication. Some subjects were either speakers
or listeners, while others alternated roles. Training constituted
a total of five hours for a duration of three weeks. Subjects were
eleven to twelve years old. It was believed that children embarking
upon the formal operational period might make optimal gains in
training because of the transitional nature of their development.
There were sixty-four subjects, half of them comprised a control
group and the other half the experimental group. The latter was
subdivided into different training groups. Both pretests and follow-
up tests were administered.

Three hypotheses were explored in this study. The learning
hypothesis simply stated that improved effectiveness at communication would subsequently be evident in similar tasks. This expectation was confirmed. Major gains were made especially in that
speakers learned to be briefer in their communications, largely as
a result of their having learned to eliminate extraneous information. However, such gains are assessed as being quite limited in
relation to the many possible criteria that were exercised in
evaluating adequacy of communication. The generalization hypothesis predicted that even in dissimilar communication tasks there
would appear significant signs of improvement. It seems that the
only noteworthy gain was the transfer of brevity in communicating
on tasks making requirements other than those in the training
situation. An increased capacity for supplying information relevant
to the new task was not observed. The role-taking hypothesis
anticipated that subjects who rotated speaker and listener roles
would show greater improvement than subjects who remained
in one or the other role. There was no evidence of this whatsoever.
Fry concludes by suggesting that listener feedback to the speaker
is as effective as role rotation for enhancing competence in communication.

Fry (1969) has criticized his own methodology in the earlier study. He proposes the notion that training the subjects on discrimination tasks (i.e., communicating information to listeners which will assist them in selecting the one correct picture out of many) favors improvement in the direction of the diminution of useless information, but does not promote the tendency to provide increasingly more useful information. To remediate this methodological deficiency, the second study utilized three different types of tasks. It was believed that the tendency toward promoting only brevity would be corrected for by using a variety of tasks, only one of which was based on discrimination. It was further believed that being trained on tasks which imposed different listener requirements would afford the subjects an increased opportunity to practice role-taking.

The sample in this study was comprised of thirty-seven fifth grade students, nineteen of whom were in the experimental group and eighteen of whom were in the control group. These subjects were brighter than those in the preceding study conducted by Fry. All subjects who received training rotated between speaker and listener roles.

Unfortunately, the results of this more extensive training program proved to be essentially negative, as had been the case with the previous attempt. Introducing a variation of training tasks and rotating the roles of all subjects did not seem to produce any significantly favorable result beyond the first study. Flavell (1968) has offered some cogent remarks in an attempt to explain these failures. Although acknowledging that there may be some deficits in the measuring procedures, he rules this out as a major contributing factor. He believes that the deficiency accounting for the failures inheres in the training procedure itself. The source of learning in the studies was the spontaneous interaction between speaker and listener. Flavell describes it succinctly, ". . . the speaker delivers his message into a tape recorder, the tape is played back one or more times, the listeners attempt to perform on the basis of it, and afterwards discuss and criticize the message with the speaker" (p. 202). In other words, Fry did not play an active role in shaping the learning experiences of the children in the training situation. Had he been more active he might have consistently and specifically directed attention to inadequate messages and possibly even provided cues to more appropriate ones. Furthermore, since Fry did not record instances of spontaneous educational experiences of the sort that might be expected to lead to improvement, it was not possible to seek a relation between those who actually demonstrated improvement and those who might have received such experiences. Flavell draws his critical comments to a close by suggesting that training in role-taking and communication skills may ultimately prove to be resistant to all efforts even under the best of conditions.

Shantz and Wilson (1972) have conducted a training study with more favorable results than Fry had obtained. They worked with an experimental group of seven to eight-year-old children containing twelve students from a suburban public school. A control group of the same number was also used. The two tasks in which the subjects were trained included one involving description, in which the listener had to reproduce a design on the basis of the hopefully full account offered by the speaker. The second task was a discrimination one, requiring only that the speaker convey essential information so that the listener may make the correct choice. All subjects rotated among speaker, listener, and observer roles. The age of the subjects to be used was determined by Piaget's earlier findings that children show a marked shift from egocentric to sociocentric speech at about age seven. It was hypothesized that children would manifest significant improvement on both tasks they were trained on, as well as in their performance on dissimilar tasks to which the gains would transfer. A total of six training sessions were given over a three-week period with the aim of bringing about this effect. The twelve subjects were evaluated at a pretest and, on the basis of the results, were formed into four subgroups. Each subgroup was comprised of one subject of high communication ability, one of medium, and one of low. By so structuring the training design, Shantz and Wilson sought to assure that each of the four trios would have a role model who would exemplify effective communication.

The general conclusion drawn from this study is pointedly

summed up by Glucksberg, Krauss, and Higgins (1975): "Small but reliable practice effects were obtained, and a moderate degree of transfer to dissimilar tasks was also obtained, although not on every measure in each of the three transfer tasks used" (p. 335). Analysis of the data suggests that few repetitions are necessary for improvement to register in descriptive tasks and that feedback is not a requisite. In contrast, more repeated trials appear necessary for making gains on the discrimination tasks. This is interpreted as supporting a previous assertion by Flavell (1968) to the effect that skill in conveying only what is necessary and screening out useless information is not simply a baseline possession, but is actually an acquisition of an advanced order in the communication process.

Shantz and Wilson offer some reasons why they may have achieved some success in their training attempt in contrast to Fry who met with essentially negative results. They point out that Fry used different materials when changing from one type of task to another. The Shantz and Wilson study did not vary the materials even when varying the task. A result of this may have been to draw the speaker's attention to the listener variable, since the materials were held constant. A second reason was that the experimenters assumed a more active role in directing the educational experience of the subjects, whereas Fry played a passive role in the communication training of his subjects. The age difference of two samples was considerable, although it is presently a moot question as to what this contributed, if anything.

The above attempts at increasing communication skills in children through laboratory means has dealt with normal populations. There have been a few highly significant attempts to offer training in role-taking skills and referential communication to deviant populations of children. Chandler (1972) has reported the results of role-taking assessment procedures conducted with normal and emotionally disturbed children. His conceptual analysis is distinctly Piagetian, viewing role-taking activity as one of the specific functions facilitated by the development of the ability to decenter. As egocentrism declines, perspectivism ascends. Measures of assessment were drawn from Feffer and Flavell. Procedurally, the subjects were required to coordinate their own perspective with that of a cartoon character who appeared in a series of cartoons displayed to the child. The subject has previously been provided with information the cartoon character could not possibly have from his vantage point. The experimenter observed the extent to which the subject would attribute knowledge to the cartoon character which only he, the subject, could possibly possess. There were three groups of subjects. One group was comprised of seventy-five normal children who ranged in age from six to thirteen years old. There were also fifty subjects who were in a residential setting for emotionally disturbed children and fifty long-term delinquents. The ages of these children ranged from eight to thirteen. The backgrounds of the emotionally disturbed and delinquent youngsters revealed a consistent pattern of social dysfunction. A comparison of these children to the normal group indicated that in contrast to the latter, the former did not display a systematic age-related progression of development in role-taking skills. Egocentric errors persisted in distorting the perspective of the deviant group members, preventing them from separating their own viewpoint from that of others. Chandler points out, however, that egocentrism was not pervasive among all of the emotionally disturbed or delinquent children. He states, ". . . children who had been severely brutalized by their environments and were hyperalert to and suspicious of the motives of others tended to be not at all egocentric" (p. 572). An examination of this observation highlights the special role that the environment may play in promoting perspectivism. Although the source of development in such cases is highly undesirable in the extreme, it is clear, nevertheless, that the social-environment of these children placed a survival value on the acquisition of role-taking skills. The abused child who learns to infer the thoughts, feelings, and intentions of a brutalizing parent may sometimes at least be able to outmaneuver, dissuade, or avoid his attacker. It was also found that, in another subgroup, egocentrism prevailed only in matters bearing directly upon the fundamental character of the children's conflict. Chandler is not clear in his report as to who these children are, referring to them only as "certain transitional subjects."

Chandler, Greenspan, and Barenboim (1974) mounted an experimental intervention program with exciting results using emotionally disturbed children from two residential settings. Role-taking and referential communication skills of 125 institutionalized children were assessed. The forty-eight children with the poorest performance, exclusive of openly psychotic and retarded children, were selected for the experiment. The total of 125 had scored significantly behind developmental gains generally reported for normal subjects of the same age in the same two task areas under examination. Despite a diversity of admitting diagnoses, most all of these children were described as antisocial and socially incompetent. They came from families of a predominantly low socioeconomic level, 86 percent of whom were caucasian. There was a mean age of eleven and a range from nine to fourteen years.

The forty-eight subjects were subdivided into three different groups. The first received training in role-taking, the second in referential communication, and the third received no training. The project covered a span of ten weeks. A pretest and posttest were administered and a follow-up was conducted twelve months later. The follow-up was based on reports from staff observers upon the behavioral performances of the subjects in interpersonal exchanges.

Training in role-taking exposed the subjects to experiences in video filming which required that they alternate in portraying various dramatic characters. The rationale, of course, was that by deliberately assuming another's role the subjects would automatically be practicing the taking of perspectives other than their own. In referential communication training a heavy emphasis was placed on offering subjects feedback in order to induce cognitive conflict when confronted with their own inadequate communication. It was expected that this would facilitate a process of equilibration which would lead to the construction of increasingly more adequate messages. The experimenters encouraged the subjects to compare their messages to peers and to playback tape recordings of their statements for self-evaluations. However, the experimenters did not directly criticize the messages of the subjects. Training, therefore, pursued a philosophy of promoting self-correcting action as opposed to content-oriented teaching by another person.

Results of the study substantiated significant postintervention improvement in both experimental groups as compared with the control group. It is of particular interest, however, that while the subjects trained in referential communication demonstrated marked gains in both that area and role-taking tasks, those trained in role-taking tasks exhibited improvement only in the area that they trained in. Chandler et al suggest that this is possibly due to the fact that the opportunity to acquire skill in applying inferences made about another's attributes to nonegocentric verbal communications is afforded by training in referential communication but not by the training given in role-taking. If accurate, this interpretation serves to emphasize the final phase of Flavell's model which was designated "application." Alternately, they propose that role-taking may be viewed as a necessary, but not sufficient condition for competent referential communication. The follow-up evaluation that occurred twelve months later indicated that the subjects in the training groups improved in social competence moderately in relation to the control group. The data did not reach a statistically significant level when analyzed, although it approximated doing so. Chandler et al are certainly justified in pointing out that countervailing familial and institutional pressures would very likely have suppressed any major gains achieved in the training project. A revised program, if it could be arranged, would be to discharge trained subjects to a benign environment where they could live throughout the twelve month follow-up period. Observations of enhanced interpersonal competence may then prove to be marked.

In closing, it is worth citing a passage from Chandler et al (1974) regarding the extension of Piagetian sociocognitive concepts to the psychopathological sphere. They state, "Taken in combination these findings lend additional weight to the initial orienting assumption that constructs and methods originally developed for the normative study of sociocognitive development may be usefully transported into the study and possible amelioration of serious social and emotional disorders of childhood" (p. 552).

CONCLUSION

The present chapter has focused upon adaptive communication with special emphasis upon the work of Piaget, Vygotsky, Flavell, Bernstein, Alvy, Fry, Shantz, and Chandler and the referential communication theorists as covered in their own survey by Glucksberg, Krauss, and Higgins. In addition to basic issues, attention was drawn also to the role of socioenvironmental factors and training studies in the development of effective interpersonal communication. Contemporary literature in the cognitive-developmental field has been turning increasingly toward extending the basic concepts of Piaget's Geneval School on the construction of knowledge in the physical world to the social matrix. Future trends are likely to witness an even more specific application of Piagetian work to an understanding of antisocial behavior from the viewpoint of dysfunctional communication based on the arrested development of perspectivism. As knowledge in this and the complementary area of reducing egocentric levels grows, we are likely to see the innovation of increasingly more effective strategies of intervention.

9

COGNITIVE-
DEVELOPMENTAL
PSYCHOPATHOLOGY

There does not exist at present a systematically integrated body of knowledge based on an application of the work of the Geneva School to the field of psychopathology. Piaget, himself, although a student of the subject as a youth, chose to consistently explore the normal evolution of intelligence. He informs us in his autobiography (Piaget 1976) of the following:

> Indeed, I have always detested any departure from reality, an attitude which I relate to . . . my mother's poor mental health; it was this disturbing factor which at the beginning of my studies in Psychology made me intensely interested in questions of psychoanalysis and pathological psychology . . . I have never felt any desire to involve myself deeper in that particular direction, always much preferring the study of normalcy and of the workings of the intellect to that of the tricks of the unconscious (p. 116).

Nevertheless, despite his own lack of concentration in this area throughout a long, prodigious and brilliant career, Piaget (1975) has recently stated that he sees on the horizon a new interdisciplinary science grappling to pull together a synthesis of knowledge to be known as *Developmental Psychopathology*. Although seemingly optimistic, he does not hesitate to assert that before this can be done an enormous amount of creative effort must be brought to bear in the face of many obstacles. In this chapter, the author proposes to make a modest attempt to survey some of the literature that has been appearing in journals and, on occasion, in books over the last couple of decades.

As a prelude to embarking upon an exploration of the literature on cognitive-developmental psychopathology the reader may be alerted to a conceptual classification which should prove useful. Briefly, there are four basic approaches employed either separately or in combination, which will be encountered. They are, in random order, as follows:

1. *Assimilation-Accommodation.* Adaptation requires an appropriate balance of these two processes. An excess predominance of one over the other, unless corrected by an equilibrating or auto-regulative process, can result in grossly dysfunctional behavior.
2. *Egocentrism-Decentration.* A developmental failure to appropriately differentiate between subject and object prevents one from achieving a genuine grasp of reality and precludes mature interpersonal relationships.
3. *Stage Arrest.* Some psychopathological manifestations can be directly related to subjects not having progressed normally through age-appropriate stages and periods of cognitive development.
4. *Preoperational Characteristics.* A good deal of the unrealistic and magical thinking typical of many abnormal subjects represents more than an average amount of adherence to such preoperational aspects of thought as animism, realism, and participation.

It should be obvious that these categories are not mutually exclusive and that they are highly interrelated. Often, in fact, the same phenomenon could be examined through the prism of any one of them, the difference being primarily a matter of emphasis.

EGOCENTRISM AND SCHIZOPHRENIA

Lidz (1973) has produced a major attempt at explaining schizophrenia in adolescence through Piaget's concept of egocentrism. An exposition of his work will be presented here. Schizophrenia, for Lidz, is not a disease possessed by the patient, but the result of a process of enculturation within a family which trains the child in irrationality through the influence of language and parental roles. It is a form of egocentrism in the parents which prevents the child from learning through the family matrix the meaning system subscribed to in the broader culture outside of the home. Parental egocentrism further blocks the child, once he becomes an adolescent, from successfully navigating through the developmental stages necessary to mature adulthood. When this occurs, the result is cognitive regression and schizophrenia. Lidz conceptualizes the family of an adolescent schizophrenic into either one of two types—the skewed or the schismatic. The skewed family appears harmonious at first glance, but further familiarity reveals that the apparent harmony is won at the expense of one of the spouses living in compliance to the will of the other. The ideas of the dominant spouse are characterized as often being bizarre and strange. It is generally the mother who carries this role. The schizophrenogenic mother is insensitive to her spouse and children as individuals with needs and wishes that exist independently of her own. In relation to her son, who becomes the patient, she constantly probes into his world and seeks fulfillment through him. She monitors all of his activities and manages to get across to him that he is central to her existence, which would be futile without him. His attempts toward independence are blocked by her and he senses this. The son is not permitted to individualize his own feelings and claim them as separate from the mother's. Those of his feelings which are not congenial to the mother's security are ignored or distorted by her. The father is an inadequate husband and parent who offers the son little in the way of coping skills.

In the schismatic family there is found a network of relationships in open conflict. Parental discord is compounded by the fact that both parents belittle each other to the children and seek to rally the children's support for themselves. The schizophrenic adolescent in this family is usually a female. Both parents have low self-esteem and have little emotional sustenance to offer their children. The female patient receives a message from the mother signifying the futility of life. Deprived of maternal attention when she was a child herself, the mother now has little warmth to extend to her own daughter. She becomes preoccupied with her daughter's adolescent sexual attitudes and activities. The father in such a family is inflexible, disturbed, distrustful and seeks emotional gratification from his daughter rather than his wife. The adolescent daughter cannot resolve the conflict between her parents and, should she attempt to favor or meet the needs of either one, she runs the risk of alienating the other. In the schismatic family egocentrism is an attribute of both parents, who fail to perceive the separate needs of their daughter and strive to have her conform to their own needs. The schizophrenic adolescent then has either one or two egocentric parents. He or she becomes parent-centered, ". . . viewing the world according to the parents' feelings, needs, and defenses, and living to protect and complete the lives of persons from whom he has not properly differentiated" (Lidz 1973, p. 48).

In Lidz's view, the peculiar, nonshared meanings and reasoning adopted by the schizophrenic represent his attempt at escaping the situation imposed upon him by an untenable family system. In doing this, however, he foregoes cooperative social life and effective adaptation to the environment at large. The patient not only fails to surmount the egocentrism specific to adolescence, but actually undergoes a cognitive, as well as emotional, regression to forms of egocentrism especially characteristic of the preoperational period. Egocentric is used in a strictly Piagetian sense here and does not connote selfishness or narcissism. The schizophrenic is said to be overinclusive in an egocentric manner in that he does not accommodate to reality, but instead assimilates and distorts it to meet his own needs. Passing and incidental comments by others are perceived as related to him. Events accidental to his experience are construed as integrally associated to him. We see this in paranoia, in which the patient may think that the FBI or an agent of that organization is diabolically engaged in activities designed to destroy him. On the other hand, Lidz points out that there is the catatonic patient who remains absolutely rigid, for fear that any shift in his body will adversely affect the world.

Lidz reviews the process through which language is acquired, stressing how the child moves from using words in a subjective, private way to employing them in terms of their public meaning.

In families of schizophrenic patients, however, the meanings of words are not properly taught. The words are contorted to meet the needs of the parent(s), and the child is unclear as to which are his own needs and which are his parents'. The normally responsive mother is aware of the needs of the two year old who uses words subjectively and she verbalizes the appropriate, that is, the publicly shared vocabulary and syntax when he does not. Gradually the child acquires language and meaning which have been adopted by the sociocultural environment outside the family boundaries. The schizophrenogenic mother is not fully capable of this because of her own egocentrism. In general, the parent(s) lacks a capacity to maintain ego boundaries and denies realistic facets of the environment in order to maintain internal security. The child is trapped in the net of the parents' diffuse ego boundaries and is constrained to invalidate his own perceptions of reality in order to preserve the parents' security.

Lidz states that most adult schizophrenics attain completely the level of concrete operational development and some even become completely formal operational with highly sophisticated abilities at abstraction. They do, however, have trouble in the struggle for separation and independence, feeling that success would be destructive to their parent(s). It is the egocentrism, developmentally speaking, that emerges at adolescence which Lidz sees as crucial to a sounder understanding of the schizophrenic. At this time the young person acquires second order operations. He can think about his own thought. He is no longer limited to applying operational thought to concrete or familiar objects, but can now reason about the many possible alternatives in the universe. Ideals and utopias are mentally generated with great gusto. In the first blush of this new form of egocentrism, the adolescent is unperturbed by the constraints of social and physical reality, often becoming visibly annoyed and impatient with those who do not share his vision. Decentration and the accompanying decline of this egocentrism come from renewed social interaction in which one's ideas are repeatedly challenged, as well as from the environmental demands of the work world which the young person must ultimately enter. Lidz

(1973) observes, however, that "The period contains the particular danger that the youth can get lost in mental operations, fantasying potential futures for himself and the world without becoming involved in the tangible measures required to make them become real" (p. 78). The young person who becomes schizophrenic fails to negotiate the developmental hurdles involved in separation and attaining autonomy which most adolescents succeed in doing. Rather than moving naturally in the direction of decentration, the preschizophrenic becomes increasingly and excessively egocentric. External events are inappropriately referred to the self. Blocked from going beyond adolescent egocentrism, the young person cognitively regresses to preoperational forms of it. Chance occurrences are not recognized as such, but are seen as meaningful events. Desire and reality are not differentiated. The word and the object are once again confused. It is once more believed that one's own thoughts can influence external and even distant things. Thinking may revert to a preconceptual level and show evidence of syncretism, in which a string of thoughts are woven together into a tangled conglomerate.

The above picture is, perhaps, overdrawn. Lidz emphasizes that the schizophrenic does not lose whatever former cognitive gains he had made before the regression. The issue, he suggests, is not whether the individual any longer has a conceptual ability, but rather under what circumstances he uses it as opposed to what circumstances induce overinclusive egocentrism in his thinking.

It has perhaps been observed in the above review of the work by Lidz that the four classifications involving egocentrism, adaptation, stages, and preoperational characteristics have already become intertwined, as indeed they would be difficult to separate in any such discussion. They will appear later in a similar medley.

THE CONCEPTUAL DEFICIT

Schizophrenia is commonly viewed as a thought disorder. The exact nature of the conceptual deficit involved, however, has not met with common agreement and various hypotheses have been advanced to explain it. Cameron (1938, 1939, 1944) maintained that the thinking of schizophrenics tended to be overinclusive. In examining the language of schizophrenic patients, he noted the propensity to eschew an organization of content based on logical and causal grounds. Instead, material that was meaningful only in terms of the patient's private associations would be included in his verbal productions. The inappropriate content could be drawn from perceived objects in the environment that have no bearing on the theme or from objects in the patient's own past, that are equally irrelevant. Goldstein (1936, 1944, 1959) has maintained that the schizophrenic's thinking is deficient primarily in that his capacity for abstraction has been impaired, which results in his functioning at a concrete level. The ability to consistently classify objects in an accurate fashion would consequently be absent, as this activity requires abstracting a common element which is then applied uniformly across all objects to be classified, which conform to the abstracted attribute. (The reader is cautioned here not to equate the use of the word concrete as employed by Goldstein with the use of the term by Piaget in referring to the concrete operational period. Remember that classification is precisely one of the major achievements of that period.) Cameron argued that if sufficient care is taken in working with the schizophrenic patient, it will be demonstrated that he has not lost the ability to function at an abstract level. Shimkunas (1972) in summarizing the literature on the subject has the following to say: "The bulk of this research has indicated that schizophrenics are not abnormally concrete, but that they verbalize peculiar and idiosyncratic concepts" (p. 149). Shimkunas reinterprets Goldstein and while rejecting the notion that a deficit in astraction leads to thinking in concrete concepts, he holds that there is an impairment in the capacity to abstract, which results in overabstraction. Although we shall not delve further into the formulation by Shimkunas, it should be noted that he believes that through an extension of the abstraction capacity, idiosyncratic and autistic thinking is introduced.

A position advanced by Von Domarus (1944) and elaborated upon by Arieti (1955) which has merited a considerable amount of discussion states that schizophrenic thinking is paralogical. Such thought processes are said to contain an abundance of logical flaws in that they deviate from the canons of formal Aristotelian logic. In interpreting the Von Domarus principle, Arieti has called it paleologic, suggesting a profound regression to the type of thought characteristic of primitive peoples and children. In the Von Domarus-Arieti view, the schizophrenic will go so far in his thinking as to equate objects on the basis of having only some attributes in common. What is involved here is not simply erroneously including an object in an array of objects being classified, but actually regarding two partially similar objects as being identical. The paralogic hypothesis by Von Domarus has been criticized, not because schizophrenics do not deviate from the laws governing formal logic in their thinking, but because of the prevalence of such deviations even among normal populations. Maher (1966) stresses that research continues to validate that personal affective material will influence the thinking of individuals, but that this is true for both schizophrenic and normal people. A careful analysis of the actual thinking process of the schizophrenic person, however, does not support the Von Domarus position, he contends.

The brief summary above was based on traditional research literature. Presently we shall examine a few attempts at understanding the thinking of schizophrenics through an application of Piagetian tasks. In effect, these efforts have been aimed at a cognitive-developmental diagnosis and comparison between subgroups of schizophrenics or between schizophrenics and other groups, such as children and normal adults. An aspect of testing which proves to be illuminating is not only the developmental level of the testee, but also the manner in which he relates to the testing situation.

Trunnell (1964, 1965) has reported two attempts at examining the developmental level of schizophrenic patients, the first being a pilot study and the second a replication study. Three groups were used in each study, including adult schizophrenics, children, and normal adults. A variety of Piagetian tasks were employed primarily involving classification and seriation tasks.

We shall discuss three of them here. One is a similarities test
in which the subjects were required to determine whether, out of
a large array of stimuli, groups of three, two, or no objects
could be classed together. For example, could the subject select
car, bicycle, and train to be grouped together, based on the
common element of transportation? In all of the tasks administered,
the experimenter was as interested in the subject's reasons for
his conclusions, as in the conclusions themselves. A second task
involved cross multiplication or conjunctive classes. For example,
a task taken directly from Piaget's early work is as follows:
An animal with long ears may be either a mule or a donkey. An
animal with a thick tail may be either a mule or a horse. Now
think of an animal with long ears and a thick tail. Is it a horse,
donkey, or mule? Note that a conjunction represents two statements connected by "and." Therefore, the statement "A mule has
long ears and a thick tail" is a conjunctive one. A third type of
task involved seriation or ordering of elements by intensity. Again
drawing from Piaget, the subject is asked such questions as
Edith is fairer than Suzanne who is darker than Lilli. Which of
the three is darkest? It is predicted that in the similarities test
schizophrenics and children would be likely to select either two
elements or none for classification, whereas the normal adults
would more frequently select an appropriate grouping of three
elements based on a common attribute. Trunnell anticipated that
the schizophrenics and children would center on partial aspects
of objects in the stimulus array and that they would be riveted
to specific physical characteristics of the objects. It was further
anticipated that even when they selected the three appropriate
objects that would go together, they would provide different
explanations for having done so than would the normal adults,
hence, indicating a difference in thought processes behind their
performance. It was further predicated that adult normals would
offer more correct answers and that their explanations would be
more logically complete. Both cross multiplication and seriation
require that the subject be able to effectively decenter and,
thereby, maintain two characteristics of the objects in mind
simultaneously. Therefore, Trunnell anticipated that schizo-

phrenics and children would focus more on one attribute of an object or relationship. Even in the case of having guessed correctly that the imaginary animal is a mule, as in the previously described task, the schizophrenic or child may say that the fact of the animal having a thick tail is the reason he made this particular selection. The explanation, of course, does not supply an adequate rationale, as an animal with a thick tail may be either a mule or a horse. A sufficient explanation must cite both the thick tail and long ears which would then include only the mule, but would exclude the horse and donkey. In fact, all of the normal adult subjects cited both attributes in naming the mule as the solution to the problem.

The schizophrenic population in the replicated study numbered twenty-four; twelve females and twelve males. Diagnostic criteria utilized relied essentially upon the traditional features of autism, ambivalence, association, and affect. All subjects in this group had some college education, most were in ongoing psychotherapy, and the majority were described as being well integrated at the time of the study on a behavioral plane. In general, the hypotheses formulated by Trunnell were confirmed. It was possible to distinguish a group of twenty-four schizophrenic patients from a group of twenty-four controls comprised of normal adults matched on dimensions of education, sex, and age. The distinguishing criteria were based on test performances and explanations derived from Piagetian cognitive tasks. In addition, there were significant similarities between task performance and underlying thought mechanisms of adult schizophrenics and children. There were also, however, important differences. The children involved ranged in age from six to eleven years, were twenty-four in number, and were also divided into twelve females and twelve males. The schizophrenics did perform in a superior manner to children on tests requiring verbal responses because of their more extensive language experience, although the actual quality of cognitive thought was not at a level comparable to that of the adult control group. In the tasks requiring the sorting of objects into classes and in combinatorial analysis, neither of which require verbal responses and both of which are more complex logically than the tasks requiring verbal responses, there were no differences between schizophrenics and children in performance.

Trunnell speculates that a child growing up in a family in which viewpoints of one or both parents are inconsistent and ambiguous would have great difficulty in learning to decenter from his own viewpoint and, therefore, in coordinating his own viewpoint with those of others. Since conjunctive thinking involves joining two attributes of an object or relation, Trunnell suggests that the interpersonal deficit which the schizophrenic experienced as a child with his parent(s) would possibly lead to a deficiency in thinking conjunctively. Poor communication models in the family can lead to very specific types of cognitive limitations. Furthermore, social interaction is usually accelerated as the child enters the concrete operational period, for it is then that he begins his school career. The child whose propensity for such interaction is markedly diminished will not be as likely to engage with peers in activities which would promote being able to handle two attributes or multiple perspectives simultaneously. It should be noted, however, that Trunnell discounts the possibility that responses of the schizophrenics could be based on social withdrawal characteristic of their condition. There is, first of all, the specificity of one type of response over another. That is, in the similarities test there was a consistency in linking two rather than three congenial items, or rather than a blatant negativism rejecting the task or stating that none of the items go together. The patients voiced opinions that the tasks were preferable to work on rather than submit to the usual hospital routine and they seemed very involved in trying to effect a solution to the problems.

Trunnell (1965) has commented on the characteristic of the schizophrenic patients in attempting to handle the problems. He states, "One is impressed with non sequiters, inappropriate responses, personalized reasons, and figural configurations which usually accompanied the more sophisticated response in the schizophrenic" (p. 14). In contrast to the control group, the schizophrenics took about one half hour longer, on the average, to complete the tasks. The schizophrenic tends to center on his own personal past experiences and, hence, his responses are often idiosyncratic and poorly adapted to the reality of the test material. While he still may have some tendencies toward centration, the child is clearly going through a more balanced process of assimilation and accommodation, as he concentrates more on the physical properties of the materials utilized for the test.

Attitudinal differences while being tested appear strikingly significant. The children were indifferent to success or failure, whereas the schizophrenics were preoccupied with the outcome. They made constant inquiries about the consequences for them of either succeeding or failing. Despite their concerns, they had previously been informed that their performances would have no bearing on their hospitalization and that the outcome would not be conveyed to the administration. In contrast, the focus of the children's concern was interpersonal. In essence, the children seemed to want to satisfy the experimenter and to be perceived as a good boy or girl.

In making some general comments, Trunnell stresses that flawed cognitive development may very readily derive from poor communication patterns within the family matrix. However, the specificity of interaction between child and parent from one family to another may vary considerably. For example, in one family a child faced with confusing and unclear parental communications may react passively, whereas in another family a child may assertively persist in attempting to improve communications, thereby minimizing his own chances of growing up with gross cognitive deficiencies. Many other permutations of communication patterns are possible with differing cognitive-developmental consequences. Trunnell (1965) is especially sensitized to the perennial problem of dichotomizing thought and feeling in psychological circles. He suggests, "The disturbance in schizophrenic thinking may be neither primary nor secondary to the emotional conflicts and intrapsychic dynamics. Both contribute to the essence of what constitutes schizophrenia" (p. 16).

In keeping with Trunnell's findings that adult schizophrenics do less well on Piagetian tasks than normal adult subjects, Lerner, Bie, and Lehrer (1972) discovered a similar outcome with a group of mentally disturbed youths ranging from fifteen to twenty-three years of age. The subjects were all hospitalized. Diagnostically, there were twelve chronic phychotics, nine borderline psychotics, and fourteen acute psychotics said to be in partial or total remission. No differences on the basis of diagnosis were reflected on either of the two types of tests administered. In one type, subjects were tested on their ability to handle conservation of substance, weight, and volume. In the other type, subjects were tested on their level of arithmetic achievement. The IQ scores ranged from 50 to 118. There were fourteen subjects out of thirty-five whose IQ was below 80. As would be predicted from earlier Piagetian reports, conservation of amount and weight were easier than conservation of volume. No subject advancing judgments reaching a concrete operational period on the volume task, offered preoperational level responses on conservation of amount or weight tasks. Difficulties between the amount and weight task were not apparent, but subjects received much lower scores for their explanations on conservation of volume than on amount or weight. For a response to be considered concrete operational it had to be based on at least one well-established operation such as identity, inversion, or compensation. Preoperational explanations either centered on one perceptual cue, such as length, over another, such as width, or invoked ontological egocentric responses of an animistic, finalistic, or artificialistic variety. There were twenty-one subjects whose IQ's exceeded 80, and nineteen of them offered responses to the conservation of amount and weight that were at the concrete operational level. Yet only eleven of the twenty-one provided responses at that level to the volume task. In contrast to generally reported findings that normal subjects can handle conservation of volume tasks, offering one or more concrete operations as justification, almost 50 percent of subjects in this study with a normal IQ could not do so. Regarding the arithmetic achievement scores, not fully reported in the research report, there is a close tie in between them and conservation performance. For example, those whose responses to amount and weight conservation were confined to a preoperational level could not perform beyond a third grade level on arithmetic achievement. Those who gave preoperational responses to volume (but presumably concrete operational responses to amount and weight, although this is not stated) were limited to a ceiling of seventh-grade level in arithmetic achievement.

An exception to this general link between arithmetic achievement and conservation resided in three subjects who received high scores in arithmetic, but responded with preoperational justifications to conservation problems. These youths had formerly done well in class before the onset of their illness, but were doing porly in their regressed state at the time of testing. Lerner, Bie, and Lehrer conclude that there was a greater vulnerability for these subjects in concrete operational areas, in the face of regression, than in arithmetic skills. The exclusion of artithmetic skills from the scope of regression in these three instances is not adequately explained by the authors, although they suggest that while reasoning at the concrete operational level may be a necessary condition for acquiring arithmetic skills, it may not be necessary in the actual execution of complex arithmetic.

Kilburg and Siegel (1976) hypothesized that schizophrenics would not perform as well in formal operational tasks as normal adults and that process schizophrenics would not perform as well as reactive schizophrenics. The Lunzer Analogies Test developed by Lunzer (1965) to test formal operational reasoning through verbal and mathematical analogies was adopted as an objective measurement. Invoked by the test are what are called second order relations, in which the thinker grasps relations between relations as opposed to relations between objects. The latter is more readily found in the concrete operational period, whereas the former has been proposed by Piaget as a defining characteristic of formal operations. An earlier report by Lunzer, disclosed that, from a group of nine to ten year olds, a decisively concrete operational age range, only 22 percent could attain even the minimum criterion signifying an elementary level of formal operational thinking. The patient population in the present study included fifty-five patients who were hospitalized at a state hospital. They were between the ages of twenty-one to fifty and all were Caucasian. Early senility, chronicity in alcoholism, drug pathology, and organic brain damage were all ruled out from the diagnoses.

The group of normal adults (fourteen) was drawn from a local trade union.

The Lunzer Analogies Test had four subtests utilized in this study. In each the predicted direction of scores was confirmed. Using the mean, the normal adult group outperformed the reactive schizophrenic group, and similarly, the reactives outperformed the process schizophrenics. Differences were of statistical significance. In a comparative statement, Kilburg and Siegel (1976) report, ". . . our normal adults (lower middle class machinists) were comparable to Lunzer's bright 13-14 year-olds on all four subtests and the total Lunzer Analogies test score. Similarly, reactives performed at a level intermediate between Lunzer's 9-10 and 11-12 year olds, and process schizophrenics consistently obtained lower scores than did Lunzer's 9-10 year-olds (with the exception of their performance on the simple analogies)" (p. 147).

A question that arises frequently in discussions on the cognitive deficit in schizophrenia is whether there is a particular kind of cognitive flaw which is specific to that diagnosis. Strauss (1967) has argued that excessive concreteness is responsible for the basic intellectual impairment in schizophrenic functioning, but that this phenomenon has its roots in normal development and, although present in exaggerated form among some schizoprhenics, it is not unique to them. He based his conclusions on a study of both acute and chronic schizophrenic patients and a comparative control group of normal adults. It was not only the case that Strauss found no type of reasoning to be specific to the patient populations, but it was also the case that some of the schizophrenics in the sample did not demonstrate the cognitive impairment that was found in varying degrees across all groups. The chronic schizophrenic participants numbered twenty-one and each had to have been in the hospital for a minimum of one year at the time of the study. There were fourteen acute schizophrenic subjects. Any patient who had been ill for one year or more was not permitted in this group. The fifteen control subjects were medical patients with no known mental illness. All subjects from each group were hospitalized at a Veterans Administration hospital. Patients with known brain pathology were excluded from the study and all who were included did so voluntarily. The subjects in the acute group were considerably younger than those of the other two groups. They had a mean age of 28.5 whereas the chronic and control groups had mean ages of 47.5 and 50.8 respectively. Years of education varied greatly with the mean number varying as follows: acute 13 years, chronic 10.4 years, control 7.6 years.

Four types of tests were administered. Three were Piagetian and the fourth was taken from the picture arrangement test of the Wechsler Adult Intelligence Scale (WAIS). The aim was to explore how the excessive concreteness of the schizophrenic, so often reported in the literature, effects the capacity to infer causal and explanatory aspects of phenomena. Complex thinking involving acquisition of knowledge through integrating perceived variables is tested by employing the tasks which will now be described.

The apparatus of the first task consisted simply of a tube, a bottle, and various cards. The tube was placed vertically over the bottle and subjects observed water flowing into the bottle from the tube. Naturally what they saw was that as the amount of water in the tube diminished, the amount in the bottle increased with a corresponding rise in the water level of the bottle. One set of five cards displayed, on each, the tube and bottle in different states with respect to the flow of the water. The task of the subject was to place the cards in serial order showing an accurate progression of the water leaving the tube and entering the bottle. Another set of ten cards was used. Five were pictures of the tube at various states of decreasing water levels and five were of the bottle at various states of increasing water levels. The task was to select the one card from those displaying bottles which would properly match the card with the tube one-third full. Lastly, each of the ten cards were to be matched so that the water levels of the bottles were matched with those of the tubes, after which each of the five resulting pairs were to be arranged in consecutive order. In performing correctly on these problems the subject was required to comprehend the simultaneous shift in water levels and, in so doing, demonstrate an ability to cordinate two perceived variables.

The second task involved an inverted Y-shaped tube. Beneath

each of the two sections of the tube was a beaker, each beaker varying in diameter, but not in height. Water from the tube flowed in equal amounts at the same pace into the two beakers. What the subject observed, of course, was that, as the water level of the tube diminished, the water levels in the two beakers increased. However, the water level of the narrower beaker would be higher at all times than the water level of the wider beaker throughout the process. Before the water flowed, the subject was asked to predict which of the two beakers would fill up first. He was later asked whether the beakers began and finished filling simultaneously, whether the same amount of water was found in each beaker upon completion of the demonstration, and to predict the water level that would appear if, after emptying one beaker, the contents of the remaining one were poured into the empty one.

The third Piagetian task dealt with integrating ratios of time, distance, and speed. Two toy cars are aligned along parallel tracks. They are put in motion to travel at different speeds, traversing different distances, and stop at different times from one another. In one demonstration a car goes faster and further than the other, but the other which is going slower and covering less distance continues in motion when the car that had outdistanced it stops. In an alternate demonstration both cars stop simultaneously, but one has traveled over a greater distance by moving at a faster rate. In both cases, the subject is questioned about which of the two cars stopped first, which was in motion for a greater period of time, and why one car traveled over more distance than the other.

On the basis of analyzing the subjects' responses once the tasks were administered, Strauss identified two major errors. In one the subjects would note a perceived variable and draw a conclusion from that alone, failing to make an inference derived from two or more variables at their disposal. Strauss calls this "equating the derived with the perceived variable." For example, some subjects stated in the task with the two beakers of unequal diameter that the one with the higher water level had a greater amount of water in it. They ignored both the fact that the beaker with the lower water level had a larger diameter and that the water had flowed into both beakers simultaneously. Had they processed this information which was available to them, they could have derived the abstract variable, quantity, correctly. Strauss comments that, in some instances, subjects actually rejected their own previous observations regarding the water flowing into the beaker at the same pace, in order to be able to more "logically" assert that there was more water in the beaker with the higher water level. Similarly, in the task involving the toy cars which stopped at different times, some subjects said that the one which had traveled further was also in motion for a longer time, despite their own observations that the one which traveled less distance was still moving when the quicker and further traveling car had ceased moving. In this case, duration is the abstract variable and it is mistakenly equated with distance, the perceived variable. A correct solution to the problem would, of course, require coordination of speed, time, and distance. The second major error was designated by Strauss as "equating two perceived or perceivable magnitudes." An example of this was demonstrated in the task requiring the arrangement of a series of cards in which each pair would show a tube of water above a bottle. Instead of showing a steady diminution of water in the tube and a corresponding increase of water in the bottle across the series, subjects making this error would match cards displaying equal water levels in both tube and bottle. They obviously exhibited no understanding of the relationship between a simultaneously decreasing water level in the tube and an increasing water level in the bottle, even though they had observed this occurring immediately prior to being asked to arrange the cards.

There were few differences in performance between the acute schizophrenic patients and the control group. The chronic schizophrenics made a significantly greater number of the types of errors discussed. However, these errors were found among members in all three groups and there was no type of error found exclusively among schizophrenics. Strauss views the excessive concreteness or attention to a single perceptual variable to be in some ways diametrically opposed to the overinclusion said to be characteristic of schizophrenic thinking. However, he believes that both excessive concreteness, as seen in his own subjects, and overinclusion, as described by Cameron (1939), are marked by a focusing impairment. The problem is in the individual's incapacity to derive complex ideas from an appropriate selection and coordination of available perceived data. Since the chronic schizophrenic group manifested significantly more errors, as opposed to the acute and control groups, Strauss emphasizes the importance of research ventures which differentiate within patient populations, to avoid overgeneralization. Strauss notes that the errors of excessive attention to a single perceptual variable are also characteristic of young children. Nevertheless, he goes on to urge explorations which will attempt to discern whether there may not be qualitative differences between these thinking errors as observed predominantly among the chronic schizophrenics and the manner in which the limitation is to be found in young children. Regarding the chronic population, he suggests that the subjects' tendency to commit these errors could be either derived from prolonged hospitalization or are possibly indicative of chronic schizophrenia being a separate illness and not merely the end result of chronic hospitalization for acute schizophrenia.

SENSORIMOTOR ROOTS

This section will present material selectively from the sensorimotor period with reference to both normalcy and pathology in development. Practical intelligence is developed on a behavioral level throughout this period which ultimately culminates in the acquisition of a capacity for symbolic thought at one and a half to two years of age. Gains made on a behavioral level will later have to be reconstructed on a conceptual level. For example, the child who learns to navigate competently on a physical plane in his environment needs to develop more complex cognitive structures before he can symbolically recreate that environment in the form of a map. The child's integrated comprehension of reality is constructed in such areas as time, space, causality, intention, object permanence, play, and imitation. In this section special attention will be given to causality and object permanence.

The normal route of development in the sphere of causality will be offered here because of its central role in adaptive living. Many adults identified as dysfunctional or mentally ill lack an appropriate sense of the source of causality in the world. They may either fail to see themselves as the locus of causality when it is appropriate to do so or they may see themselves as a cause agent influencing events over which they have no control at all. Either or both of these errors will result in grossly maladapted behavior. Yet it is developmentally in the sensorimotor period that the child first organizes his activities in relation to the world so that he learns to distinguish between things and events which he can influence and those which he cannot. Piaget (1936/1971) in stages 1 and 2 characterizes primitive causality as a fusion of efficacy and phenomenalism. During these first two stages, the infant's behavior revolves around looking, grasping, and sucking reflexively, as well as the primary circular reactions of these reflexes. In a primary circular reaction, the activity is repeated by the presence of a stimulus accidentally come upon. A child sucks from the nipple, swallows, then has the sucking mechanism triggered off again by the presence of the nipple. In this way there is strengthening of the response and a beginning accommodation to reality. At the same time that the accommodation is occurring, the child is, of course, assimilating the external world, which he does not perceive as such, into his reflex schemas. The external world upon which he acts at this stage is experienced as an extension of his own activity. The infant experiences a diffuse sense of efficacy, but this feeling is not of himself as a separate entity. Piaget (1936/1971) states, "Primitive causality may therefore be conceived as a sort of efficiency or efficacy linked with acts as such, always with the reservation that such feelings are not considered by the subject as coming from himself but are localized in perceptual aggregates constituting the point of departure for objects in general or for the body itself" (p. 257). Eventually the efficacy will become a clear internal sense of the self's own power and the phenomenalistic aspect becomes a full realization of the external world as separate from the self and as constituting a network of independent causality. In brief, efficacy becomes psychological causality and phenomenalism becomes physical causality.

In the third stage the infant makes some progress but remains characterized by what Piaget calls "Magico-Phenomenalistic efficacy." The essence of this is the child's sense of his own movements being the cause that creates effects even of events residing at some distance from his body. There are three main areas that the child observes—movements of his own body, movements which depend on his bodily activities, and movements in the external world which are not dependent on his activities. In the previous two stages, cause and effect were not differentiated but experienced together in a single perceived act. However, from the third stage onward the child internalizes a sense of his causal efficacy and the effect is externalized when he acts. The flaw in his behavior is in attempting to produce the sound of his rattle by merely waving his hand, having previously triggered off the sound when his hand had accidentally come in contact with the rattle. The child can be obsessed with looking at his own hand under these circumstances, with a studied expression as if his hand movements should be the sole source of causing the rattle to effect a sound. On some vague level the child is becoming conscious of purposefulness. He is beginning in the third stage to perform what Piaget calls secondary circular reactions. When his own actions accidentally trigger off an interesting sight or sound, the child will reproduce the action to make the interesting spectacle last. However, he does not necessarily bother to make spatial contact and, therefore, is not always successful. Thus efficacy and phenomenalism are still not completely differentiated at this magico-phenomenalistic stage. The secondary circular reaction reflects a movement away from the body toward things in the external world, whereas the primary circular reaction involves body-centered activities. The child still does not have a sense of self as separate from the rest of the world, however. Piaget raises an interesting question in attempting to determine whether the child at stage 3 has as yet developed a recognition of objects outside of himself as a source of independent causality. Supposing A is observed causing B. Will the child who wishes to continue experiencing the effect B attempt to act on A by touching or pushing it once it stops causing B? Piaget set up circumstances in which this could be observed and he concluded that the child does not. For example, if the experimenter swings an object several times and then stops, the child may revert to magico-phenomenalistic actions such as arching his back or swinging his hand at the air while loking at the object as if to see it repeat its former effect. Alternately, the child may direct his attention to the experimenter's hand, possibly only striking it and then looking to see if the object is again repeating the effect. However, he does not make any attempt to steer the experimenter's hand toward the object so that it may perform causally. The hand is simply not viewed by the child as an independent causal agent, but merely as causally subordinate to the child's own efficacy. Regarding the movement of the child's own body, generally, the actions of his body directly upon other objects, and the action of an external object upon another, Piaget (1936/1971) comments, ". . . in these three cases it is to the dynamism of his own activity that the child attributes all causal efficacy, and the phenomenon outside, however removed it may be from his own body, is conceived only as a simple result of his own actions" (p. 281). It is perhaps plausible at this juncture to entertain the notion that schizophrenic persons who have an unreal sense of omnipotence with respect to their control over the universe may have become arrested developmentally at stage 3 in the area of causality, or may have regressed to it. There are also features of this in the ontological egocentrism of the preoperational period and where one is to pinpoint the arrest or regression would depend on the degree of primitiveness of the belief. Since the areas of development in the sensorimotor period are inter-dependent aspects of the same growing person, it is likely that any such arrest or regression would not be limited to a single area. For example, the schizophrenic person who is functioning at least partially in stage 3 of causality is also likely to have a grossly deficient concept of object permanence.

Piaget has made some particularly interesting remarks about the role of the person in the child's environment at this stage. In Piaget's view another person in the environment is subject to the same attitude and behavior in the realm of causality as are inanimate objects. There is a reality in the child's life which lends some credence to such a relation to the person, for the child has often only to cry or perform other acts and the other person's behavior is fairly predictable. An adult or older sibling will frequently comply with the child's attempts to get him to do its bidding. There is an essential method, however, which is unique to how the child may attempt to produce an effect in the other person through imitation. In the third stage the child can only imitate behaviors which are already in his behavioral repertoire. When he imitates the other person with the intention of producing a repetition of the same act in that person, he merely experiences the other person's actions as an extension of his own performance. In general, throughout development during the sensorimotor period, Piaget places great importance upon the role of the person in fostering the child's cognitive growth. He notes that the child is more animated in the presence of other people and states, ". . . contact with persons plays an essential role in the processes of objectification and externalization: the person constitutes the primary object and the most external of the objects in motion through space" (Piaget 1936/1971, p. 285). It is the person who represents the most prominent and dominant locus of causality outside of the child and, therefore, constant interaction with the other person facilitates the child's detachment from causality as inhering only in his own activity.

In the fourth stage the child does in fact dissociate causality and his own actions. The two are no longer inseparable. External objects are viewed as being a source of independent causality, yet are in some way still contingent on the child's activities. Another person can act as an independent cause agent, but requires the action of the child to set him in motion. Therefore, while external objects have now acquired partial objectification and spatialization, they require the intervention of the child's actions to be put in motion as causal agents. The child is now observed taking another's hand and placing it by a toy to be swung, even going on to attempt to get the exact action desired by manipulating the person's fingers to provide momentum. Note that, while this still provides a significant role to the child in activating the other's causality, it is an important advance over the previous stage when he would simply strike the other's hand as if this would make the toy swing. Similarly, in the fourth stage the child relates to inanimiate objects in the same way. He will give them a push or strike them and then wait to see them go into action.

The fifth stage ushers in a total objectification and spatialization of causality in the external world. The child after the first year of life no longer acts as if animate or inanimate objects in his world are links to his actions before performing causally. External objects are seen as being independent sources of causality. The child is now observed placing a ball at the top of an incline, then allowing it to act in accord with its own nature. Piaget observes about his own daughter's behavior in this stage while playing with a toy, "Jacqueline, instead of pushing the object or even giving it a shake by a simple touch, makes every effort to put it down as rapidly as possible and to let go of it immediately, as though her intervention would impede the toys spontaneous movement instead of aiding them!" (1936/ 1971). The source of causality now inheres in the object. The same shift, of course, is seen in relation to people. For example, when Jacqueline wants her father to resume blowing in her hair after he stopped, she merely places her head next to his lips and awaits expectantly for him to initiate the action. Previous to this stage she would literally manipulate his lips, as if her own action were necessary before he could blow on her again. Two major achievements arise during the fifth stage which have great bearing on the furthering of the causal notion. They are the tertiary circular reaction and the invention of new means through active experimentation. In the tertiary circular reaction the child searches for the novel and shows an objective interest in exploring the properties of objects as they exist independently of himself. This forces a greater accommodation to objective reality than previously experienced. In the process of inventing the new means, the child gropes with the object through a series of trial and error behaviors, but the groping is goal-directed and not merely random. The child has increasingly come to recognize that there is a world of cause and effect independent of himself and that maximum adaptation requires of him a certain amount of submission to these phenomena. Piaget (1936/1971) asserts, "Whereas up to now the child has commanded nature, he now begins to do so only by 'obeying it'" (p. 330). It is worth noting here that obeying nature is not to be enslaved by it, but by understanding its laws one gains a greater command over it. There now exists a reciprocal relationship in which the child is acted upon by external causes and also acts upon those causes in the objective world, as well. He comprehends himself behaviorally as one of a series of causes existing in the world.

In the sixth stage the child acquires representation in causality. He no longer is solely reliant upon direct perception, but can now infer causes from observed effects and conversely can anticipate the effect of a contemplated causal action derived from an object in the environment. The emergence of the capacity for symbolic thought gives rise to causal deduction, which frees the child from the sensorimotor limits of direct perception. As in all stage phenomena, it should be realized that limitations of former stages persist, despite the capacity to perform at the symbolic level. They may be especially manifest in the face of problems that are more than moderately novel and which pose exceptional difficulty.

Goulet (1974) has researched the causal development of the very young child in relation to his reaction to strangers. He points out that while there is general agreement on the observation that sometime during the second year, the child begins to manifest a fear reaction in the presence of a stranger, disagreement revolves around how to understand the meaning of this event. Tracing the development of the causal concept, Goulet pauses at the fifth stage to emphasize that Piaget suggested that at this stage the child will regard objects with an apprehensive expression because he no longer thinks they are predictable. He now has a greater tendency to take note of the novel in his environment. Goulet speculates that prior to this stage of causal development, fear of new or strange aspects of the environment is not likely. A scale of causality was constructed to diagnose the child's causal level based on Piaget's work. There were thirty-two subjects, eight in each of the following age groups: thirty-two weeks, forty weeks, forty-eight weeks, and fifty-six weeks. The mother is present and visually accessible throughout the experiment, although she remains inactive. The stranger, the experimenter, acts in a normal manner while moving through a series of graded steps to bring him into closer contact with the infant. The subject's reactions were observed in terms of facial expression, motor activity, and vocal sounds. Basically, reactions could be classified as positive, negative, or neutral. One facet of the findings was that from among the oldest infants (fifty-six weeks) there were only two of the eight who showed positive reactions. In the other three groups, a majority of the infants responded positively. In general, when comparing responses across age groups in relation to certain positive and negative reactions, there were twice as many infants behaving negatively in the oldest age category than in the other three groups. Negative behavior included such reactions as attempts to avoid contact, crying, or even striking out at the approaching stranger. The oldest infants were also ranked at the highest level of causal development, as one would expect. Nevertheless, when the sample was analyzed from the standpoint of specific causal stages for each subject in relation to whether the global score of responses in the presence of a stranger was positive, negative, or neutral, it was found that there was no correlation. Hence, Goulet concluded that the infants' stages of causal development did not correspond with their affective reaction to the presence of a stranger. The findings convey that for an infant to express fear of a stranger it is not necessary that he be at a high level of causal development, as fear of a stranger was found in a few infants who were only at stage 3. These results were not expected. In analyzing the data further, Goulet discovered that there is, however, a unique role played by stage 5 development. Some subjects seemed positive when the stranger was present, but at a distance, shifted to an intensively negative reaction when being approached or touched by the stranger. All of these subjects were at stage 5 or 6, although not all subjects at stage 5 or 6 reacted negatively to such stranger behavior. Goulet (1974) puts it succinctly, ". . . approach or contact would constitute an inherent threat in the eyes of the child only if he has acquired a thoroughly objectified and spatialized concept of causality" (p. 93). Goulet theorizes that, viewing objects as capable of autonomous causal action, independent of the child's own activity is responsible for his fear as the stranger approaches or touches him. While motionless at a distance, the stranger poses no threat. It is not his presence, but his behavior that produces anxiety in these infants. The behavior is a necessary, but not a sufficient condition, for not all infants at stage 5 or 6 will react apprehensively in these circumstances. However, only infants who reach stage 5 will show a capability for such a response under the conditions described.

Brossard (1974) has conducted a study similar to Goulet's, in which he sought to discover whether there is correspondence between the infant's development in object permanence and his response to strangers. The reader will recall that for the youngest infant there exists no concept of a permanent object which is independent and durable irrespective of the infant's own perception and actions. It is only through gradual stage transitions that he can finally deal with complex, invisible displacements of an object. His ability to deal with invisible displacements is due to the development of representation, which enables him to make deductions about the object even though he, himself, is neither perceiving nor acting upon the object. Brossard stresses that the problem he is researching is an interpersonal one, because the stranger is, in fact, an animate and not an inanimate object. The distinction is a developmentally important one for, as Piaget has noted, there is a décalage in which children will be observed to arrive at stage 6 in relation to the substantiation or permanence of a person before they arrive at an object concept for inanimate objects. The scoring of positive and negative reactions utilized by Bossard were the same as those utilized by Goulet. Both research attempts were part of a larger project and were presented in a volume by Décarie et al (1974). Bossard found no correlation between the infants' affective reaction to the presence of a stranger and their stage of object permanence with a person. However, further analysis reveals that of a total of thirty-two subjects, there were sixteen who changed affective tone when the stranger moved toward them and/or touched them. Further, fourteen of the sixteen proved to be at stages 5 or 6 in object permanence in relation to a person. There was also a marked tendency for those who did not show an affective change to be in the lower levels of object permanence development. Those who shifted in affect almost invariably changed in the direction of a negative response, hence signifying that the situation was being interpreted as a threatening one.

Décarie (1974) dares to speculate upon the findings of Goulet. She points out that only two of the subjects who manifested a change in affective tone from positive to negative were at stage 5 in relation to attributing causality to inanimate objects. The other three subjects who manifested this behavior were already at stage 6. Since an infant will experience a décalage in development, first acquiring a causal concept in relation to persons and later acquiring it in relation to inanimate objects, Décarie suggests that it is entirely possible that the two subjects at stage 5 in relation to objects may already be at stage 6 with regard to persons. If this should be the case, all five subjects who changed from reacting positively when the stranger remained at a distance to reacting negatively when he moved toward them or actually touched them, would be at stage 6 in relation to attributing causality to persons. More specifically, this would mean that they had reached the stage of representative thought and were conceptually capable of anticipating and making inferences that would take them beyond the immediately perceivable. At a distance, the stranger is merely an unfamiliar, but interesting sight, which poses no threat. Upon approaching the infant at stage 6, the stranger may trigger off an anticipation of a fearful event. The infant at a stage prior to the sixth does not have the capacity to imagine such an event. The infant at stage 6 may infer that the stranger is about to pick him up and that this will cause the mother to leave or he may infer that the stranger is going to pick him up because his mother is planning to leave. Décarie emphasizes that either interpretation of the event will very likely stimulate anxiety in the child. She points out that this imagined sequence is not at all uncommon for infants to have experienced, as when a baby sitter arrives, picks up the child, and then the mother leaves.

PERSON AND OBJECT PERMANENCE

The phenomenon of a décalage in development regarding object permanence has been carefully studied by Bell (1970) who has indicated some diagnostic significance to it. An earlier attempt at researching Piaget's hypothesis that person permanence would precede inanimate object permanence was conducted by Saint-Pierre (1962), who found a confirmation in twenty-three of thirty infants studied. There were cases, however, in which either no décalage occurred or where the sequence was reversed. Recognizing the mother as central to the infant's interaction with his environment, Bell sought to examine her role in relation to the child's development of the object concept. In particular she wished to ascertain whether the nature of the child's attachment to his mother exercised any influence over the sequence with which person permanence and object permanence appeared. Bell worked with a population of twelve females and twenty-one males, totalling thirty-three infants, of middle-class background. Each was measured on developmental level in relation to object permanence and separately in relation to person permanence. The sample was divided into three groups, designated positive décalage, negative décalage, and no décalage. If an infant evidenced a décalage favoring person permanence it was considered in the positive group and in the negative group if it favored object permanence. Attachment to the mother was determined by structuring situations in which the infant would be separated from the mother for several minutes and then brought back to her. Behavior of the infant would be observed and scored. It should be noted that, during the separations, the infant would be in an unfamiliar situation in the presence of a stranger. There were basically three groups of children classified according to their tendencies to explore the surroundings during the phases of the study and to seek closeness to the mother. Interviews were held with the mothers to obtain data about their attitudes and activities with the children.

In accord with Piaget's previous observations, a majority of the subjects evidenced positive décalage. There were twenty-three infants who were more advanced in person permanence than in object permanence. The negative décalage category had seven subjects and for three subjects no décalage was found. Each of the infants was tested three times between the ages of eight and one half and eleven months and a portion of them was tested once again at thirteen months. The décalage for those favoring person permanence was relatively constant over the testing period and was not eliminated until both person and object permanence reached the most advanced level sometime after the experiment. Infants with a negative décalage, however, moved more rapidly in closing the gap, so that by the time of the third testing session all but two subjects had eliminated the discrepancy. Therefore, Bell points out, being scored as having no décalage may simplify signify that the infant is being tested at a particular point in development when that condition obtains, but it does not signify that there has never been a décalage.

What can be said of the relationship between mother attachment and object concept? There were twenty-four infants assigned to group B, which was characterized by the subjects' ability to use the mother as an anchor point of security in order to venture forth to explore the environment prior to the brief separation phase of the study. Further, infants so classified displayed clear attempts to interact and gain closeness with the mother once reunited. Of these twenty-four subjects, Bell reports that twenty-three were scored as having a positive décalage and one had no décalage. Group A contained five infants. Their characteristic behavior was to avoid person contact and to focus upon interaction with objects in the environment. The negative décalage classification claimed four of these subjects and one exhibited no décalage. In group C there were four children who showed maladaptive coping behavior in the unfamiliar situation and were ambivalent toward the mother in her presence. All four scored a negative décalage. One of them had registered no décalage until tested at thirteen and one half months at which time the negative décalage was apparent. Significantly, the only subjects who demonstrated a positive décalage were those who had a close attachment to the mother, but who also felt secure in leaving her side to explore their surroundings. A comparative analysis was also performed in relation to the developmental level of object permanence for both the positive décalage group and those with either negative or no décalage combined together. In general, by the age of thirteen and a half months it appears that infants in the positive décalage group have also acquired a concept of object permanence which is more advanced than that of those infants in the negative décalage group. Bell asserts that the quality of interaction between mother and child during the first months of life will directly influence the nature of attachment and development of person permanence. She has made some general comments based on the interviews with the subjects' mothers which are worth quoting at length.

> Mothers of babies in the positive décalage group tended to go on frequent outings with their babies and to avoid even brief daily separations from them. They tended to comment only on the baby's positive features, and never showed physical rejection or mistreated the infant in front of the observer. Mothers of negative décalage infants instead were significantly rejecting . . . they were prone to express disapproval and rejection through inappropriate use of physical punishment, refusal to establish contact with the baby, or abrupt interference with his ongoing activity (1970, p. 309).

Bell has highlighted through her impressive study, the singular importance of a good mother-child interaction in contributing to adaptive cognitive functioning and the development of symbolic activity. (Read Clarke-Stewart 1973, for a well documented review of the influence of mother-child interaction upon the child's cognitive functioning.) The child who has a negative décalage will also be observed to have a less sound structure of object permanence than the child with a positive décalage. We shall now turn to a developmental issue of the sensorimotor period bearing on mental representation as defined by Piaget and to the early hallucinatory experience as described by psychoanalytic theorists. Piaget's findings on the construction of the object concept have been confirmed independently by Décarie (1965) and Escalona (1968). What seems to be a subject of debate is whether the early hallucinatory image is a phenomenon of true mental representation, given that its appearance is posited by most psychoanalysts at a time in development prior to the time that Piaget claims for the emergence of genuine representation. Vitally linked to this problem is the relationship between the psychoanalytic concept of object constancy, first introduced by Hartmann (1964) and the Geneva School's concept of object permanence, introduced by Piaget (1936/1971). Major attempts have been made by Décarie (1965) and Fraiberg (1969) to place the psychoanalytic and Genevan positions into a conceptually consistent framework. The following formulation will rely heavily upon their insightful efforts.

It would seem that depending upon whose definition and understanding of the concept is being honored, object constancy may generally be found to first appear anywhere between five months to thirty-six months (Kaplan 1972). The nature of object constancy will vary depending upon which theorist is being accepted. The issue is whether object constancy requires object permanence in the Piagetian sense or whether it may predate Piaget's concept. Anna Freud has not used the concept of object constancy in the cognitive sense to denote the capacity to evoke absent objects, on a symbolic plane, which have substantial existence independently of the child. Her emphasis is on the stability of the emotional attachment or libidinal cathexis of the child for the mother. Prior to object constancy the child undergoes a "need-satisfying" phase during which the object is cathected only in times of need and frustration. During this period the object has no existence when there is no need. Further, cathexis is withdrawn from the disappointing or thwarting object. In the subsequent period of object constancy the cathexis is maintained regardless of the child's need state or the frustrating actions of the mother. The emphasis is upon libidinal attachment throughout and not upon the separate existence of the loved object as an independent entity in itself. According to Décarie's interpretation of Anna Freud, the first appearance of object love, but not object constancy itself, appears between five to six months. From then on there is a gradual progression toward object constancy. Décarie (1965) states, "The kind of object constancy which is implied in the continued cathexis of the absent object does not really appear before the beginning of the third year" (p. 116).

On the other hand Spitz (1957, 1965) specifically relates object constancy to mental representation in the strict cognitive sense. (Colbiner, in the appendix to Spitz 1965, presents an extended discussion from the psychoanalytic perspective.) He pinpoints stranger anxiety at eight months and explains it through mental representation. The stranger's face is compared to the infant's internal image of the absent mother. Recognition that the stranger is not his mother and that she is not presently available to him produces anxiety. Fraiberg (1969) reports that through an exchange of correspondence, she received confirmation from Spitz that he views object constancy as present in the infant by eight months and that he intends to assert that the child of that age has the capacity to evoke an image of the object not present to him. However, Spitz acknowledges in the correspondence that the object involved here is specifically the mother and that the circumstances are especially stressful for the infant. Whether the infant could perform similarly with consistency and under less stressful conditions remains a moot question for him. Nevertheless, it should be apparent that placing mental representation at eight months of age poses a problem when examined in the light of Piaget's position, confirmed by subsequent researchers, that this capacity appears between eighteen months to two years of age. It is true that Piaget holds that person permanence appears prior to the permanence of inanimate objects, but one would not expect a time lag of such proportions.

Mahler (1975) clearly links object constancy to mental

representation, but does not see it as fully developing until between twenty-five and thirty-six months. Because of the special nature of the interaction between the child and his mother, as opposed to the interaction between the child and less emotionally charged objects, the mental representation of the mother may occur more swiftly, but may be less stabilized at first than is the case with inanimate objects (Pine 1974). The stringent position adopted by Mahler (1975) is reflected in her own words:

> It is only after object constancy is well on its way, which according to our conceptualization does not seem to occur before the third year . . . , that the mother during her physical absence can be substituted for, at least in part, by the presence of a reliable internal image that remains relatively stable irrespective of the state of instinctual need or inner discomfort (p. 110).

Fraiberg (1969) suggests that theorists who date object constancy from eight months to eighteen months are construing libidinal cathexis in terms of some form of mental representation. When object constancy is seen as emerging at eighteen months, Piaget's stage 6 criterion for mental representation is invoked. In the case of Mahler, who does not place object constancy before twenty-five months, Fraiberg states that even more restraining criteria are being utilized to account for the sustained image of the mother which the child can manage even in the face of internal disruption. It is precisely the meaning of the term "mental representation" in psychoanalytic usage which remains variable and vague in the literature. Fraiberg sets out to clarify matters by offering a distinction between the terms "recognition memory" and "evocative memory." Recognition memory is triggered by the sight of some sign which, in turn, points to further detail that is recalled. For example, seeing an old friend may bring to mind a series of past experiences which one might not have otherwise imagined. However, representing these events in the total absence of any triggering stimulus would be an example of evocative memory. Fraiberg cogently argues that the anxiety Spitz observed in the infants he studied at eight months can be explained by recognition memory and need not invoke an interpretation of evocative memory. Responding to Spitz's comment that the mother is felt to be "lost" to the child when he fails to find her upon comparing her image to the stranger's face, Fraiberg (1969) states, "On the contrary, if a mother is 'lost' when she is not perceived, this may be taken as evidence that the mental image of the mother is still unstable, is not independent of perception, requires affirmation from visual experience" (p. 24). In the child's visual experience there is a repeated presentation of the joyous sight of the mother. When the "expectation" of still another repetition is disconfirmed for the eight-months-old child, this could produce an unsettling affect. The expectation need not be predicated upon evocative memory at all. Further, Fraiberg asserts, "The child who is capable of evocative memory can sustain the image of the mother *not* present in perception which should theoretically diminish the disturbing effect of a strange face" (p. 24). She then predicts that, in fact, one would find a corresponding basis in cognitive development that would account for diminishing stranger anxiety at about twelve to thirteen months old, which she suggests is supported by Piaget's observations and theories. In her argument, Fraiberg emphasizes the possibility that the very absence of a stable and well-developed mental representation is the source of anxiety for the child who has become so libidinally cathected to the mother. Its presence would offer a sense of security.

What of the image in relation to the early hallucinatory experience which gratifies an intense need or wish? Is this a genuine case of mental representation? The child in the absence of food and in a state of intense hunger may hallucinate the breast, taking it to be the real object. There follows at least partial gratification. Décarie (1965) adopts the position that this hallucinatory event is not to be equated with full mental representation of stage 6 development in the object concept. In Fraiberg's terms it is recognition memory. It lacks the complete evocative character of Piaget's stage 6. Instead it is more like stage 4 in which the screen behind which a ball may be hidden from a child is the sign that leads him to retrieve it. Even though the ball is no longer in sight, the child still depends on visual cues to locate it. When still at this stage, in fact, if the ball previously located at position A is seen being removed to position B, the child will only look for it where it had been previously found. He can not as yet deal with either visible displacements (stage 5) or invisible displacements (stage 6). In referring to the hallucinatory image, Décarie (1965) contends, "This is not yet true representation but rather analogous to representation in stage 4, in which visceral hunger sensations play a role of perceptual indicators of a forthcoming feeding and lead the infant to believe that the object is already present" (p. 206). She further points out that the image in these circumstances is described by Rapaport (1954) as being vague, diffuse, and undifferentiated. Hence, it lacks the distinct and precisionlike form of mental representation as appearing at stage 6. It also lacks the independent, substantiated existence of an object in the Piagetian meaning of complete object permanence. To the contrary, its appearance is subjectively rooted in the temporal and sporadic need system of the infant rather than being grounded in external reality and accorded continuity of existence. To qualify as evocative memory, a more advanced form of mental representation, it must sunder its roots from the stimulus of need, just as the child eventually transcends his dependence on visual cues related to the external world. This is an essential point advanced by both Décarie (1965) and Fraiberg (1969).

Kaplan (1972) has advanced the observation that, despite the wide range along which the appearance of object constancy is placed by varying psychoanalytic theorists, there are many who view it as a gradually developing phenomenon. Elaborating upon this position, she has proposed that the development of object constancy can be followed through adolescence. Her contention is that the various phases can be understood in the light of stage properties and décalages as in Piaget's system. Achievements at one level are reconstructed at a later and more advanced level where they are integrated with the newly evolving structures of development. Kaplan (1972) concludes, "The process of new structure formation and reorganization of adolescence should modulate the intensity of libidinal ties and identifications of the past without eradicating them" (p. 333). Taking this long-range view, Blatt (1974) has maintained that adult depression may have as its source the impairment of object constancy and mental representation at one of the earlier developmental stages. It is suggested by him that as long as the object is present in the individual's actual environment, the problem may not be apparent. However, upon removal from or loss of the object, such as a parent, the flawed capacity for object representation fails to offer the needed internalized images for support. Absence of the cathected object on both an external and internal plane then produces fertile grounds for depression. Despite the more differentiated and discrete nature of the image at stage 6 of the sensorimotor period, it is not until the outset of formal operations, age eleven or twelve, that representation is comprised of a sharply etched image. Blatt points out that prior to this time, children have difficulty in recalling vividly even familiar faces and places. Once the individual moves into advanced levels of cognitive development, he has at his command a meaningful and broad repertoire of images and memories which he may evoke rather than to become depressed. The type of depression, ancaclitic or introjective, is said to be determined by the level of representational impairment.

Blatt and Wild (1975) have drawn heavily from Piaget in their developmental approach to schizophrenia in terms of boundary differentiations. Their concern is with the individual's capacity to differentiate between his own self and the external world, as well as between his internal representations and that which is represented. The individual who differentiates boundaries appropriately does not mistake the image or word for that which it signifies. Objects that are separate in reality are not fused in the mind. Boundary disturbances are likely to result in poor differentiation within the intrapsychic, cognitive, and interpersonal domains, according to Blatt and Wild. Yet these disturbances are not to be found in equal proportions among all schizophrenics. The authors' premise is that paranoid subgroups invoke defense strategies which are designed to combat boundary problems. Projection in particular is viewed by Blatt and Wild as a defense which serves to differentiate between self and object. In general, they have found that poor cognitive, perceptual, and interpersonal boundaries are maintained by chronic, undifferentiated, process schizophrenics. However, in contrast, Blatt and Wild (1976) assert, "The paranoid's hyper-alertness, overly focused attention and perception, fragmented thinking, extreme constriction, excessive autonomy and interpersonal distance, preoccupation with power and control, and guarded and suspicious behavior can all be understood, in part, as exaggerated defensive efforts to prevent the dissolution of boundaries and accompanying experiences of merging and fusing" (p. 229). They believe, also, that the extent of boundary disturbance may serve as a measure of pathological severity. There is a positive correlation between early disruption of interpersonal relationships and the maintenance of poor boundaries. Patients with such a history and current boundary problems will have a more difficult time sustaining personal relationships in the present. Among the more impaired schizophrenics there is a greater likelihood of mothers having been either cold and distant or intrusive and enveloping from the patients' early life onward. The patients as children failed to differentiate between self and parent. They are marked by a desire to merge with the parent; a primitive struggle for separation ensues, which goes beyond the normal adolescents' struggle between independence and dependence.

The genesis of boundary disturbances are to be found in very early cognitive development. Radical egocentrism of the sensorimotor period is gradually surmounted through the infant's interaction with the environment. This interaction enables the child to defeat the most primitive boundary limitation of all in which there is, in the beginning, no sense of either self or external world. Behavior suggesting that the infant construes the object as being a part of his own activity is finally surrendered, as the object is accorded an independent existence apart from the child's own activity or perception. It is the gradual construction of a stable mental representation which makes this possible. It is necessary, however, that the image or verbal signifier in representation be distinguished from that which it stands for, if genuine boundary

differentiation is to be maintained. The infant progressively re-
linquishes behavior which expresses the self as the exclusive
locus of causality. By the end of the sensorimotor period, the
infant differentiates between causality residing in the self and
that which derives from people and objects outside the self.
A further distinction is made between cause and effect, as the
infant by stage 6 can infer one from the other, going either from
cause to effect or from effect to cause. Effectual parenting gives
due recognition to the child's own feelings and promotes his
capacity to differentiate between what he is feeling and desiring
from that which the parent feels and wishes. Blatt and Wild further
emphasize that schizophrenics have great difficulty in maintaining
a realistic time orientation. This is especially true of nonparanoid
schizophrenics. They lack an appropriate sense of sequencing and
of the relationship among past, present, and future. The origins of
a sense of time are to be found in the sensorimotor period, as
Piaget (1936/1971) has informed us. A primitive sense of time
is related at first to the infant's own subjectivity in terms of its
efforts, satisfaction, and expectations. By the end of the sensorimotor period, the infant's time sense has become spatialized and
objectified. The development of a sense of objective duration,
of the relationship among past, present, and future, is inseparable
from isomorphic developments in the spheres of causality, object
permanence, and space.

Anthony (1956) cites his observations bearing on the sensorimotor roots of childhood psychosis. He tells of a severely disturbed
child, mute and vegetative, who attempts to pick up pictures
of food that appear in a journal. The effort is a serious one and
the child exhibits frustration at his failure. Yet when the page is
turned, thereby concealing the illustrations, he does not attempt to
restore the previous situation. He obviously has an inadequate
sense of the continued existence of the "food." In a similar
observation, the child is playing aimlessly with two objects. The
first two objects are removed and replaced by two other objects,
with the identical activity persisting. When one of the second
pair of objects is surreptitiously removed, the child evidences
no sense of loss. He initiates no effort to seek the missing

object. It is as if it had never existed. In still another observation the child, in a state of hunger, eagerly moved toward a piece of candy he spots on a table. Before he can reach it, however, a cloth is thrown over it so that it is no longer visible. Once the candy is out of sight he immediately stops moving in that direction and begins another activity. To test whether he was possibly inhibited from removing the cloth in the presence of the observer, he is left alone. Despite this, he makes no attempt to obtain the candy. In another situation, twelve pieces of candy are separately placed under twelve corresponding cups. As each cup is removed by the observer, the child will take the candy. He makes no attempt himself, however, to remove a cup. There appears to be no inference that the remaininig cups may conceal a piece of candy. The impairment of object permanence and the ability to anticipate is clear in these examples. Confusion between what constitutes a two dimensional image and a real object is also apparent. Anthony emphasizes that while there were varying degrees of a poor object concept among the psychotic children he observed, they were all rooted to the sensorimotor level. Bettelheim (1967) observes that the autistic child is well-known for his persistent efforts to keep the environment the same. Perhaps, Bettelheim urges, the autistic child has faulty object permanence development and is striving to achieve a level of constancy in the external world to compensate for his inability to maintain images internally. In fact, it does seem that objects exist for the autistic child only when visually perceived or found in customary surroundings. The infant at stage 4 equates the object with a place. Once having located it at a particular place, he will look for it there again, even if he has seen it displaced to another location. Bettelheim stresses that the autistic child must always have his familiar objects in the same location, as if "place" were a part of its definition and permanence. By insisting on constancy as he knows it, the autistic child is assuring his own security. Bettelheim (1967) cogently comments, "Through his insistence on sameness the autistic child makes his most immediate surroundings a bit predictable, but without any comprehension or belief in the permanence of objects. This eliminates the need to understand the nature of the object. If the object is an Object-in-a-certain-place I need not know its intrinsic nature to predict the vagaries of existence" (p. 449). He suggests that normally a child will have a wish for the mother to return when she is out of sight and that this wish eventually gives rise to the image which sustains him in her absence. The development of person permanence in this manner will soon extend to less significant objects in the environment. However, for the autistic child the mother does not generate secure feelings and is a threat. Therefore, he does not possess a wish for her to return when she is absent for he is actually better off without her. There then exists no basis for the image to be constructed in the autistic child and he, consequently, lacks object permanence. Central to Bettelheim's view is that the autistic child refuses to interact normally with the environment, to assimilate and accommodate to it, because he finds it destructive in the form of his mother. Further, the child fails to interact beyond the sensorimotor period with others in the environment and, therefore, lacks the experience of testing out his perceptions and cognitions against those whose view of reality differs. Changes does not occur. Development is impeded.

Freeman and McGhie (1957) have also reported from their studies of chronic and deteriorated schizophrenic patients that the psychopathology observed can largely be understood as an expression of flawed sensorimotor development. They have made observations of hebaphrenic adult patients who exhibit object concept development at the level of a very young infant. In the case of one patient, he would often ask for cigarettes, but whenever one would drop from his line of vision he made no attempt to retrieve it. Yet he had a strong desire for cigarettes, which were the only environmental objects he showed an interest in. If he placed a lighted cigarette off to the side on a table, he would request another shortly, but never think to go back to the original one. Freeman and McGhie state succinctly, "It appeared to us that, like the infant, once the object passed out of his immediate perceptual field it had disappeared" (p. 182). They note that the other behavior of chronic schizophrenic patients reflects activity similar to the primary and secondary circular reactions of the infant. It is the aspects of not having a goal in mind at the outset and of being influenced by chance happenings by which Piaget characterized primary and secondary circular reactions that seem to also describe much of the behavior of patients observed by Freeman and McGhie. They further report that many of their chronic schizophrenic patients do not clearly distinguish ear, mouth, and eye. The authors relate this to an early stage in the development of imitative capacities, in which Piaget (1946/1962) points out that the infant can only imitate with parts of his body which he can see.

There appears to be ample basis for acknowledging that the construction of reality by the child during the sensorimotor period serves as a foundation for normal adaptation to the environment. Impaired development in structures of space, time, causality, object concept, and person permanence can result in poor boundary differentiations and the painfully chaotic world in which the schizophrenic is so often found to live.

E. J. ANTHONY ON PSYCHOPATHOLOGY AND CHILDREN

A pioneering attempt, possibly the best available, to extend Piaget's system to a clinical understanding of children has been made by Anthony (1956). He characterizes Piaget's developmental psychology as an ego psychology dealing, as it does, with the conflict-free sphere. Although establishing the fact that for Piaget cognition and affect are indissociable, Anthony suggests that the ego-ideal of the system might well be considered the "logical machine." The adaptive processes of assimilation and accommodation are presented as the dynamic structure of the system. An imbalance of these functions, in which assimilation predominates could lead to fantasy, egocentrism, and autism. To the contrary, excessive accommodation could lead to undue lability with an ever-changing personality, always seeking to conform to something outside the self.

Anthony highlights the similarity between the syncretistic thinking of the preoperational child and the paranoid psychotic.

Syncretistic thought fuses unrelated elements and subscribes to causal forces that are nonexistent. Connections and relationships are seen when only chance occurrences are operating. The tendency for transductive thinking, in which elements tend to be equated on the basis of predicates has also been found in both children and schizophrenics. For example, if an avocado, which is green, is ripe, then a banana, which is green, must be ripe. The accidental attribute of green signifies an equation of ripeness in both foods. Transductive reasoning is especially prevalent just after the sensorimotor period and is a preconceptual phase which is conducive to syncretic thought, as it permits unrelated thoughts to be fused.

Anthony identifies the concept of immanent justice as one which persists longer and has greater intensity among subgroups of children. Immanent justice is the belief found among pre-operational children that wrongdoing may be automatically punished by external forces inherent in nature. Children with phobias of paranoid content are especially vulnerable to this expectation, as are disturbed children who have difficulties with masturbation. One may also speculate that the paranoid expectations of some adults could be based on the persistence of the immanent justice notion, so that they expect retaliation from nature for a "sinful" deed or thought.

Animism is a powerful turn of thought in the young child's development and Anthony suggests that for a time it protects him from facing the fact of death. The endowment of all things with at least potential life is characteristic of the very young child. As development progresses he gradually constricts the range of types of objects to which he is willing to ascribe life or its properties. Unclear at first about the nature of death, the child abandons animistic thinking at about ten or eleven years of age and this sets the groundwork for a new kind of fear. The younger child, of course, is vulnerable to fearfulness of objects in his environment because he has unrealistically endowed them with life. The present author, for example, is familiar with a young child who was terrified when in the presence of a loudly functioning old-fashioned vacuum cleaner. Given a dash of animism and a bit of imagination, the vacuum cleaner has all the makings of a first rate monster. Anthony believes that animism is largely responsible for many of the fears and fantasies of the child under seven years, whereas afterward the anxieties expressed seem to derive more from the social arena. In normal young children, Anthony's studies show, animism generally becomes prominent at night. The dream or nightmare is the bearer of many of these fantasies. It should be remembered that the preoperational child's thought is characterized by realism, in which psychic events are accorded external, substantial existence. Therefore, if in a dream the child may be prone to imbue an inanimate object with life, which might render it fearful, the child genuinely believes that it exists within the room and not in his head. Psychotic children were found by Anthony to show extensive animism in which objects such as the moon, lights, and shadows become feared. Clinically, Anthony has found that interpretations offering intellectual explanations are not useful if the child's fears derive from animism. The reader should not conclude from this discussion that fear responses are intrinsic to animism. Innumerable examples to the contrary can be cited. In one entertaining protocol, Piaget tells of a child observing a twisted string unwinding with a weight at the bottom. The child remarks that the string knows it is twisted and is deliberately unwinding itself.

Anthony dwells little upon the more logical and formalized components of Piaget's system. He does urge, however, that a systematic and penetrating developmental diagnosis of children's reasoning is useful, especially with those suffering from learning disabilities. He comments in closing, "Within the new discipline of *genetic epistemology* one must look more closely at the whole process of the acquisition of ideas. It is not sufficient to understand the dynamics of feeling; we must also understand the genetics of thinking, after which we may claim with greater truth that we really understand our patients" (Anthony 1956, p. 34).

DECENTERING AND THE FEFFER MODEL

The interpersonal model advanced by Feffer has been extended by him to account for symptoms in psychopathological behavior. Feffer (1967) contends that, when sequential decentering pre-

vails over simultaneous decentering, such characteristic manifestations of symptoms as "isolation, exaggeration, and fluctuation"
will be evident. Sequential decentering offers only a partial
correction of distortion, while simultaneous decentering provides
complete correction of distortion. An example of this is seen in
the Piagetian classification problem in which there are twelve
wooden beads, ten of which are brown and two of which are
white. The preoperational child can center on the total class and
know that there are twelve wooden beads. He can also center
on the two subclasses and know that there are more brown beads
than white beads. However, when asked if there are more brown
beads or more wooden beads, he cannot coordinate the decentration,
simultaneously taking into account the relationship between part
and whole, even though he has been able to shift sequentially
from whole class to subclass. Instead, he centers on the perceptually salient aspect of the brown beads and claims that there
are more of them than wooden beads. Feffer believes that the
same cognitive limitation inherent in this problem involving
physical materials can also be applied to the interpersonal world
to explain symptom behavior. The essence of this primitive form
of cognition is that aspects of a reality are viewed in isolation,
sequentially in time, without any reciprocal interaction coordinating the various aspects. Feffer, drawing upon a passage
from Bleuler (1951), suggests that a lack of simultaneous coordination between means and end in striving to attain a goal
would be indicative of immature cognitive functioning and isolating
the two so that neither can reciprocally modify the other leads to
dysfunctional behavior. In the interpersonal realm, an individual
can modify his own anticipated behavior by first taking the role
of the other and assessing how that behavior would be reacted to
by the other if carried out. Feffer, in analyzing a passage from
Cameron (1951) attempts to further extend the decentering
principle to symptom expression. He illustrates this by citing
delusional thinking in which the schizophrenic patient imagines
himself being the recipient of a hostile aggressor. In this hypothetical situation the patient is virtually assuming two roles in
fantasy, those of the hostile aggressor and of the victim. Whereas

in adaptive interpersonal relations the individual can view himself subjectively from his perspective and objectively from the perspective of the other, the delusional thinker isolates the various perspectives of victim and aggressor. This is true, even though both roles, those of victim and aggressor, are contained within the same person. The roles take on an exaggerated character because the isolation precludes modification or correction of distortion. The delusional person fluctuates between the two roles, never coordinating them through simultaneous decentering. The key to this condition is that the hostile role is one that is ego-alien and consequently externalized by projection. The patient must defensively isolate himself from it. Defensive isolation from role-carrying attributes that are ego dystonic has been studied at greater length by Lowenherz and Feffer (1969) in an ingenious experiment utilizing the Role Taking Test and Thematic Apperception Test. A comparison was made of cognitive levels, based on decentering capacity, between subjects' ability to role take in situations involving defensively isolated attributes as opposed to nonisolated attributes. It was found that when subjects were required to take the role of characters who had attributes which were not ego syntonic to them, the subjects tended toward sequential decentering. Contrary to this, subjects role-taking in situations where the attributes of the other were ego syntonic tended toward simultaneous decentering. Specifically, where defensive isolation was not involved, a subject could invoke an internal orientation in describing one character of the story and coordinate this with an external orientation of another character. For example, the subject assuming the role of a wife in the story may describe her as angry because her husband came home late that evening and consequently the dinner was burned; while the same subject may, in assuming the role of the husband, describe him as realizing his wife is angry, but feeling he had no choice because of an emergency situation that developed at work at the last minute. In cases of defensive isolation, however, there was a higher incidence of responses favoring simple refocusing, in which the subject goes from the viewpoint of one character to the other's without preserving continuity or consistency. Hence, in the example cited, the subject may describe the wife as angry when assuming that character's role, and when assuming the husband's role may describe him as viewing his wife as pleased. There is clearly no coordination between the internal and external perspective of the wife's behavior.

Feffer (1967) suggests that the notion of primitive decentering may also be applied to impulse and control behavior in the neurotic. An example may be an exaggerated impulse toward destructive or aggressive behavior which is countered by an equally exaggerated defense of reaction formation in which the neurotic adopts an excessively sweet and kindly attitude. Feffer cites the well-known example of the exaggerated impulse to soil, which is countered by an excessive control mechanism and cleanliness. In commenting generally on this phenomenon, he states simply, "The impulse and control are clearly separated: rather than serving to modulate each other, they are expressed as fluctuating polarities . . ." (p. 24). Regardless of the etiology of the problem, it is the isolation precluding reciprocal modulation which is central to Feffer's position. Feffer seems willing to accept that the motivation to avoid anxiety stimulates defensive measures, but he holds that it is not the avoidance of anxiety which accounts for the exaggerated and fluctuating manifestations of symptomatology. Rather, it is the isolation of the subsystems which produces the symptom expression.

Feffer believes strongly that his formulation holds promise for bridging the gap between Piaget's essentially impersonal application of cognitive structures and his own interest in applying cognitive development to the interpersonal sphere. The concept of decentration is admirably suited to serve as a foundation for the bridge, as it is structurally isomorphic between physical and social domains. In an attempt to pursue that promise further, Suchotliff (1970) set out to discover whether the same construct, decentration, can contribute to an understanding of the schizophrenic's cognitive impairment in both social and nonsocial contexts. It was hypothesized that the forty schizophrenic patients would perform less adequately because of an apparent deficiency in decentering skills than a control group of twenty normal subjects. It was further hypothesized that, within the patient population, there would be a positive correlation between the low scores anticipated on both the socially oriented and the non-socially oriented tasks. In other words, schizophrenics would be deficient in decentering when compared to normals and the deficiency would constitute a formal property of their thought in all cognitive domains, whether social or nonsocial. The social task involved communication in which a subject had to select a word from a list which would offer the recipient an associative cue to a target word which the donor knew, but the recipient did not. The donor had to use the feedback from the recipient in order to make more effective selections of clue words on sub-sequent trials. Basically the task required that the donor decenter in order to simultaneously take into account the referent or target word, the clue word, and the feedback. By isolating these elements and focusing on only one of them, the subject would minimize his chances for effective communication. The schizo-phrenic patients did not adequately take into account differential feedback. They responded to feedback as if they were taking an individual word association test, reports Suchotliff, simply ignoring the referent word itself. In general, the hypotheses tested were confirmed. Decentering impairment cut across the communica-tion and nonsocial tasks in the schizophrenic group, which in turn could not come up to the decentering competence demonstrated in the performance of the control group. Suchotliff's findings would seem to support Feffer's conviction about the vital importance of decentering in both personal and impersonal realms.

THE GENEVA SCHOOL

There has been a flurry of research activity over the last fifteen years emanating directly from the Geneva School in Switzerland. Inhelder (1943/1968) has spearheaded this break-through with the publication of a major volume on retardation. Very little of what has been done, however, has yet been reported in English and as far as this author can ascertain, what has been studied is in a stage remote from any state of synthesis. What

appears in this section represents merely a fleeting acquaintance
with what, it is hoped, will eventually emerge as a comprehensive
presentation of the Geneva School's findings on cognitive-
developmental psychopathology. Much of the research (Inhelder
1966, 1971; Schmid-Kitsikis 1973) has been conducted through a
collaborative effort with the staff of the Geneva University
Psychiatric Clinic. Investigations have covered not only the
mentally retarded, but also psychotic, dysphasic, and dyspraxic
children. In addition, congenitally blind children were compared
with those who were blinded four years or more after birth.
Senile dementia and adult schizophrenia have been studied as well.
Material in this section will be devoted exclusively to observations on the psychotic child.

Inhelder (1971) has described the results of studies conducted
with a group of psychotic boys, ranging in age between ten to
fifteen years, who had been in some form of treatment for
approximately ten years. Types of tasks utilized tested the children
on classification, conservation, and chance. A cognitive diagnosis
placed the children along a continuum from a beginning stage
of concrete operations through a transitional phase to formal
operations. The sample contained a small subgroup whose members
seemed to be characterized by an integrated thought structure and
who did not fall below expected developmental level for their
age. The vast majority of the subjects, however, had incompletely
integrated and unstable structures. In all cases subjects could not
deal with tasks involving chance phenomena, the solutions to
which would have required invoking probabilistic thinking. The
children with integrated thought structures were insistent that
causal laws were operative and when they could not adequately
explain what was happening through those laws, they shied away
from the problem. Inhelder's main point is that these particular
children possess the necessary operations to resolve tasks involving
chance, but that this is their characteristic reaction when confronted with stark uncertainty. The bulk of the children, those
with only partially integrated structures, fall back upon invoking
magical explanations. Those who do not do so suggest that they
have been deceived by the experimenter. Generally in normal

development, it is the preoperational child who has no grasp of the differentiation between chance and nonchance. As Flavell (1963) points out, "Nothing is deductively certain and nothing is genuinely fortuitous for him; his thought is forever at midstream between these poles" (p. 342). The concrete operational child recognizes the differentiation between chance events and those determined by necessary causality, but cannot adequately bring to bear his rationality upon chance factors. It is at the time of formal operations when the adolescent develops operations of combinatorial analysis and proportionality that he can resolve chance problems. Flavell (1963) cites a simple task of this sort at which only the adolescent excels as entailing the prediction of the distribution of twenty pairs of marbles drawn randomly from a bag in which there are twenty red and twenty blue marbles. What are the probabilities of obtaining more homogenous pairs of one color or the other, or of obtaining more mixed pairs? Inhelder reports further that the psychotic children with only impartially integrated structures did not perform as well in conservation of matter tasks as they did with those pertaining to logical inclusion. Such a décalage or lag in development is not generally found among normal populations. Also, the psychotic children seemed to revert back to nonconservation responses even after a time when it appeared, somewhat deceptively, that the ability to conserve had become crystallized. It is most unusual for this to occur normally, as logical certitude and stability are major criteria of genuine development. It is also noteworthy that psychotic children who seemed stabilized in their conservation responses relied almost exclusively on reasoning involving identity explanations. Inversion responses were rare occurrences and compensatory responses were never introduced.

The last major type of deficiency discussed by Inhelder is that of the psychotic child's inability to make an imaginative assumption which is socially shared. Granted that a child has a rich fantasy life, for the psychotic child it is encapsulated in his private world. To share a pretended experience with another is a social act which he has little capacity for. Inhelder believes that sharing a make-believe world involves the symbolic function, that is, the ability to differentiate between signified and signifier. However, it is precisely the ability to distinguish between reality and the symbol which represents it, which is impaired in the psychotic child.

In summary, Inhelder suggests that a study of radically psychotic children can promote illumination of normal development and, conversely, a knowledge of normalcy in cognitive development will shed light on pathological mechanisms and structures.

Elsa Schmid-Kitsikis (1973) has made a contribution to the understanding of psychotic children's thought mechanisms by analyzing the self-regulating or equilibrating process among them. Her sample was of fifty psychotic youngsters ranging from seven to twelve years of age, who were administered conservation, classification, and relation tasks.

A striking aspect of the psychotic child's reasoning is the co-existence of preoperational and operational responses to a variety of conservation tasks. These responses may be detected in sequential statements which contradict one another or they could actually be built into a single statement. Schmid-Kitsikis indicates that, in dealing with conservation of weight, some subjects have been observed saying, "It's the same weight; it's thinner than the other so it weighs less." There is no apparent awareness of the contradiction inherent in the responses of these subjects and the oscillation between the two levels of reasoning does not eventuate in a more stable equilibrium of operational explanations. She further observes that these children tended to seek homogeneity of the experimental materials. For example, after one of two balls of clay had been made into a sausage during a conservation of weight task, the children would often seek to have the remaining ball transformed into a sausage so that identically shaped elements could be compared. Schmid-Kitsikis cites a further example of this propensity to duplicate the model in a different type of task and she stresses that when the children are not permitted to do as they wish in this area they become disturbed and often cannot succeed at performing the task. Still another tendency is the resistance to predicting the outcome, but instead insisting on the task being executed first in order that they may observe the results before commenting. In other words, in a conservation of weight task, for example, the psychotic child will frequently request that the two items simply be weighed, rather than anticipate which would weigh more if they were to be weighed. Schmid-Kitsikis sees in this an inclination toward avoiding conflict, as is also manifest in the children's observable attempts to alter the experimental conditions so that there is conformity to concrete reality as they imagine it. In characterizing the behavior of the psychotic children when facing the various Piagetian tasks, Schmid-Kitsikis (1973) states, "Thus it would be possible to interpret the basic avoidance and reality transformation mechanisms as a fundamentally affective need for non-contradiction by annulment of too obvious conflicts, which would lead to a more reasoning state" (p. 704).

AFFECTIVE REALISM

Odier (1956) has made one of the earliest attempts at an extensive application of the Piagetian system to the field of psychopathology. He had been a psychiatrist and psychoanalyst of French-Swiss background, whose untimely death prevented his work from reaching its final stage of evolution. Nevertheless, some of the speculative formulations introduced in his book will be presented below.

The concept of objective relativism, borrowed from Piaget, is seen as central to the psychoneurotic's thought pattern. The neurotic has not achieved objective relativism to the degree that the normal adult has and, therefore, his thought is characterized by three basic limitations. One of these is his tendency to accord objective and external existence to some of his own private psychic events. Another is his propensity to make absolute his own viewpoint, failing to recognize that any other could exist. The third limitation is to imbue an absolute existence to aspects of reality which actually exist only by virtue of their relational nature or the perspective from which they are seen. In brief, the neurotic negates objectivity, reciprocity, and relativity in some areas of his thinking. This state is predicated upon infantile realism and Odier (1956) comments upon it as follows, "The existence of several possibilities creates the necessity for hypotheses and a respect for objective proof, but infantile realism is by nature the enemy of hypotheses and experimentation as well as of relativity of thought" (p. 18).

Although Piaget's concept of realism emphasized intellectual aspects, such as reasoning and judgment, Odier stresses that the same principle can extend to the affective realm, covering needs, instincts, and feelings. In fact, he contends that affective realism lasts longer than intellectual realism and is an even more clear exemplar of adualism, the inability to differentiate between internal and external. The reader, of course, will immediately recognize the term adualism as synonymous with egocentrism. The main point is that even well-educated and intelligent adults, who have surmounted intellectual realism, may continue to be characterized by affective realism and the attendant immaturity that would go along with it. The decline of affective realism leads to a sense of internal security, self-value, and autonomy or independence. These three achievements signify a dualism or de-centration in the psychic organization. Together they comprise the ego functions, in Odier's framework, and working in harmony they produce a sense of "ego well-being." Disharmony among these three spheres is responsible for the individual suffering a sense of inadequacy and inferiority. The neurosis in Odier's view is not a new experience for the person, but a reexperience of affective realism. The distinction between intellectual realism and affective realism is central to the position Odier (1956) is expositing. He states, "As we know, adolescents become familiar first and most easily with the principles and laws of intellectual logic. The logic of interpersonal relationships, the necessity of applying this logic to family and social life, may escape them for a long time . . . the resulting lag remains the specific feature of many adult neuroses" (p. 29).

Odier's book contains many highways and byways. We will travel only one of them in the remainder of this section, however, hoping that perhaps the reader will wish to travel further on his own at some later time. The "neurosis of abandonment" is one to which Odier devotes lengthy consideration. An abandonee is a person who, although he has not usually experienced real abandonment, suffers from a subjective feeling of having been abandoned in a relationship with another person. Abandonism is in direct proportion to an internal sense of insecurity. The abandonee fears most of all that he will be rejected. Any omission of overt attention on the part of the other is interpreted as a lack of love by the abandonee. His fear in fact generates imagined rejections. He requires the certitude that he is loved in order to achieve or maintain any semblance of security. The obsessive thoughts of abandonment lead to many undesirable interpersonal dynamics ranging from obsequiousness in order not to lose the other person to alienating the other by imputing to him motives of wishing to abandon. Odier goes into some detail to demonstrate that while the abandonee desires only security, his neurosis precipitates constant crises and conflicts in relationship with a spiraling effect of intensified insecurity. We will focus on one aspect of the problem here.

A characteristic line of reasoning pursued by the abandonee reveals the egocentric nature of it. A woman feels that since the man with whom she is involved does not have the kind of consideration for her that she expects, he cannot possibly love her any longer. A man who has not received a desired telephone call concludes that the woman from whom he expects it is detached. Another man reasons that the woman with whom he is involved did not come to visit him even though she knew he would be at home; therefore, he is now unimportant to her. In still another instance, the woman deduces that since the man forgot her birthday, he must be angry at her. Finally, a woman observed that the man was pleased when they were last together, but seemed displeased when he returned; therefore, she reasons that he is going to terminate the relationship. The general description of what is taking place is worth quoting at length.

> Clearly the needs and demands, desires and fears of S are expected to magically dictate O's thoughts, words and acts. O has to partake in the affective life of S; this intimate participation

arising intuitively between the two is the fundamental cause for
their relationship. If S has a desire, O has to have it too. He must
love or dislike the same things and the same people. Difference
is confused with disagreement and the latter with disunion. Everything that threatens this participation produces a sudden decrease
in S's feelings of value and security (Odier 1956, p. 226).

The three principles undergirding this type of egocentric
reasoning pivot around the lack of objectivity, relativity, and
reciprocity. The abandonee does not inquire into the objective
reasons behind the other person's behavior. Difference or disagreement not being countenanced, the abandonee simply abso-
lutizes his own conviction that he is in some way being abandoned.
Further, his own needs and feelings are not seen as relative to
another's in the relationship, hence there is no realization that
there must be mutual regulation and adjustment between the two
participants. Finally, the abandonee's own affectivity impedes
him from taking the role of the other. The partner to the abandonee
is not permitted to act either spontaneously or independently without being accused of indifference and unfaithfulness. In brief, the
partner must fuse his emotions in conformity with those of the
abandonee, a restraint having been placed on the differentiation of
feelings. Odier believes that the mature choice of an appropriate
partner proceeds from self-esteem and security. The abandonee
reverses this process and hopes to achieve these attributes as end
products of the relationship. Unfortunately, however, the developmental presence of affective realism, which prevents objective
relativism in the emotional domain, does not allow this painfully
sought goal to be obtained.

CONCLUSION

There has been a décalage, undoubtedly, between Piaget's
study of normal cognitive development and similar attempts at
acquiring knowledge of cognitive-developmental psychopathology.
The content of this chapter remains to be assimilated and ac-
commodated by the complex structure that, it is hoped, will someday
be constructed through integrating psychoanalysis with the work

of the Geneva School. Of course, what is contained in this chapter is merely a springboard to much more theorizing and research activity which remains to be carried out. In closing, two basic notions will be reemphasized. The first is that, in view of Piaget's contention regarding the indissociability of affect and cognition, neither normal nor pathological development can be adequately understood by centering on only one of these components. There should be no allowance made for an egocentric partisanism which insists on absolutizing one to the exclusion of the other. The second is the notion attributed earlier to Inhelder, that a better understanding of psychopathology will enhance our understanding of normalcy and that, reciprocally, the reverse is also true.

REFERENCES

Alvy, K. T. Relation of age to children's egocentric and co-operative communications. *Journal of Genetic Psychology,* 1968, 112, 275-286.

————. The development of listener adapted communication in grade-school children from different social-class backgrounds. *Genetic Psychology Monographs,* 1973, 87, 33-104.

Anthony, E. J. The significance of Jean Piaget for child psychiatry. *British Journal of Medical Psychology,* 1956, 29, 20-34.

————. The system makers: Piaget and Freud. *British Journal of Medical Psychology,* 1957, 30, 255-269.

Arieti, S. *Interpretation of Schizophrenia.* New York: Robert Brunner, 1955.

Armsby, R. E. A reexamination of the moral judgments in children. *Child Development,* 1971, 42, 1241-1248.

Barnes, E. Punishment as seen by children. *Pediatric Seminar,* 1894, 3, 235-45.

————. Growth of social judgment. *Studies in Education,* 1902, 2, 203-17.

Bearison, D. J. and Cassel, T. Z. Cognitive decentration and social codes: communicative effectiveness in young children from differing family contexts. *Developmental Psychology,* 1975, 11, 29-36.

Bell, S. M. The development of the concept of object as related to infant-mother attachment. *Child Development,* 1970, 41, 292-311.

Bernstein, B. Some sociological determinants of perception. *British Journal of Sociology,* 1958, 9, 159-174.

————. A public language. *British Journal of Sociology,* 1959, 10, 311-326.

————. Elaborated and restricted codes: An outline. *Sociological Inquiry,* 1966, Spring, 254-261.

References   285

————. A sociolinguistic approach to socialization with some reference to educability. In J. Grumperez and D. Hymes (Eds.), *Directions in Sociolinguistics*. New York: Holt, Rhinehart, and Winston, 1972.

Bettelheim, B. *The Empty Fortress*. New York: The Free Press, 1967.

Blatt, S. J. Levels of object representation in anaclitic and introjective depression. *Psychoanalytic Study of the Child*, 1974, 29, 107-157.

————— and Wild, C. M. *Schizophrenia: A Developmental Analysis*. New York: Academic Press, 1976.

Bleuler, E. The basic symptoms of schizophrenia. In D. Rapaport (Ed.) *Organization and pathology of thought*. New York: Columbia University Press, 1951, 581-649.

Bloom, L. *Language Development: Form and Function in Emerging Grammars*. Cambridge, Mass.: MIT Press, 1970.

————. *One Word at a Time: The Use of Single-word Utterances Before Syntax*. The Hague: Mouton, 1973.

Borke, H. Interpersonal perception of young children: Egocentrism or empathy? *Developmental Psychology*, 1971, 5, 263-269.

————. Chandler and Greenspan's "Ersatz Egocentrism": A rejoinder. *Developmental Psychology*, 1972, 7, 107-109.

————. Piaget's Mountains Revisited: Changes in the Egocentric Landscape. *Developmental Psychology*, 1975, 240-243.

Boszormenyi-Nagy, I. and Sparks, G. N. *Invisible Loyalties: Reciprocity in Intergenerational Family Therapy*. New York: Harper & Row, 1973.

Boyle, D. G. *A Student's Guide to Piaget*. New York: Pergamon Press, 1969.

Brainerd, C. J. and Hooper, F. H. A methodological analysis of developmental studies of identity and conservation and equivalence conservation. *Psychological Bulletin*, 1975, 82, 725-737.

Breger, L. *From Instinct to Identity: The Development of Personality*. Englewood Cliffs, N.J.: Prentice-Hall, 1974.

Brodzinsky, D. M. and Jackson, J. P. Effects of stimulus complexity and perceptual shielding in the development of spatial perspectives. Paper presented at the meeting of the Society for Research in Child Development, Philadelphia, 1973.

————, ———— and Overton, W.F. Effects of perpetual shielding in the development of spatial perspectives. *Child Development,* 1972, 1041-1046.

Brossard, M. D. The infant's conception of object permanence and his reactions to strangers. In T. G. Décarie (Ed.) *The Infant's Reaction to Strangers.* New York: International Universities Press, 1974.

Bruner, J. S. The course of cognitive growth. *American Psychologist,* 1964, 19, 1-15.

Byrne, D. Role-taking in adolescence and adulthood. Unpublished doctoral dissertation. Harvard University, 1975.

Cameron, N. Reasoning, regression and communicatoin in schizophrenia. *Psychological Monograph,* 1938, 50, 1-34.

————. Deterioration and regression in schizophrenic thinking. *Journal Abnormal Social Psychology,* 1939, 34, 265-270.

————. Schizophrenic thinking in a problem-solving situation. *Journal Mental Science,* 1939, 1012-1035.

————. Experimental analysis of schizophrenic thinking. In J. Kasamin (Ed.) *Language and Thought in Schizophrenia.* Berkeley, Calif.: University of California Press, 1944.

————. Perceptual organization and behavior pathology. In R. R. Blake and G. V Ramsey (Eds.) *Perception, an Approach to Personality.* New York: Ronald Press, 1951.

Chandler, M. J. Egocentrism in normal and pathological childhood development. In F. J. Monks, W. W. Hartup, and J. D. Wit (Ed.) *Determinants of Behavioral Development.* New York: Academic Press, 1972.

———— and Greenspan, S. Ersatz egocentrism: A reply to H. Borke. *Developmental Psychology,* 1972, 7, 104-106.

————, ———— and Barenboim, C. Assessment and training of role-taking and referential communication skills in institutionalized emotionally disturbed children. *Developmental Psychology,* 1974, 10, 546-553.

Chaplin, M. V. and Keller, H. R. Decentering and social interaction. *The Journal of Genetic Psychology,* 1974, 124, 269-275.

Charlesworth, W. R. and Zahn, C. Reaction time as a measure of the comprehension of the effects produced by rotation on objects. *Child Development,* 1966, 37, 253-268.

Clarke, J. The concept of "aliveness" in chronic schizophrenia, *British Journal of Medical Psychology,* 1969, 42, 59-66.

Clarke-Stewart, K. A. Interactions between mothers and their young school children: Characteristics and consequences. *Society of Research in Child Development Monograph,* 1973, 38.

Cohen, B. D. and Klein, J. F. Referential communication in school age children. *Child Development,* 1968, 39, 597-609.

Cromer, R. F. The development of language and cognition: the cognitive hypotheses. In B. Foss (Ed.) *New Perspectives in Child Development.* Baltimore: Penguin Books, 1974.

Dale, P. S. *Language Development: Structure and Function* (2nd ed.). New York: Holt, Rhinehart and Winston, 1976.

Décarie, T. G. *Intelligence and Affectivity in Early Childhood.* New York: International Universities Press, 1965.

————. *The Infant's Reaction to Strangers.* New York: International Universities Press, 1974.

Dodwell, P. C. Children's understanding of spatial concepts. *Canadian Journal of Psychology,* 1963, 17, 141-161.

Durkin, D. Children's concepts of justice: A comparison with the Piaget data. *Child Development,* 1959a, 30, 59-67.

————. Children's acceptance of reciprocity as a justice principle. *Child Development,* 1959b, 30, 289-296.

————. Children's concepts of justice: A further comparison with the Piaget data. *Journal Educational Research,* 1959c, 52, 252-257.

————. Sex differences in children's concepts of justice. *Child Development,* 1960, 31, 361-368.

————. The specificity of children's moral judgments. *Journal Genetic Psychology,* 1961, 98, 3-13.

Elkind, D. Piaget's conservation problems. *Child Development,* 1967, 38, 15-27.

_____. *Children and Adolescents: Interpretive Essays on Jean Piaget*. New York: Oxford University Press, 1974.

Escalona, S. K. *The Roots of Individuality*. Chicago: Aldine, 1968.

Evans, R. I. *Jean Piaget: The Man and His Ideas*. New York: E. P. Dutton and Co., Inc., 1973.

Feffer, M. H. The cognitive implications of role-taking behavior. *Journal of Personality*, 1959, 27, 152-167.

_____. Symptom expression as a form of primitive decentering. *Psychological Review*, 1967, 74, 16-28.

_____. Developmental analysis of interpersonal behavior. *Psychological Review*, 1970, 77, 197-214.

_____ and Gourevitch, V. Cognitive aspects of role-taking in children. *Journal of Personality*, 1960, 28, 384-396.

_____ and Suchotliff, L. Decentering implications of social interactions. *Journal of Personality and Social Psychology*, 1966, 4, 415-422.

Fishbein, H. D., Lewis, S. and Keiffer, K. Children's understanding of spatial relations: Co-ordination of perspectives. *Developmental Psychology*, 1972, 7, 21-33.

_____ and Osborne, M. The effects of feedback variations on referential communication of children. *Merrill Palmer Quarterly*, 1971, 17, 243-250.

Flavell, J. H. *The Developmental Psychology of Jean Piaget*. Princeton, N.J.: D. Van Nostrand Co., 1963.

_____. The development of inferences about others. In Mischel (Ed.) *Understanding Persons*. Great Britain: Basil Blackwell, 1974.

_____, Botkin, P. T., Fry, C. L., Wright, J. W., and Jarvis, P. E. *The Development of Role-Taking and Communication Skills in Children*. New York: John Wiley & Sons, 1968.

Fraiberg, S. Libidinal object constancy and mental representation. *Psychoanalytic Study of the Child*, 1969, 24, 9-47.

Freeman, T. and McGhie, A. The relevance of genetic psychology for the psychopathology of schizophrenia. *British Journal of Medical Psychology*, 1957, 30, 176-187.

Fry, C. L. Training children to communicate to listeners. *Child Development,* 1966, 37, 674-685.

————. Training children to communicate to listeners who have varying listener requirements. *Journal of Genetic Psychology,* 1969, 114, 153-166.

Furth, H. G. Research with the deaf: Implications for language and cognition. *Psychological Bulletin,* 1964, 62, 145-164.

————. *Thinking Without Language.* New York: The Free Press, 1966.

————. *Piaget and Knowledge,* Englewood Cliffs, N.J.: Prentice-Hall, 1969.

————. On Language and Knowing in Piaget's Developmental Theory. *Human Development,* 13, 1970, 241-257.

————. Linguistic deficiency and thinking: Research with deaf subjects 1964-1969. *Psychological Bulletin,* 1971, 74, 191-211.

————. *Deafness and Learning: A Psychosocial Process.* Belmont, Cal.: Wadsworth, 1973.

———— and Youniss, J. The influence of language and experience on discovery and use of logical symbols. *British Journal of Psychology,* 1965, 56, 381-390.

Gardner, H. *The Quest for Mind.* New York: Alfred A. Knopf, 1972.

Glucksberg, S. and Krauss, R. M. What do people say after they have learned how to talk? Studies of the development of referential communication. *Merrill Palmer Quarterly,* 1967, 13, 309-316.

————, ———— and Higgins, T. The development of communication skills in children. In F. Horowitz (Ed.) *Review of Child Development Research,* Vol. 4. Chicago: University of Chicago Press, 1975.

Goldman, R. J. *Religious Thinking from Childhood to Adolescence.* London: Routledge and Kegan Paul, 1964.

Goldschmid, M. L. Different types of conservation and non-conservation and their relation to age, sex, I.Q., M.A. and vocabulary. *Child Development,* 1967, 38, 1229-1246.

_____. The relation of conservation to emotional and environmental aspects of development. *Child Development,* 1968, 39, 579-589.

_____. The role of experience in the rate and sequence of cognitive development. In D. R. Green, M. P. Ford, and G. B. Flamer (Eds.) *Measurement and Piaget.* New York: McGraw-Hill, 1971.

Goldstein, K. The modification of behavior consequent to cerebral lesions. *Psychiatric Quarterly,* 1936, 10, 586-610.

_____. Methodological approach to the study of schizophrenic thought disorder. In J. S. Kasamin (ed.) *Language and Thought in Schizophrenia.* Berkeley: University of California Press, 1944.

_____. Concerning the concreteness in schizophrenia. *Journal Abnormal Social Psychology,* 1959, 59, 146-148.

Goulet, J. The infant's conception of causality and his reactions to strangers. In T. G. Décarie (Ed.) *The Infant's Reaction to Strangers.* New York: International Universities Press, 1974.

Graham, D. *Moral Learning and Development: Theory and Research.* New York: John Wiley & Sons, 1972.

Gruen, G. E. Note on conservation: Methodological and definitional considerations. *Child Development,* 1966, 37, 977-83.

Hall, V. C. and Kingsley, R. Conservation and equilibration theory. *Journal of Genetic Psychology,* 1968, 113, 195-213.

Hartmann, H. The mutual influences in the development of ego and id. *Essays on Ego Psychology.* New York: International Universities Press, 1964, 155-182.

Hess, R. E. and Shipman, V. C. Early experience and the socialization of cognitive modes in children. *Child Development,* 1965, 36, 869-886.

Hickey, J. Stimulation of moral reasoning in delinquents. Unpublished doctoral dissertation. Boston University, 1972.

Hoffman, M. L. Moral development. In P. H. Mussen (Ed.) *Carmichael's Manual of Child Psychology.* Vol. 2. New York: John Wiley and Sons, 1970.

Hollas, M. and Cowan, P. Social isolation and cognitive development: Logical operations and role-taking abilities in three Norwegian social settings. *Child Development,* 1973, 44, 630-641.

Inhelder, B. Cognitive development and its contribution to the diagnosis of some phenomena of mental deficiency. *Merrill-Palmer Quarterly,* 1966, 12, 299-321.

————. *The Diagnosis of Reasoning in the Mentally Retarded* (W. B. Stephens, et al, translators). New York: Chandler, 1968. (Originally published, 1943.)

————. Developmental theory and diagnostic procedures. In D. R. Green, M. P. Ford, G. B. Flamer (Eds.) *Measurement and Piaget.* New York: McGraw-Hill, 1971, 148-171.

———— and Piaget, J. *The Growth of Logical Thinking from Childhood to Adolescence.* (A. Parsons and S. Milgram, translators). New York: Basic Books, 1958. (Originally published, 1955.)

———— and ————. *The Early Growth of Logic in the Child.* (E. A. Lunzer and D. Papert, translators). New York: W. W. Norton & Co., 1969. (Originally published, 1959.)

———— and Sinclair, H. Learning cognitive structures. In P. H. Mussen, J. Langer, and M. Covington (Eds.) *Trends and Issues in Developmental Psychology.* New York: Holt, Rhinehart, and Winston, 1969.

————, ———— and Bovet, M. *Learning and the Development of Cognition* (S. Wedgwood, translator). Cambridge, Mass.: Harvard University Press, 1974. (Originally published, 1974.)

Jensen, L. and Rytting, M. Effects of information and relatedness on children's belief in immanent justice. *Developmental Psychology,* 1972, 7, 93-97.

Johnson, R. C. A study of children's moral judgments. *Child Development,* 1962, 33, 327-354.

————. Early studies of children's moral judgments. *Child Development,* 1962, 33, 603-605.

Kaplan, L. J. Object constancy in the light of Piaget's vertical décalage. *Bulletin of the Menninger Clinic,* 1972, 36, 322-334.

Kenniston, K. Student activism, moral development, and morality. *American Journal of Orthopsychiatry,* 1970, 40, 577-592.

Kilburg, R. R. and Siegel, A. W. Formal operations in reactive and process schizophrenics. In R. Cancro (Ed.) *Annual Review of the Schizophrenic Syndrome.* New York: Bruner/Mazel, 1976.

Kohlberg, L. Moral development and identification. In H. Stevenson (Ed.) *Child Psychology. 62nd yearbok of the National Society for the Study of Education.* Chicago: University of Chicago Press, 1963a, 277-332.

_____. The development of children's orientations toward a moral order. 1. Sequence in the development of moral thought. *Vita Humana,* 1963b, 6, 11-33.

_____. Stage and sequence: The cognitive developmental approach to socialization. In D. A. Goslin (Ed.) *Handbook of Socialization Theory and Research.* Chicago: Rand McNally, 1969.

_____. Early education: A cognitive developmental view. In Sears, P. S. (Ed.) *Intellectual Development.* N.Y.: John Wiley & Sons, 1971a. (Abridged and reprinted from *Child Development,* 1968, 39, 1013-1062.)

_____. From is to ought: How to commit the naturalistic fallacy and get way with it in the study of moral development. In L. Mischel, (Ed.) *Cognitive Development and Epistemology.* New York: Academic Press, 1971b.

_____. Stages of moral development as a basis for moral education. In C. M. Beck, B. S. Crittenden, and E. V. Sullivan (Eds.) *Moral Education.* New York: Lewman Press, 1971c.

_____. Continuities and discontinuities in childhood and adult moral development revisited. In Kohlberg, L. *Collected Papers On Moral Development and Moral Education.* Spring, 1973a.

_____. *Collected Papers on Moral Development and Moral Education.* 1973b.

_____ and Elfenbein, D. The development of moral judgments concerning capital punishment. *American Journal of Orthopsychiatry,* 1975, 45, 614-640.

_____ and Kramer R. Continuities and discontinuities in childhood and adult moral development. *Human Development,* 1969, 12, 93-120.

_____, Yaeger, J., and Hjertholm, E. Private speech: Four studies and a review of theories. *Child Development,* 1968, 39, 691-736.

Krauss, R. M. and Glucksberg, S. The development of communication: Competence as a function of age. *Child Development,* 1969, 40, 255-266.

Kurtines, W. and Grief, E. B. The development of moral thought: review and evaluation of Kohlberg's approach. *Psychological Bulletin,* 1974, 81, 453-470.

Langer, J. *Theories of Development.* New York: Holt, Rinehart and Winston, 1969.

Laurendeau, M. and Pinard, A. *The Development of the Concept of Space in the Child.* New York: International Universities Press, 1970.

Lee, L. C. The concomitant development of cognitive and moral modes of thought: A test of selected deductions from Piaget's theory. *Genetic Psychology Monographs,* 1971, 83, 93-146.

Lerner, S., Bie, I., and Lehrer, P. Concrete-operational thinking in mentally ill adolescents. *Merrill Palmer Quarterly,* 1972, 18, 287-291.

Lewis, M. M. *Language, Thought, and Personality.* New York: Basic Books, 1963.

Lickona, L. Piaget misunderstood: A critique of the criticisms of his theory of moral development. *Merrill Palmer Quarterly,* 1969, 15, 337-350.

Lidz, T. *The Origin and Treatment of Schizophrenic Disorders.* New York: Basic Books, 1973.

Loevinger, J. *Ego Development.* San Francisco: Jossey-Bass 1976.

Looft, W. R. Egocentrism and social interaction across the life span. *Psychological Bulletin,* 1972, 78, 73-92.

Lowenherz, L. and Feffer, M. Cognitive level as a function of defensive isolation. *Journal of Abnormal Psychology,* 1969, 74, 352-357.

Lunzer, E. S. Problems of formal reasoning in test situations. *Monographs of the Society for Research in Child Development,* 30 (Serial No. 100), 1965.

Maher, B. A. *Principles of Psychopathology.* New York: McGraw-Hill, 1966.

Mahler, M., Pine, F., and Bergman, A. *The Psychological Birth of the Child.* New York: Basic Books, 1975.

Masangkay, Z. S., McCluskey, K. A., McIntyre, C. W., Sims-Knight, J., Vaughan, B. E., and Flavell, J. H. The early development of inferences about the visual percepts of others. *Child Development,* 1974, 45, 357-366.

McKechnie, R. J. The influence of story structure and behavioral area on the moral judgment of the child. M.Sc. thesis, Leeds University, 1971.

————. Between Piaget's stages: A study in moral development. *British Journal of Educational Psychology,* 1971, 213-217.

Medinnus, G. R. Immanent justice in children: A review of the literature and additional data. *Journal of Genetic Psychology,* 1959, 94, 253-262.

Mehrabian, A. *An Analysis of Personality Theories.* Englewood Cliffs, N.J.: Prentice-Hall, 1968.

Miller, P. H., Kessel, F., and Flavell, J. H. Thinking about people thinking about people thinking about . . .: A study of social cognitive development. *Child Development,* 1970, 41, 613-623.

Miller, S. A. Extinction of conservation: A methodological and theoretical analysis. *Merrill Palmer Quarterly,* 1971, 17, 319-334.

Modgil, S. *Piagetian Research: A Handbook of Recent Studies.* New York: Humanities Press, 1974.

Neale, J. M. Egocentrism in institutionalized and noninstitutionalized children. *Child Development,* 1966, 37, 97-101.

Odier, C. *Anxiety and Magic Thinking.* New York: International Universities Press, 1956.

Otaala, B. *The Development of Operational Thinking in Primary School Children.* New York: Teacher's College Press, 1973.

Peill, E. J. *Invention and Discovery of Reality: The Acquisition of*

References 295

Conservation of Amount. New York: John Wiley & Sons, 1975.

Piaget, J. *The Language and Thought of the Child* (M. Gabain, translator). Cleveland: Meridian Books, 1955. (Originally published, 1923.)

————. *The Child's Conception of the World* (J. and A. Tomilson, translators). Totowa, N.J.: Littlefield, Adams & Co., 1960. (Originally published, 1926.)

————. The general problems of the psychobiological development of the child. In J. M. Tanner and B. Inhelder (Eds.) *Discussions on Child Development,* Vol. 4. *The Proceedings of the Fourth Meeting of the World Health Organization Study Group on the Psychobiological Development of the Child.* New York: International Universities Press, 1960.

————. *Play, Dreams, and Imitation in Childhood* (C. Gattegno and F. M. Hodgson, translators). New York: W. W. Norton & Co., 1962. (Originally published, 1946.)

————. *The Origins of Intelligence in the Child.* (M. Cook, translator). New York: W. W. Norton & Co., 1963. (Originally published, 1936.)

————. Development and learning. In R. E. Ripple, and V. N. Rockcastle (Eds.) *Piaget Rediscovered.* Ithaca, N.Y.: School of Education, Cornell University, 1964, 7-20.

————. The development of mental imagery. In R. E. Ripple and V. N. Rockcastle (Eds.) *Piaget Rediscovered.* Ithaca, N.Y.: School of Education, Cornell University, 1964, 21-32.

————. *The Moral Judgment of the Child.* (M. Gabain, translator). New York: The Free Press, 1965. (Originally published, 1932.)

————. *The Child's Conception of Number* (C. Gattegno and F. M. Hodgson, translators). New York. W. W. Norton & Co., 1965. (Originally published, 1941.)

————. *Psychology of Intelligence* (M. Piercy and D. E. Berlyne, translators). Totowa, N.J.: Littlefield, Adams & Co., 1966. (Originally published, 1947.)

————. *Six Psychological Studies* (A. Tenzer, translator). New York: Vintage Books, 1968. (Originally published, 1964.)

_____. *Judgment and Reasoning in the Child* (M. Warden, translator). Totowa, N.J.: Littlefield, Adams, & Co., 1969. (Originally published, 1924.)

_____. *The Child's Conception of Physical Causality* (M. Gabain, translator). Totowa, N.J.: Littlefield, Adams & Co., 1969. (Originally published, 1927.)

_____. *The Mechanisms of Perception*. New York: Basic Books, 1969. (Originally published, 1961.)

_____. *The Child's Conception of Time* (A. J. Pomerans, translator). New York: Ballantine, 1971. (Originally published, 1927.)

_____. *The Construction of Reality in the Child* (M. Cook, translator). New York: Ballantine, 1971. (Originally published, 1936.)

_____. *The Child's Conception of Movement and Speed* (G. E. T. Holloway and M. J. Mackenzie, translators). New York: Ballantine, 1971. (Originally published, 1946.)

_____. Intellectual evolution from adolescence to adulthood. *Human Development,* 1972, 15, 1-12.

_____. Affective unconscious and cognitive unconscious. In *The Child and Reality*. New York: Grossman Publishers, 1973.

_____. *Understanding Causality* (D. and M. Miles, translators). New York: W. W. Norton & Co., 1974. (Originally published, 1971.)

_____. In foreword of *Explorations in child psychiatry* (E. J. Anthony, Ed.) New York: Plenum, 1975.

_____. Autobiography. In (S. Campbell, Ed.) *Piaget Sampler.* New York: John Wiley & Sons, 1976, 115-147.

_____, and Inhelder, B. *Le Développement des Quantités Physiques Chez L'Enfant.* Neuchâtel: Delachaux et Niestlé, 1941.

_____, and _____. *The Child's Conception of Space* (F. J. Langdon and J. L. Lunzer, translators). New York: W. W. Norton & Co., 1967. (Originally published, 1948.)

_____, and _____. *The Psychology of the Child* (H. Weaver, translator). New York: Basic Books, 1969. (Originally published, 1966.)

————, and ————. *Mental Imagery in the Child* (P. A. Chilton, translator). New York: Basic Books, 1971. (Originally published, 1966).

————, and ————. *Memory and Intelligence* (A. J. Pomerans, translator). New York: Basic Books, 1973. (Originally published, 1968.)

————, ————. *The Origin of the Idea of Chance in Children.* (L. Leake, Jr., P. Burrell, and H. D. Fishbein, translators). New York: W. W. Norton & Co., 1975. (Originally published, 1951.)

————, ————, and Szeminska, A. *The Child's Conception of Geometry* (G. A. Lunzer, translator). New York: Harper & Row, 1960. (Originally published, 1948.)

Pimm, J. B. The clinical use of Piagetian tasks with emotionally disturbed children. In G. I. Lubin, J. F. Magary, M. K. Poulsen (Eds.) *Proceedings of the Fourth Annual U. A. P. Conference on Piagetian Theory and the Helping Professions.* Los Angeles, February, 1975, 199-213.

Pine, F. Libidinal object constancy: A theoretical note. In Goldberger and V. H. Rosen (Eds.) *Psychoanalysis and Contemporary Science,* Vol. 3. New York: International Universities Press, 1974, 307-313.

Pulaski, M. A. S. *Understanding Piaget.* New York: Harper & Row, 1971.

Rapaport, D. On the psychoanalytic theory of thinking. In R. R. Knight (Ed.) *Psychoanalytic Psychiatry and Psychology,* Vol. 1. New York: International Universities Press, 1954, 259-273.

Rawls, J. *A Theory of Justice.* Cambridge, Mass.: The Belknap Press of Harvard University Press, 1971.

Rosenberg, S. and Cohen, B. D. Referential processes of speakers and listeners. *Psychological Review,* 1966, 73, 208-231.

Rubin, K. H. Extinction of conservation: A life span investigation. *Developmental Psychology,* 1976, 12, 51-56.

———— and Schnider, F. W. The relationship between moral judgment, egocentrism, and altruistic behavior. *Child Development,* 1973, 44, 661-665.

Saint-Pierre, J. Etude des differences entre la recherche active

298 References

de la personne humaine et celle de l' object inanime. Master's dissertation, University of Montreal, 1962.

Salatas, H. and Flavell, J. H. Perspective taking: The development of two components of knowledge. *Child Development,* 1976, 47, 103-109.

Schallenberger, M. Children's rights. *Pediatric Seminar,* 1894, 3, 87-96.

Schmid-Kitsikis, E. Piagetian theory and its approach to psychopathology. *American Journal of Mental Deficiency,* 1973, 77, 694-705.

Selman, R. L. The relation of role-taking to the development of moral judgments in children. *Child Development,* 1971a, 42, 79-91.

————. Taking another's perspective: role-taking development in early childhood. *Child Development,* 1971b, 42, 1721-1734.

————. Social-cognitive understanding: A guide to educational and clinical practice. In T. Lickona (Ed.) *Moral Development and Behavior.* New York: Holt, Rinehart, & Winston, 1976, 299-316.

———— and Byrne, D. F. A structural-developmental analysis of levels of role-taking in middle childhood. *Child Development,* 1974, 45, 803-806.

Shantz, C. U. The development of social cognition. In E. M. Hetherington (Ed.) *Review of Child Development Research,* Vol. 5. Chicago: University of Chicago Press, 1975.

————, Asarnow, J, and Berkowitz, M. Situational and intellectual factors influencing perspective-taking performance in children. Paper read at the Southeast regional meeting of the Society for Research in Child Development, Chapel Hill, North Carolina, 1974.

———— and Watson, J. S. Assessment of spatial egocentrism through expectancy violation. *Psychonomic Science,* 1970, 18, 93-94.

———— and ————. Spatial abilities and spatial egocentrism in the young child. *Child Development,* 1971, 42, 171- 181.

_____ and Wilson, K. Training communication skills in young children. *Child Development,* 1972, 43, 693-698.

Shimkunas, A. M. Conceptual deficit in schizophrenia: A reappraisal. *British Journal of Medical Psychology,* 1972, 45, 149-157.

Sinclair, H. Piaget's theory and language acquisition. In M. F. Rossokopf, L. P. Steffe, and S. Taback (Eds.) *Cognitive-Developmental Research and Mathematical Education.* Washington, D.C.: National Council of Teachers of Mathematics, 1971.

Sinclair-de-Zwart, H. Developmental psycholinguistics. In D. Elkind and J. H. Flavell (Eds.) *Studies in Cognitive Development.* New York: Oxford University Press, 1969.

Smedslund, J. The acquisition of conservation of substance and weight in children. I Introduction. *Scandinavian Journal of Psychology,* 1961, 2, 11-20 (a).

_____. The acquisition of conservation of substance and weight in children. II External reinforcement of conservation of weight and of the operations of addition and subtraction. *Scandinavian Journal of Psychology,* 1961, 2, 71-84 (b).

_____. The acquisition of conservation of substance and weight in children. III Extinction of conservation of weight acquired "normally" and by means of empirical controls on a balance scale. *Scandinavian Journal of Psychology,* 1961, 2, 85-87 (c).

_____. The acquisition of conservation of substance and weight in children. IV An attempt at extinction of the visual components of the weight concept. *Scandinavian Journal of Psychology,* 1961, 2, 153-155 (d).

_____. The acquisition and conservation of substance and weight in children. V Practice in conflict situations without external reinforcement. *Scandinavian Journal of Psychology,* 1961, 2, 155-160 (e).

_____. The acquisition of conservation of substance and weight in children. VI Practice on continuous versus discontinuous material in conflict situations without external reinforcement. *Scandinavian Journal of Psychology,* 1961, 2, 203-210 (f).

_____. Concrete reasoning a study of intellectual development. *Monograph social research child development,* 1964, 29.

Spitz, R. A. *No and Yes: On the Genesis of Human Communication.* New York: International Universities Press, 1957.

_____. *The First Year of Life.* New York: International Universities Press, 1965.

Steinfeld, G. J. Piaget's concept of decentering in relation to family process and therapy. G. I. Lubin, J. F. Magary, M. K. Poulsen (Eds.) *Proceedings of the Fourth Annual U. A. P. Conference on Piagetian Theory and the Helping Professions.* Los Angeles, February, 1975, 280-287.

Strauss, J. The classification of schizophrenic concreteness. *Psychiatry,* 1967, 30, 294-301.

Stuart, R. B. Decentration in the development of children's concepts of moral and causal judgment. *Journal of Genetic Psychology,* 1967, 111, 59-68.

Suchotliff, L. C. Relation of formal thought disorder to the communication deficit in schizophrenics. *Journal of Abnormal Psychology,* 1970, 76, 250-257.

Sullivan, H. S. *The Interpersonal Theory of Psychiatry.* New York: W. W. Norton & Co., 1953.

Tomilson-Keasey, C. and Keasey, C. B. The mediating role of cognitive development in moral judgment. *Child Development,* 1974, 45, 291-298.

Trunnell, T. Thought disturbances in schizophrenia: Pilot study utilizing Piaget's theories. *Archives General Psychiatry,* 1964, 11, 126-136.

_____. Thought disturbances in schizophrenia: Replication study utilizing Piaget's theories. *Archives General Psychiatry,* 1965, 13, 1-18.

Von Domarus, E. The specific laws of logic in schizophrenia. In J. Kasanin (Ed.) *Language and Thought in Schizophrenics.* Berkeley, Calif.: University of California Press, 1944.

Vygotsky, L. S. *Thought and Language* (E. Hanfmann and G. Vakar, translators). Cambridge, Mass.: The MIT Press, 1962. (Originally published, 1934.)

INDEX OF NAMES

INDEX OF SUBJECTS